FULFILMENT

To our beloved daughter, Nancy, whose untimely death is the great tragedy of our lives.

FULFILMENT

MEMOIRS OF A CRIMINAL COURT JUDGE

DAVID VANEK

DUNDURN PRESS
TORONTO · OXFORD

Editor: Carrie Whithers
Design: Scott Reid
Printer: Transcontinental Printing Inc.

Canadian Cataloguing in Publication Data

Vanek, David
Fulfilment: memoirs of a criminal court judge
Copublished by the Osgoode Society for Canadian Legal History.
ISBN 1-55002-325-X
1. Vanek, David. 2. Ontario. Provincial Court, Criminal Division — Biography. 3. Judges — Ontario — Biography. 4. Criminal justice, Administration of — Ontario. I. Osgoode Society for Canadian Legal History. II. Title.

KE416.V36A3 1999   345.713'05'092   C99-932711-9   KF345.Z9V34 1999
1   2   3   4   5   03   02   01   00   99

THE CANADA COUNCIL | LE CONSEIL DES ARTS
FOR THE ARTS | DU CANADA
SINCE 1957 | DEPUIS 1957

We acknowledge the support of the **Canada Council for the Arts** for our publishing program. We also acknowledge the support of the **Ontario Arts Council** and we acknowledge the financial support of the Government of Canada through the Book Publishing Industry Development Program (BPIDP) for our publishing activities.

Care has been taken to trace the ownership of copyright material used in this book. The author and the publisher welcome any information enabling them to rectify any references or credit in subsequent editions.

J. Kirk Howard, President

Printed and bound in Canada.

Printed on recycled paper.

Dundurn Press	Dundurn Press	Dundurn Press
8 Market Street	73 Lime Walk	2250 Military Road
Suite 200	Headington, Oxford,	Tonawanda NY
Toronto, Ontario, Canada	England	U.S.A. 14150
M5E 1M6	OX3 7AD	

CONTENTS

Acknowledgments

This book is comprised of my recollections refreshed in various instances by personal letters and other materials close to hand that I accumulated over the years. Otherwise I did no research of any kind. In retirement, there was no staff upon which to rely, not even a secretary. With uncertain fingers, laboriously, I operated my out-dated computer, which I used as a word processor. It was highly fortuitous, therefore, when I divulged to my nephew, Jonathan Speigel, that I was in process of writing my memoirs. He immediately volunteered to serve as my editor. I accepted the offer with gratitude and made the appointment on the spot. Jonathan is a bright, able and busy legal practitioner with special skill in the operation of the computer, an aptitude particularly useful in preparing a book for publication. Despite his numerous other responsibilities, somehow he found the time to bring his uncle's project to fruition. In the process he managed to cure my errors and excesses of language. I particularly appreciate that he exercised his editorial function in an attitude of moderation without affecting the thought or style of the writing. Rather, he enhanced the text and made it more readable. I wish to express my heartfelt thanks to Jonathan, the number two son of my sister, Mary.

A few years after my retirement from the Bench, Peter Oliver invited me to participate in the oral history program of the Osgoode Society for Canadian Legal History. I gave three interviews for this program, which were tape-recorded. A transcript of the interviews was prepared, which I edited. I understand that the tapes and transcript are presently filed in the Archives of Ontario for safekeeping and future research. I am considerably indebted to Christine Kates, the interviewer for the oral history program. The transcripts of her interviews prompted me to write a considerably expanded version and virtually served as a blueprint for these memoirs.

I also acknowledge the contribution of The Honourable Mr. Justice Paul Reinhardt of the Ontario Court of Justice who examined my manuscript and responded immediately with enthusiasm and support. He also encouraged me to make revisions and additions that I believe have added substantially to the quality of the book.

Finally, I express my appreciation to Joyce, my dear wife, for her forbearance and support. We have been together so long that it was not possible to tell my story without interweaving a good part of hers as well. Joyce examined the work chapter by chapter as it was written and gave me the benefit of her comments. I am pleased that the fruits of this undertaking have been accorded her stamp of approval, which is the ultimate reward for my labours.

Foreword

The purpose of The Osgoode Society for Canadian Legal History is to encourage research and writing in the history of Canadian law. The Society, which was incorporated in 1979 and is registered as a charity, was founded at the initiative of the Honourable R. Roy McMurtry, a former attorney general for Ontario, now Chief Justice of Ontario, and officials of the Law Society of Upper Canada. Its efforts to stimulate the study of legal history in Canada include a research support program, a graduate student research assistance program, and work in the fields of oral history and legal archives. The Society publishes volumes of interest to the Society's members that contribute to legal-historical scholarship in Canada, including studies of the courts, the judiciary and the legal profession, biographies, collections of documents, studies in criminology and penology, accounts of significant trials, and work in the social and economic history of the law.

Current directors of The Osgoode Society for Canadian Legal History are Jane Banfield, Tom Bastedo, Brian Bucknall, Archie Campbell, J. Douglas Ewart, Martin Friedland, Charles Harnick, John Honsberger, Kenneth Jarvis, Allen Linden, Virginia MacLean, Wendy Matheson, Colin McKinnon, Roy McMurtry, Brendan O'Brien, Peter Oliver, Paul Reinhardt, Joel Richler, James Spence, Harvey Strosberg and Richard Tinsley.

The annual report and information about membership may be obtained by writing: The Osgoode Society for Canadian Legal History, Osgoode Hall, 130 Queen Street West, Toronto, Ontario. M5H 2N6.

We are very grateful to Judge David Vanek for offering us the opportunity to publish his memoirs. In Ontario provincial court judges are the workhorses of the judiciary, carrying out a huge range of tasks and bearing an enormous burden. Most students of Canadian legal history are familiar with the book written by that notorious character, George T. Denison, who published his own *Recollections of a Police Court Magistrate* in 1920. In that volume Denison told his sometimes astounded readers that the concern of his court was not law but justice. "I never follow precedents," he related, "unless they agree with my views." From his appointment in 1877 until the end of 1919 there were 650,000 cases. "The majority of these have been dealt with by me, as for the first twenty years I had no assistant."

As David Vanek makes clear, the work of the provincial court has changed greatly since George Denison's day and David Vanek's courtroom was characterized by high standards of legal professionalism. What has not changed since the late nineteenth century, however, is the significance of the so called "lower courts" and Judge Vanek and his colleagues dealt on a daily basis with a large and sometimes startling range of cases.

This marvellously readable book offers wonderful windows into the travails of a Jewish immigrant family living in the Toronto area in the inter-war years, a frank yet humorous record of Mr. Vanek's experiences, military and otherwise, during World War II, and behind-the-scenes accounts of the struggle to reform and win new stature for provincial court judges in Ontario in the 1960s and 1970s. The book also discusses a number of David Vanek's significant cases including the case of the baby deaths at the Hospital for Sick Children in Toronto. This engaging book, charming and insightful, makes a significant contribution to both social and legal history.

R. Roy McMurtry
President

Peter N. Oliver
Editor-in-Chief

Preface

As the Chief Judge of the Provincial Court from 1990 to 1999, the history of the court has been one of my personal interests. To this end I have worked with the Ontario Judges Association and the Ontario Family Law Judges Association, now merged into the Ontario Conference of Judges, in a joint venture with the Osgoode Society to preserve the history of our court through oral history interviews with the members of the court. I am proud that this work has resulted in some 45 interviews to date, principally by oral historian Christine Kates, including an interview with David Vanek. What is even more rewarding for me is that David Vanek, in part as a result of his oral history interview, has been inspired to take the next step and write his memoirs. All of us who care about the Provincial Court, and the people who serve on it, are in his debt.

Once I started reading this manuscript I could not put it down. It provides a window on a period when Toronto was evolving into the diverse and sophisticated city it has become. It tells with clarity and good humour the story of an immigrant family's journey in coming to Canada and finding a way to succeed and achieve. It provides valuable insight into the experience of growing up Jewish in southern Ontario in the first half of this century. Most of all, it reveals the experience, wisdom and humanity of a very remarkable Provincial Court judge.

David Vanek became a judicial officer at a time of great change in the

Provincial Court, as it made the transition from a Magistrate's Court many of whose members were non-lawyers to full fledged Criminal Court made up of highly trained legal practitioners with a parallel criminal jurisdiction to the County and District Courts. This evolution of the court has placed great demands on the individual judges who served as trial judges during this period, as well as on those judges who took leadership roles in court administration, or in the judges' associations. No reader could ever doubt the challenges of Ontario Provincial Court work in the 80's after reading David Vanek's description of his experiences as the preliminary inquiry justice in **Regina v. Susan Nelles** - Chapter 20. In my view, those challenges have actually increased in the 90's. Judge Vanek brings a special perspective to his discussion of these years and the administrative issues that arose due to his service as an executive member of the judges association and President from 1979 to 1980, as well as his role as chair of the Provincial Criminal Court Judges Special Committee on Criminal Justice in Ontario which produced a Report, released on the 2nd of January, 1987, commonly referred to as the "Vanek" Report. Under David Vanek's leadership, the Report was the work of a broadly based group of judges including The Hon. Norman Nadeau, Vice-Chair, and judges W. D. August, P.R. Belanger, C.R. Merredew, G.E. Michel, R.D. Reilly, W.S. Sharpe, J.D.R. Walker and Anton Zuraw.

It has been my responsibility as Chief Judge to oversee many of the institutional changes that were necessary to meet the challenges foreshadowed in the "Vanek" Report and the experiences of Provincial Court trial judges during Judge Vanek's career on the bench. That these changes were discussed, studied and reported on by the Special Committee of the Judges Association provides a valuable historical record of the analysis and recommendations of the judicial leadership of the day.

Like many provincial judges who have come before and since, David Vanek's career has been one of service to his community. It is truly fortunate that David Vanek has decided to once again serve his community by writing this book. Judge Vanek is a gifted writer and story teller, and although a lawyer, academic and judge who has written in legal journals and in his judgments on many legal topics for the benefit of other lawyers and judges, he has written a book that is accessible and understandable to the non-lawyer.

Because of David Vanek's skill as a writer this book will be rewarding not only for students and teachers, lawyers and judges, but for the general public, as well. It deserves to be read by a diverse audience. I hope that it will be, because it has a great deal to say.

Sidney B. Linden
Chief Justice, Ontario Court of Justice
April 21st, 1999

One
Just a Farm Boy

The celebrated French philosopher, Rene Descartes, is credited with establishing the fact of human existence when in the seventeenth century he wrote in Latin "cogito ergo sum" "I think, therefore I am." Personally, I have always taken my own existence for granted, but it is comforting to know that one's assumptions have been corroborated. I have been more concerned, however, to learn about the circumstances associated with my birth and existence. In this regard I received considerable assistance, by way of hearsay evidence, a number of years ago on the occasion of the "briss" of my brother Morris' eldest son.

This was an occasion just after the end of World War II, in about 1946 or 1947. By then I had been demobilized. I had my own family and we were living in our first modest dwelling, perhaps a mile or two from my brother's small bungalow. I was acutely conscious of my own importance and respectability as a recently appointed lecturer in Law at the University of Toronto. Morris' wife, Feige, had presented him with his first offspring, a fine, healthy baby boy. This, in the Jewish tradition, is a most happy event, and calls for a *briss*, which is the ritual circumcision of the male child, and a *pidyon ha ben*, the redemption of the first born male child from the priestly class. My brother had scheduled the briss to be held at his home on a Sunday morning.

It turned out to be a warm, sunny, summer day. Upon awaking, I dressed and leisurely made my way to my brother's dwelling where, to my surprise, I found no one at home. I was certain this was the correct time and place, so I sat down on the concrete steps leading to the front entrance and waited for something to happen. In due course a car arrived, seemingly packed with people, and out came Morris and Feige and assorted other family members, as well as an elderly gentleman with a long grey beard. They proceeded to file into the dwelling with barely a word passing between us. The elderly gentleman fixed me with a piercing glance as he passed by. I assumed, of course, that he was the "moile," a religious Jew who was authorised to perform the surgery, and well qualified to conduct the religious ceremony associated with the circumcision. Gradually the guests arrived and soon the small livingdining room area where the event was to take place was filled to the point of overcrowding.

Then the drama unfolded. The hubbub of many voices was suddenly hushed as the mother brought in the baby, who was lying on a cushion. There were mingled oh's and ah's from the assembly. Now the elderly gentleman took over the conduct of the proceedings in strict accordance with the requirements of Jewish law and tradition. He intoned the customary prayers. The baby was prepared for THE EVENT. Then, one swift cut of the sharp knife, and it was over. The baby cried; the guests shouted "mazel tov," tears flowed, and the baby was fed a drop of wine, which seemed to quiet him. Then, the elderly gentleman, flushed with his success in this exercise, turned to his audience and, in a strong voice, declaimed:

"So you think this was a briss! You should have been there when I performed the briss on THIS ONE!" To my astonishment, he accompanied this statement with a finger pointed directly at me.

"*Oy hot es geblust*," (Oh how the wind howled), he continued in Yiddish. "*Oy, schnee bis zum knee.*" (snow up to the knees). "*Oy war es kolt!*" (How freezing cold it was!).

In this manner, to my utter discomfiture, he made a public declaration of the very personal circumstances surrounding my own circumcision that happened many years ago and were not even a remote memory. He told how he was summoned to the farm at Pine Orchard where I was born in the year 1915. How he travelled from the big city of Toronto as a religious duty and "mitzvah" to Jewish people in the country who were cut off from civilization and all the hardships he endured in the process. Obviously, this had made a deep impression on his mind. For me, this episode was most embarrassing. However, it did instil a latent yearning to visit the farm, something I only managed to do many years later.

Who ever heard of Pine Orchard? Recently, a friend, who had been assigned the task of formally introducing me at a gathering of people with whom I was already well acquainted, called me on the telephone.

"David," he complained, "I have been reading your curriculum vitae. Where is Pine Orchard? I can't find it anywhere."

I had to laugh. "Of course you won't," I replied. "It's not on any map. It is not a municipality. It's a postal address."

Actually, the birth certificate that I carry adopts a broad geographical view of the matter and lists my birthplace as "Whitchurch Twp. York Co." However, the farm where I was born, and that was my first home, was apparently also known as "Cedar Valley." The farm is located about six miles east of the Town of Newmarket in the Township of Whitchurch, and lies between Newmarket and Vivian. Today, Newmarket is a thriving centre located about twenty-five miles from the northerly limit of Toronto. In 1915, it was occupied mainly by retired farmers, retail shops and other business enterprises servicing the needs of the farmers in the surrounding countryside. As for Vivian, few people would have known it even then. In those days it was likewise a mere postal station, although it gained some slight additional importance as a milk stop on the railway line that ran from Toronto through the Town of Stouffville north to about Lake Simcoe.

My memory of the farm is very dim. It is virtually confined to the fact that there was a big collie dog called "Sport" who would bring in the cows at night, a dirt lane that passed a pond, and ducks in the pond that went "quack, quack." After all I was a mere two or three years old when we moved away and I had never been back until a short while ago. At that time, I was in Newmarket and had finished my business there. I had some spare time and it occurred to me that this would be a good opportunity to satisfy my yearning to become reacquainted with the farm. I was aware of the location in a general way. After some inquiry for directions, I set off. Eventually, I came to a concession road and then a dirt lane leading from it. I turned onto the lane and found my childhood impressions confirmed. The lane passed a pond where there were ducks that went "quack, quack," and I arrived at an old farmhouse that looked to be quite unchanged. I knocked at the front door, which was opened by a young woman.

"Excuse me," I asked in a somewhat quavering voice, "Is this the west half of lot 34 in concession six east of Yonge Street, Township of Whitchurch?"

"Why yes," replied the young woman.

"Well, madam, what do you know," I stammered, "I was born here!"

The young woman was much more composed than I. "Won't you come in and have a cup of tea?" she said.

And so I did. Thus passed a pleasant visit, in conversation with the present occupant, when we discussed and contrasted living at the farm then and now. I learned that the current use of the farm was mainly for the raising of thoroughbred Arabian horses. One wall was covered with ribbons and plaques representing prizes awarded for excellence in this regard. Later, I walked about the farm to an extent. Somehow I found the visit deeply satisfying. It restored a feeling of attachment to the land and particularly the land where I was born, but which of course I never worked. Actually, I seriously doubt that my father ever personally worked the land either, although almost immediately upon his arrival in Canada he acquired and settled on the farm and apparently took up the life of a farmer.

My father emigrated to Canada from Czarist Russia in about 1913. He brought with him his eldest son Tevya — in Canada he was called Thomas or Tom. My father was then thirty-three years of age. Tom would have been thirteen years old and only recently have celebrated his bar mitzvah, marking his admission to manhood as a member of a Jewish congregation. They came from Uman, a town in the province of Kiev in the Ukraine. My mother was left behind with four younger children: Chaya (Laura), eleven years; Fanny (Faye), nine years; Abe, four years; and Moses (Morris), an infant of two years. My mother followed about a year later with the four youngsters. I shall occasionally refer to my parents as "Ma" and "Pa," the children's customary mode of address. It was not unusual in those days for the head of family to emigrate first, find work and accommodation, make all other appropriate arrangements, and then bring over his wife and children to join him. In later years, however, I am bound to report that Ma would relate a quite different version of the emigration, especially if she was annoyed or vexed with Pa, which was often the case.

According to her, one day, without warning, Pa ran out on her, taking Tom as a kind of hostage to ensure she would eventually join him in the new world. So there we have it. In one version, Pa proceeded as a normal, responsible, cautious head of household. In the other version, he abandoned his wife, virtually kidnapped her eldest male child, and left her to fend for herself and four small children. Eventually, she was thus forced, with all her children, to travel thousands of miles across the ocean to join him in a harsh existence as a pioneer farmer in the wilderness of a foreign country. According to her, what did he do on the farm? He grew potatoes – "all sour!"

To my knowledge, Pa never bothered to contradict Ma's account of the exodus from Russia and arrival in Canada. If there was a difference of opinion on this important subject, you may infer, correctly, there were also differences between them on numerous other matters. The relationship between my parents was generally characterised by turbulence and occasional open warfare, interrupted from time to time by an armistice or even blessed peace. It must have been peace that prevailed some time after Ma's arrival, which provided an appropriate climate for my birth in 1915. I have always felt grateful to Ma for coming to this country and making peace with Pa so that I could always boast, with regard to the matter of citizenship, that I am a native-born Canadian.

I never enjoyed the privilege of knowing my grandparents. Curiously, my parents were not my chief sources of information about my grandparents, life in the old country, and the circumstances surrounding the emigration of my parents to Canada. My information was gleaned from two cousins, who were each about fifteen years my senior and who came to Canada from Russia, separately, when they were about twenty years of age. Norman Oster was related in two ways: not only was he the son of my mother's brother Shalom, he was also my brotherinlaw, having married my sister Faye. Harry Clayman was the son of my father's sister whom I knew as Mima (Aunt) Sonya. The following account is mainly attributable to Harry, but was substantially confirmed and supplemented by Norman.

My paternal grandmother, Fruma, was married to Israel Nieminsky. They had a child named Esther. When Esther was about five years old,

Fruma divorced Nieminsky by a *gett* according to Jewish law. In those days, it was a legal divorce recognized by Russian civil law. Thereafter, Israel, an engineer, went with Esther to Siberia where he was employed in the construction of the TransSiberian Railway. Fruma then married my paternal grandfather, Israel Bar Vinarski, on the rebound.

At the time of his marriage, Israel was employed as a bookkeeper in a lumber camp near a *dorf* (village) called Kozlouka where Fruma lived with her parents. Why did a respectable, young, Jewish man work in a lumber camp — a pious Jew who, according to Harry, would rather have perished than to eat *chozer* (pig)? The answer is quite simple. He was hiding out! He was a draft dodger, not unlike the American youths who avoided military service in Vietnam by coming to Canada. In those days, Grandpa Israel lived in the bush as a nonlegal personality, passing himself off under a number of aliases. He was not written into the book of the living until his first child was about five years old. Then he finally decided to take a chance and go to whatever passed for the equivalent of the draft board. First, however, he took a medical precaution that was not at all uncommon. He caused himself to be crippled by arranging for the tendons of the fourth and fifth fingers of his right hand to be cut so that these fingers could not be straightened and used. In this way, he avoided the terrible obligations of long-time military service, obtained a Russian passport, and acquired legal status in Russia, albeit as a Jew.

After his legalization, he took his bride of five years and moved to Uman, about 250 miles away. Uman was then a sizeable city with a substantial Jewish population. The Jews lived in the congested central area in a gully surrounded by the gentile Ukrainian population who dwelt in the green area above. When he settled in Uman, Grandpa Israel became a *melamed* (teacher) and taught Hebrew religion and language and Yiddish, the common language spoken by Jewish people of the Diaspora (area outside Israel). Grandma Fruma was a dressmaker, and, it seems, a very good one. She dealt with and worked for the finest people in Uman. In this way, my grandparents together managed to eke out a frugal living.

My grandparents, Fruma and Israel, had three children who were born about three years apart: Jacob, my father, familiarly known as Yankel; Sheindel (Sonya), Harry's mother; and Tabel. Aunt Sonya married Nacham, the son of Gedalia Klebanov. She married late in life for those times; she was a spinster of twenty-four years when the wedding took place. She was an easygoing, amiable, and hardworking woman with surprising inner strength. Under her mother's guidance Sonya became a competent dressmaker. Nacham, a butcher by trade, was down on his luck; and never seemed to climb out of this condition. He emigrated to Canada in about 1913 at which time his name was changed to Clayman, courtesy of the Canadian Customs Service. However, he only managed to bring over his wife and children, Harry and Pearl, sometime after the Russian Revolution, in about 1921. Tabel married a man who was forced into the Russian army. Her stepsister, Esther, who was still living with Israel Nieminsky, sent for her and Tabel went to Siberia to live with Esther. Some time afterwards contact with this branch of our family was apparently lost.

Grandpa Israel was learned in Hebrew and Torah, but so also were many Jews in the Shtetels (Jewish areas) of Russia and Poland where they lived. It was their way of life to spend many hours of each day at the synagogue studying the Holy Books and engaging in discourse and argument on religious topics. Grandpa Israel was generally regarded as a very pious and learned man and was highly respected in the Jewish community. He was also, however, extremely stern, strict, unbending and subject to fits of uncontrollable temper. At the synagogue, for instance, he might suddenly take offence at some casual or relatively innocent remark, which he would make the occasion for a bitter quarrel; he would then withdraw from the synagogue in sullen and unforgiving anger and not return for months at a time. There were numerous occasions as well when he quarrelled, mainly about money, with Grandma Fruma, who was an assertive and determined woman. His earnings were always meagre; Grandma and Mima Sonya earned more than he did. He devoted himself to his teaching and studying and accepted his status in the community as the learned melamed.

My grandparents dwelt in a small threeroom house, which by modern western standards would be regarded as quite primitive. The dwelling was entered from a narrow alley that led from Nikolewska, the main street of Uman, named after the Czar. Three steps led directly into a living room, the room containing the sewing machine. Next to the living room, separated by a fireplace built into the wall, was a bedroom that contained two beds. The fireplace provided the heating for both rooms. The third room was a kitchen with a builtin oven, like a baker's oven, over which was a shelf upon which a person could stretch out and sleep. Twice each week, Grandma used the oven to bake bread. Of course, there was no running water or inside plumbing. Ewey, the *wasserfuhrer*, delivered water twice each week by horse and wagon. Ewey would carry two pails at a time and fill a large container that held about six pails of water. A shed housed the container and firewood. During the daytime, the bedroom was put into service as a classroom. A large table was set up in this room around which the students gathered. This was the *cheder* (religious school) in which Grandpa Israel practised his profession as a melamed.

In general, the children of Uman received no formal secular training even in grade school; and it was rare to have the privilege of attendance at a gymnasium, roughly equivalent to our high school, let alone any higher level of education. In these circumstances, Grandpa Israel spared nothing to ensure that his only son, Yankel, received the best training that was available, which meant that Yankel received the most intensive Jewish education that his father was personally able to provide in his cheder. Later in life, Yankel, in frustration, would sometimes complain to his mother — he would not dare complain to his father — "What has he learned me? I can hardly write my name in Russian!"

Nevertheless, thus prepared, by the time Yankel attained fifteen or sixteen years of age, he was sent from home to obtain gainful employment. He was lucky. He got a job as a clerk in a wholesale business dealing in yard goods. Behind this good fortune may readily be perceived the manipulation of a devoted and determined woman his mother. It was Grandma Fruma who, through her dressmaking, had contacts with the shops and customers, and it was she who arranged with the proprietors to take in her son so that he might learn the trade. She approached a distant relative, Ziche Mordechai, who on her entreaty, hired her son and sponsored him in Mordechai's substantial wholesale business. Bright and ambitious, Yankel, proved to be an eager worker. Within a few years he quite mastered all the facets of the business in yard goods or materials, a trade which in those days was a key area of merchandising. Garments were not then available for sale in shops readymade as they are today; people either made their own or employed a dressmaker or tailor for the purpose. The main trade was not in madeup garments but in materials. Yankel became an expert, not only as to the quality of merchandise but in all the techniques of a trading business. He also proved to be a good salesman and began to participate in purchasing. His employer sent him on buying trips to

Lodz, in Poland, where the textile centre was located and Yankel became acquainted with the sources of supply. He became well known to suppliers as well as to customers. He also began to acquire an understanding of the various methods of financing a trading business.

By the time Yankel was eighteen or nineteen years old, he was becoming known in Uman as an enterprising businessman of great promise who knew his way through all the intricacies of the yard goods trade. He was a young man who was going places. At about this time, a man named Rachlis decided to open a wholesale business in yard goods in competition with Yankel's firm. Rachlis enticed Yankel away from his old firm by giving him a raise of five rubles per week and perhaps other inducements. Ziche Mordechai went to Yankel's mother and complained bitterly to her about him. "Upon her entreaty, he had taken Yankel into his employ and confidence in a respectable business, operated by a devout and pious Jew. He had taught Yankel every aspect of the business and this was the reward? Having taken every advantage of his employment and the trust and confidence reposed in him, Yankel was now throwing over his former employer and associates in favour of a competitor who was out to ruin them!"

When Fruma heard this complaint, she joined Ziche Mordechai in wrath and indignation. She was a proud, strict and honest woman. She straightway went to the new store, went around the counter where Yankel was working, and administered two resounding slaps to his face. She ordered him to go right back to his former employment or not bother to come home. He did neither. Instead he went to the synagogue where he remained until his mother's anger had somewhat dissipated; it did not take long. Rachlis assured Fruma that he was a devout, observant Jew, and she softened and accepted the situation as a fait accompli. Indeed, as Yankel continued to work for Rachlis, my grandparents Vinarski witnessed with pride their son's further development and promotion in the world of business. Within months, his wages escalated considerably. He became the highest salaried person in the Rachlis establishment. An unmarried man, not yet twenty years old, he was earning more than most married people in Uman.

Yankel continued to work for Rachlis for two or three years. Then, just as he had left Ziche Mordechai, he suddenly abandoned Rachlis as well, taking with him another of Rachlis' clerks, a young man named Dukelski. Together they opened a new wholesale yard goods business under the name of Dukelski and Vinarski. The mainstay of the business was Yankel, who had learned the trade and knew the customers — the former clientele of the two older wholesale firms — and was well acquainted with the textile mills. In short order, Dukelski and Vinarski became immensely successful. They carried on their business on the main street of Uman, in large premises and with numerous clerks and other employees. Before long, their establishment became the chief wholesale house for the sale of yard goods in Uman. In the business world, young Yankel Vinarski had arrived.

He had arrived equally in the social world, for almost coincidental with the opening of the new business he married a girl from one of the most pious and respected families of Uman. My mother, Gissie (Jessie in English) was a very handsome young woman. She was the daughter of Shmuel, the *sofer* (scribe), as he was familiarly known in the Jewish community. My maternal grandfather's surname was Osterlitz, which in Canada became abbreviated to Oster. As a sofer, my grandfather Osterliz was a religious scholar and artist who engaged in the holy work of inscribing the words of the Torah on scrolls that were kept in the ark of each synagogue. At religious services on the Sabbath and on religious holidays and festivals, the finished scrolls were brought out with reverent care and read from to the congregation. The inscription was a delicate form of handwriting, somewhat akin to calligraphy, by use of a quill pen. My grandparents Osterlitz enjoyed a status and respect in the Jewish community perhaps second only to the rabbi.

As great as Yankel's success was in the world of business, this marriage was an equally huge success socially. It caught the imagination of the Jewish population of Uman. It was a match that seemed to have been ordained in heaven. Even so, it was actually arranged here on earth in the customary way through the services of a *shotchan* (a matchmaker). The arrangements included the negotiation of the *nodan* (dowry). This reflected the status and importance of the bride's parents and the prospects of the groom, a selfmade businessman who was regarded as "a catch." The nodan was substantial — at least 250 rubles and not less than two years' room and board with the parents of the bride. The young couple had everything going for them; they should have lived happily ever after!

However, troubles soon arose that seriously disturbed the otherwise even course of their lives — troubles associated with the business of the partnership. The new business flourished for a year or two until suddenly, my father suffered his first bankruptcy. The bankruptcy came as a shock to the entire community.

Undaunted, however, the partners effected a settlement with their creditors and opened an even larger business with stock obtained from many of the same suppliers on credit terms. The reorganized business employed fifteen to twenty people and seemed to be thriving. Unfortunately the salesmen went on strike. My father would not yield to their demands, even though he was being brought to the point of financial ruin.

My father then did something very wrong. He reported the strikers to the authorities. "So what!" you may think. Realize that this took place in Russia shortly before the Russian revolution. Jewish strikers would have been regarded as revolutionaries and dealt with most harshly by the authorities. Feeling in the community ran very high against my father. The workers threatened his life. My grandfather Shmuel interceded on my father's behalf and tried to pacify the workers. He went to the house of one worker and was attacked for his pains.

It was in this atmosphere that my father emigrated to Canada. His name became Jacob (or Jake) Vanek.

My cousin Norman Oster told me this version of my father's downfall in Uman many years later. I give this caveat regarding Norman's version of these events. Norman was only thirteen years old at the time of the strike. More importantly, towards the latter years of my father's life, he and Norman had a falling out about matters on which I cannot comment, but which could affect the accuracy of this story.

What I know for certain is that my father emigrated to Canada taking with him his eldest son; that my mother followed shortly afterwards to join him on the farm at Pine Orchard; and that she came shepherding three ambulatory youngsters and carrying a fourth child in her arms. She also brought her most precious possessions: a huge *karzibnka* (a wicker trunk) packed with downfilled comforters, cushions and assorted bedding; a nickelplated samovar; and a photograph. The photograph was of herself, her two sisters, and her only brother: Chana, the eldest; Chassie, her young sister; and Shalom, Norman's father. She also brought the crown jewel of all her possessions: two large photographs in oval mahogany frames that at all times hung in a place of honour in whatever home in which we lived. My maternal grandmother is shown wearing a plain, dark dress and a "babushka" (kerchief) round her head. My grandfather, the sofar, is seen as an ascetic elderly gentleman with sloping forehead, fine features, and a long, grey beard. He is wearing the customary "yarmulke" (skullcap) and is seated at a table with a quill pen in his hand in the act of painstakingly inscribing a scroll with the holy words of the Torah.

"By the way," I inquired, "Who was Daniel Shackman?" We were assembled in Nina's apartment "sitting shiva" on the occasion of the death of my brother Abe. "Shiva" is the traditional week of mourning of the surviving members of the family. I addressed the question to Norman.

Predictably, Norman answered my question with a question, "Why do you ask?"

I embarked upon a rather long explanation.

"When I was at the hospital and Pa was on his death bed, back in September 1955, I was given an ancient cardboard package, pouch or file, tied with ribbon, containing a variety of papers and documents that had been brought with him to the hospital. Naturally, after his death I examined the contents with keen interest and anticipation. To my astonishment, I found that it contained nothing of economic value or even of apparent sentimental value. I was intrigued to discover among the contents a number of duplicate registered copies of documents relating to the farm. Much later I happened to be in Newmarket and, out of curiosity, decided to examine the title to the farm at the Registry Office.

"I found that Pa purchased the farm, containing about one hundred acres, in September 1913, jointly with one Daniel Shackman, together with the stock and equipment associated with the farm. The purchase price was $6,000, $2,000 of which was paid in cash. The cash payment was made up of $500 advanced by Shackman and $1500 by Vanek. The purchasers also entered into a partnership agreement that provided in part that the parties would be entitled to all profits in equal shares and have the right to withdraw $4.00 per week from the business.

"The partnership did not last long. In June of the following year, Daniel Shackman released his interest in the farm upon payment of the sum of $500. Apparently, they could not get along. Pa did not remain on the farm very long after that either. In October 1916, he leased the farm, together with the stock and equipment, to Charles Emerson on terms that I think may have been fairly typical in the Ukraine, if not in Canada. It provided for the landlord and the tenant to share the crop produced in the operation of the farm. The lease contained numerous other special provisions; for example, the lessor was to have one half of all potatoes grown on the premises, but all corn and turnips were to be used as feed.

"It was at about this time that our family moved to Toronto, although I was too young to have any recollection of this event. Pa sold the farm in 1920 but reacquired it several years later by grant under the power of sale in a mortgage. He finally disposed of it in 1938 by sale to Fred Bowser of Newmarket with whom he had other business dealings."

While I was delivering this explanation, my brother Morris, who had been listening to our conversation, had obviously been pondering the mystery of the package I received from my father at the hospital. "What else did you find in that package?" he asked.

Now I am reasonably certain I had previously shown the contents of the package to any members of my family who had shown any interest in examining them. Nevertheless, once again I gave them a detailed account of the curious contents of the package.

I have looked through the package on numerous occasions. It contains the title papers to which I had already referred. There is a copy of the mortgage back on the purchase of the farm, two assignments of the mortgage, the lease to Emerson, and a chattel mortgage made between "Jake" Vanek of the Township of Whitchurch as mortgagor and William G. Widdifield of the Town of Newmarket as mortgagee. Attached to the chattel mortgage is a list of the mortgaged items:

 1 bay mare, with white spot in face, 8 years old called "Maude."
 1 Bay horse, 12 years old called, "Bill."
 2 Holstein cows, black and white, 5 years old.
 1 Durham cow, red and white, 8 years old.
 2 white cows, 6 years old; 2 red cows, 5 years old.
 2 black cows, 4 years old.
 1 black cow, 6 years old.

1 black cow with white spots in side, 6 years old.
2 blue and white cows, 6 years old
1 Holstein bull.
1 Frost and Wood Binder; 1 Mower; 1 single plow;
1 riding plow; 1 double plow No. 2 1 set disk harrows;
1 set iron harrows; 1 set wood harrows; 1 heavy wagon,
    together with neck yoke and whippletrees;
1 democrat; 1 open buggy; 1 top buggy;
1 Fanning Mill; 1 Cutting box, Peter Hamilton make;
1 scuffler; 1 Drill; 1 Cultivator; 2 sets single harness; 1 set
    double harness; 1 cutter; 1 heavy sleigh; 1 single sleigh;
Together with all other stock of horses, cattle and farm
    implements now owned or hereafter acquired by the
    Mortgagor during the currency of the Mortgage and of all
    renewals hereafter.

All of this stock of horses, cattle and farm implements was
mortgaged to secure payment of the munificent sum of $350.

In addition to the title documents, Pa's curious package includes
two letters from the tenant, Charles Emerson, written in pencil. One
letter deals with the matter of the untimely decease of one of the cows.
It is on paper so old that it has now disintegrated. The other is dated at
Cedar Valley, May 31, 1917, and reads:

Mr. Vanek. Dear Sir:

We got your letter just today and asking about the potatoes. I
got your potatoes at Vivian Station all right and have them
planted now. Seed potatoes are worth $4.00 a bag but I don't
know of anyone that has got any now. If you can get them
from the city send them on to Cedar Valley Station. Mr. Fisher
has a fresh milk cow and calf will trade them for your mare
and colt. And I don't know of anyone else that has got fresh
milk cows to sell. Sorry you are sick in bed hope you are
better now. Everything is all right up here in good order.
Regards to your wife and children.

My family must have been living at 8 Kensington Avenue at this
time because this file also contains a letter from a Mrs. Slominsky

about the rent dated March 19, which was curt and to the point. Addressed to "J. Veineck, Esq.," it is nothing if not emphatic.

Dear Sir,

I wish to advise you that the rent for 8 Kensington Ave will be $25.00 per month on and after the 20th day of April 1917. Should you not wish to pay this monthly rental kindly vacate the Premises by the 20th of April and oblige.

Pa paid up as evidenced by a receipt, also in the file, written in pencil on a slip of paper and signed, J. Slominsky, dated May 20, 1917, stating, "Received from Mr. Vinnick the sum of $25 for rent, ending June 25th, 1917."

Apart from these papers, the file contains a few documents referring to certain business transactions of days long by. An invoice from Wolfe Bros. dated January 30, 1917, addressed to "Veenik" at 8 Kensington Ave. for $54.00; a statement of account with the Georgetown Creamery (M. Saxe, Proprietor) also addressed to 8 Kensington. Another statement inexplicably addressed to H. Davis, 14 Kensington; and a credit note from Kofman Bros. and Fine dated years later in 1930, apparently representing the return of some canned goods. The rest of the package or file is taken up by a large bundle of very official looking documents in Russian.

On another occasion, I asked Norman to examine these documents for he still retained some knowledge of the Russian language. After several minutes of careful scrutiny, Norman came up with the verdict. "These are all papers dealing with business matters in which Pa was involved in Russia before the Russian Revolution. In the main, they are promissory notes given by Pa to some other person or firm or promissory notes given by others to him, stamped with official stamps, plus court documents representing efforts to recover the monies secured. In some instances, he was being sued; in other cases, he was doing the suing." Needless to say, all these documents were completely worthless after the Russian Revolution of 1917. What a ridiculous collection of memorabilia! My father was an intelligent person. He was not a sentimentalist. He was a businessman. His whole life was bound up in business. I have been trying for years to unravel the puzzle as to why he would have kept this singular and random collection of worthless papers as his most prized possession, to be turned over to me upon his death.

After I completed my long dissertation about the title to the farm and the contents of Pa's package, again I turned to Norman and said, "So what is the answer to my question? What do you know about Daniel Shackman?" I am afraid Norman got a little muddled. He was quite certain that Daniel Shackman was the son of one Gedalia, but he was mistaken. An unimpeachable authority, my cousin Nathan Shackman, a retired physician who now resides in Los Angeles, has now informed me about the correct state of affairs:

"Early in this century, five Shackman bothers who lived in the Ukraine decided to emigrate. Two went to Canada (Herschel and Philip); two went to London (I don't know their names), and my grandfather (Shmuel Chaim) went to New York. Daniel is Herschel's son."

I should explain that I have a heightened interest in the name "Shackman." My mother's younger sister, Chassie, was married to Israel Shackman whose parent, Shmuel Chaim Shackman, had settled in New York. They lived for years in Brooklyn. The Brooklyn Shackmans operated a grocery business. They had two sons, Dave and Nathan, the latter being my informant on this subject. In summary, my cousin Nathan, on my mother's side, told me about his relative Daniel, on his father's side.

The Canadian Shackmans, to whom Norman referred, belonged to my grandfather's generation. According to Norman, they were my parents' neighbours when my parents lived at Cedar Valley. Herschel Shackman owned a farm near or fronting on Highway No. 48; Philip Shackman must also have resided close by. Indeed, my parents drew comfort and companionship in those early days in Canada from friends who lived in various localities within a radius of perhaps twenty-five miles of the farm. Their friends included Mr. and Mrs. Clouth who had a retail dry goods store in Newmarket (which seemed to fit their name), Joe Caplan who operated a refreshment booth and dance pavilion at Lake Wilcox (his son Dave played in the band) and the Borinskys of the Town of Stouffville.

The elder Borinsky was an early settler in Stouffville. He had four sons: Joe, Jake, Norman and Harold. The old man was said to have put Joe in the creamery business in Stouffville and Jake into the produce business. Norman Borinsky became a lawyer. He changed his surname to Borins and was the first Jew to become an assistant Crown attorney in the Province of Ontario. Philip Shackman had a daughter Bessie, who married Joe Borinsky. For some years, Joe Borinsky was the Mayor or Reeve of Stouffville. When I was a young lad, there was a great deal of visiting between Joe and Bessie, the Borinskys of Stouffville, and my parents.

By the time we moved for good to Toronto, my parent's circle of friends had expanded considerably. It came to include, for instance, Chazan Barkin, who was a cantor and well-respected in the Jewish community of Toronto. I have a vivid image of Chazan Barkin in my memory. He was small and rotund. He had a Van Dyke beard and was dignified in bearing and bombastic in manner. Chazan Barkin was not only a strong cantorial vocalist; he was also an accomplished pianist. At informal gatherings, with a minimum of prodding, he would strike a majestic pose at the piano and perform with great flourish and considerable skill.

I asked Norman if he had personally known Herschel Shackman. Norman said he had a keen recollection of the old man and spoke of Herschel with affection. Herschel had an endearing personality. He would tell very comical anecdotes much in the manner of Shalom Aleichem. At one time, he drifted off to Detroit. After his wife died, however, he returned to the same farm. He tried to make some money out of it by giving Jewish city dwellers the opportunity of enjoying the fresh air and sunshine of the farm, including bathing in a muddy pond and heavy kosher meals, as a summer country holiday. When I queried the economic feasibility of this operation, Norman exclaimed in some exasperation, "Where then do you think your father got the idea of opening a summer resort at Lake Wilcox?"

Two
Childhood Memories

On about January 4, 1918, there occurred an event of such surpassing importance that it may have driven the news of the day about the Great War off the front page of the Aurora Banner. Of such great interest was this historic event that the item was reprinted years later under the caption "50 Years Ago." It read:

> OAK RIDGES — Mr. Vaneck and family, from Cedar Valley, have moved into the house and store lately owned by Mr. Keys, and have begun business.

In 1918, as a young toddler not yet three years of age, the world was beginning to open to me like a beautiful flower unfolding into bloom. I was not at all conscious that there had been a Bolshevik Revolution in Russia on November 7, 1917, which was followed by Russia abandoning the war against Germany by an armistice and the Peace of BrestLitovsk of March 2, 1918; nor did I appreciate that American troops were streaming into Europe to reinforce the allied force or that Germany was about to launch its last major offensive of the war. My world was confined to the house and store in Oak Ridges and their immediate environs.

Gradually I came to terms with this new and different environment. Our family home was now part of a substantial twostorey white brick building located on the northeast corner of Yonge Street Highway and a bumpy gravel side road that led for about a mile and a quarter to a small, but deep, springfed lake known as Lake Wilcox. From the part of the premises fronting on the Lake Wilcox Road my father operated a general store. The kitchen and living quarters were at the rear of the store. The bedrooms were on the second floor. I remember the kitchen well because that is where my dog Sport, brought with us from the farm, snapped at me when I was seated at the kitchen table and accidentally kicked him as he was dozing under the table. It was a somewhat traumatic experience.

We were able to boast that the property came fully serviced with central heating. The premises included a basement with a furnace and uncovered tin heating ducts. I have a vivid recollection of the heating ducts. One morning I awoke rather late in the bedroom on the second floor where I slept and was too lazy to visit the outhouse. I found an opening in the heating ducts and peed into it. Directly afterwards I learned to my dismay about the consternation that this had caused in the store below where customers remarked upon the moisture, having an unmistakable odour and appearance, dripping from the exposed pipes. The premises also included a cistern. This is also imprinted upon my memory because of a sad and tragic accident. Our cat fell into the cistern and we were unable to rescue her in due time. Poor thing; she drowned.

My father dealt in a wide variety of goods appropriate to an old fashioned general store catering to a farm trade. He sold such diverse items as groceries, tobacco products, boots and shoes, paint, feed, overalls and other apparel, and, of course, yard goods. When I began to understand the obligation of *kashruth*, the Hebrew dietary laws, I found it difficult to accept that the "pananas" that were suspended in a bunch from the ceiling were not contaminated by the ham and bacon on the counter below. My father called this fruit "pananas" and so affected my speech that it was not until I was in my late teens that I realized that "bananas" was spelled with a "b," not a "p." The stock-in-trade also included gasoline, which was dispensed from a pump in front of the store, and related products needed to service motor vehicles that were being acquired by the public in ever increasing numbers. In a shed attached to the premises, my father stored blocks of ice, covered with sawdust. The ice provided customers with refrigeration for their perishable foodstuffs during the warm weather.

Oak Ridges was mainly just a cluster of houses and cottages in the country, surrounded by farms. It lay almost midway between what was then the Town of Aurora, about three miles to the north, and the Village of Richmond Hill, five miles to the south.

Lt. Colonel John Graves Simcoe, the first Lt. Governor of the newly formed Province of Upper Canada founded Toronto, then called York, in 1793. Upon York's creation, Simcoe undertook, as one of his first projects, the construction of an arterial highway extending northward to open up the Province of Upper Canada for settlement. Simcoe had previously been the officer in command of the Queen's Rangers, a regiment that had fought on the side of Great Britain in the American revolutionary war. It was mainly his troops of the Queen's Rangers who accomplished the road building task by creating a rudimentary highway about thirty miles long. It was later extended from time to time, and has been known as the Yonge Street Highway. The new highway did, in fact, encourage settlement. Substantial tracts of land were granted to retired soldiers in recognition of their service to their country. In addition, there was an influx of settlers who came from the United States to Canada as pioneers during or after the War of Independence and whose sympathies remained with Great Britain. They became known as United Empire Loyalists. By 1918, Toronto had grown to a population of about a quarter million people, mainly of British descent, proud of their heritage and loyal to the British Crown. It was sometimes referred to, boastfully, as the "Queen City of Canada," and occasionally, perhaps disparagingly, as "Toronto the Good." Its main northerly thoroughfare, Yonge Street Highway, passed by our store at Oak Ridges and connected the outlying areas with the city.

The construction of a radial line, commencing in 1896, along the east side of Yonge Street Highway established another linkage. The radial line extended northerly past our store in Oak Ridges to a terminus at Lake Simcoe. By 1918, and certainly the 1920s and 30s, the radial line had become very popular. It was used by commuters and people attracted to a pleasant, recreational area at Bond Lake, a small but attractive lake, located about a half mile north of our store, and a summer resort area known as Jackson's Point, located at Lake Simcoe. In addition to a passenger service, the radial cars carried a certain amount of freight. The Ridge Inn, built in 1837, stood across the Lake

Wilcox Side Road from our store and also fronted on the Yonge Street Highway. It was a favourite stopover for travellers to and from Toronto. In front of the Inn on Yonge Street, there was a car stop, as well as a wooden platform that served as a milk stand and, in general, as a facility for the loading and unloading of freight. In 1918, Oak Ridges was also the junction for a spur line that was begun in 1902, which linked the radial line along Yonge Street with the Town of Schomberg, a distance northwesterly of about thirty miles. The trains using the spur line were powered by steam. The spur line continued in operation until about 1930. A rather substantial railway station of wooden construction stood at the junction. For many years, this area was often referred to by the alternative name of Schomberg Junction because of this linkage between the Yonge Street Radial and the spur line to Schomberg. Our general store enjoyed a relative monopoly of the retail trade of the surrounding area and, in addition to the train station, it was the hub and main focal point of the hamlet of Oak Ridges in 1918 and for some years afterwards.

At the rear of our store and house, apart from the usual water pump and wooden outhouse, there was a substantial area of vacant land, which my mother used for a garden. My father may dubiously have lain claim to be the farmer of the family; my mother was undoubtedly the gardener. His potatoes were always sour; hers were sweet and firm. Each spring, with the assistance of a helper, she would direct the planting. "Dig here, plant there," and invariably produced an excellent yield of a variety of vegetables that well served the needs of our family. This was but a sideline for my mother, who was always a very busy woman. She was a careful housekeeper. She was an excellent cook and even a better baker, a function she exercised as an art. She baked homemade bread and exceptional strudel, wrapped in paper-thin dough and exquisite to the taste, as well as a variety of cakes and pastries. She had this failing, however, that she was always searching for compliments on her surpassing ability as a baker. Her tactic was to complain: "I don't know what happened to the strudel and the cakes; nothing turned out right; I'm sorry." Then she had to be reassured that the strudel and the cakes were absolutely delicious. My mother also made wine for Passover, butter, cheese, and sauerkraut. For the Sabbath, the smaller children had to get out of the way while the house was cleaned and the Sabbath dinner prepared. The days preceding a holiday were a time for a thorough cleaning. Upon the commencement of the Passover, as if by magic, all the regular dishes were gone and replaced with special tableware and the *chomatz* (bread) was replaced by *matzoh*, (unleavened bread) and other products appropriate to the Passover. Amongst all her varied activities, my mother would occasionally attend to customers in the store and somehow also find the time to look after a family composed of her husband, the man of business, and six children of varying ages, of whom I was then the youngest.

In 1918 my big brother Tom was 18 years of age, Laura was 16, Faye 14, Abe 9, Morris 7, and I was 3 years old. I was the youngest of the children until I attained the age of about four years. I remember a gradual transformation occurring in the body of my mother, and then, as if by magic, the sudden entry into our household of a baby sister, Mary. I do not recall any reaction of jealousy on my part although the birth of the baby automatically resulted in a demotion and loss of status for me. From being the youngest of the family, I now had to settle for youngest of the boys, no longer entitled to special attention but expected instead to cherish, honour, protect, and care for my little sister. It should be appreciated that our family was regulated on a hierarchical basis. As the eldest, Tom was in a class by himself. For my parents, the sun rose and fell on Tom. He also commanded immeasurable respect from all the other children. Like the king, Tom could do no wrong. Of course, my older sisters were well loved. As for the rest of the family, with the exception of the little sister, we were bound to take our proper chronological place in the hierarchy. This dictated that, in later years, when we attended school, my older brother Morris was entitled to the prior use of the bathroom even if I consequently had to be late for school.

With the arrival of my baby sister, although I was by no means entirely neglected, I found myself increasingly left to my own devices for amusement. This led to a most alarming experience. A single line railway track that led easterly to Wilcox Lake lay a short distance of perhaps three hundred yards north of our store and house. I believe the Lake Simcoe Ice and Fuel Company, which for many years operated an ice-cutting station at the Lake, used the railway line. One summer day, unaccompanied by any older member of the family, I was playing at this railway line on which there stood a jigger. This was a contraption composed of a wooden platform normally propelled along the track by two persons facing each other and alternately pulling up and down on a handle connected intermediately to wheels that rested on the track. A group of youths from a camp for Boy Scouts at Lake Wilcox were playing with the jigger and it attracted my interest as well. At one stage of the game that they were playing, I was seated on the jigger. Suddenly the boys gave the jigger a stout push and I fell off. The jigger passed right over my body. Because I was so small, miraculously I was unscathed. However, this was my first and last experience with jiggers.

While I was busy getting into one kind of mischief or another, my brother Tom was busy becoming a man. My father bought a Model-T Ford car that Tom soon learned to drive. One summer, with the use of the car, Tom operated a jitney service, transporting people to and from Lake Wilcox — until he nearly wrecked the car in an accident. Apparently he was driving the car at an excessive speed as he rounded a sharp curve in the Lake Wilcox Road and the car overturned. It was not long after this misadventure that my father put Tom into business. Somehow Pa managed to find a store for rent in the most remote, depressed, and plain dirty part of Toronto. There, at the corner of St. Clair Avenue and Runnymede Road, he installed his eldest son to operate a tobacco and confectionery shop. The location was remarkable for the fact that only part of the premises actually was situated within the limits of the City of Toronto. The rest fell within the Township of York. Across the road stood a roundhouse for trains where the steam engines were cleaned. At Keele Street, about a half-mile to the east, were the abattoirs and the meatpacking centre of Toronto. The mixture of soot from the roundhouse and the sickly sweet discharge from the abattoirs was overpowering, especially when there was a breeze from the east. On the positive side, however, the residents of the area took a liking to the energetic young fellow who was trying to make a living in the corner shop. Tom helped himself by hiring children of the neighbourhood to sell and deliver newspapers for him, sponsoring teams in baseball and hockey, and general involvement in the affairs of the community. As a result, he became quite popular in the neighbourhood. His business prospered and soon he was on the way to becoming the only affluent member of our family.

After I turned five years of age, it became my time to enrol in public school. I was bundled off for my first day at the Oak Ridges School, sometimes then also known as the RR No. 1 Aurora School, a one-classroom building about a half-mile north of our store on the opposite side of Yonge Street. A single classroom accommodated all grades from one to twelve and was presided over by a single teacher. My day began auspiciously but ended with disaster. I had long curly hair, which my mother would not allow to be cut until a few years later after I put burrs into my hair to force the issue. I was seated in front of Billie Carlisle, who found my hair tantalizing. He pulled my hair and I cried. It was then that I learned a hard lesson, which I have often dwelt upon in later life. There is no absolute justice. For some reason unknown to me, Billie Carlisle was not punished. I, however, was sent home with a note to my parents stating that I was still too immature for school and would they kindly enrol me again next year after I reached six years of age.

Shortly after, I had my revenge, for we moved to Toronto and, instead of registering in the Oak Ridges School, I began grade school in Toronto.

We moved to Toronto in approximately 1921. Instead of the one-room school at Oak Ridges I commenced my education at the Annette Street Public School, a large urban school of many rooms, well organized and structured. The children were normally assembled in the playground and marched to their classrooms to the sound of music.

Our family took over a threestorey building in a connected row of buildings in the West Toronto Junction, an area amalgamated somewhat prior to our arrival with the burgeoning City of Toronto. Our new address was 3134 Dundas Street West. My father now operated the business of a shoe store on the ground floor of the building and our family occupied the apartments above the store. I have never been able to fathom what motivated my father to make this dramatic change. He gave up the thriving business of a general store in the country for a shoe store in the city for which there was a chronic lack of customers. The store, however, provided an excellent facility for playing with my little sister amongst the wooden stands and shelves on which stood mountains of boxes of shoes. As well, I was able to enjoy the excitement of witnessing the construction along Dundas Street past our store of the extension of the streetcar line from Bloor Street to Runnymede Road. This occurred about contemporaneously with our arrival to the district. As an additional bonus, our premises were located only a short distance of about two miles from my brother Tom's store at Runnymede and St. Clair, where the most delicious candy was to be found.

I became a good friend of a boy who lived next door with a widowed mother, a sister, and a much older brother. They lived in an apartment similar to ours, over a paint and wallpaper store that the older brother operated. My mother regarded this friendship with disapproval, partly because their store was dirty and smelled of paint mingled with other distasteful odours and partly because she found the occupants vastly below her high standards and unacceptable in her eyes. My mother was a proud and somewhat haughty woman. Mention their name to her and a look of disdain would appear. She would dismiss them with the single word of contempt — "prosst!" — meaning vulgar, coarse, uncouth and common. Still, she was unable to dissuade me from this relationship and my friend and I enjoyed many good times together without any substantial adverse effects in the development of my moral character, except, perhaps, for a few trifling incidents. There was one occasion, for example, when my friend showed me a fifty-cent piece he had taken from the cash register of his family's store. Although highly shocked at this disclosure, I feel obliged to confess that I nevertheless accompanied him to a pleasure park at Lambton, near the Humber River some miles from home, and joined in the spending of his pilfered proceeds. In another instance, he and I were pushing each other in the school playground; we were promptly apprehended, brought before the principal, and got the "slugs."

In those days, I tolerated the school, but I enjoyed playing in the playground during recess. The boys played a variety of games. One game was played with old, hard chestnuts tied to a string. The object of the game was to smash the other boy's chestnut. Perhaps it was because of this game, that I acquired a fondness for the stately chestnut trees that lined several of the streets near the school. These streets led to High Park, a magnificent wooded area of several hundreds of acres close by Lake Ontario that was dedicated to the use and enjoyment of the people of Toronto in perpetuity under the will of J.G. Howard. We also played a game with pocketknives, which involved tossing the blade into a wooden bench and counting the fingers between bench and handle. There was a more rugged game that we played called "pull the rider off the horse." Here an older boy would take the part of the horse and carry a younger boy on his shoulders as the rider. I was very popular as a rider because I was small and light and easy to carry.

It is not to be assumed that all was fun and games, however, because attendance at school also involved the heavy task of absorbing the instruction delivered by the teacher during an otherwise long and tedious day. Then, to aggravate this injustice, my parents enrolled me in afterschool sessions of the local cheder run by a melamed, Mr. Gringorten, from a room in his residence on Maria Street. Mr. Gringorten was a "greenhorn," a relative newcomer to Canada from somewhere in the "Old Country." Maria Street was a district comprised almost entirely of Jewish people. It ran one block north of and parallel to Dundas Street. It was a Jewish settlement centred round an orthodox synagogue in which the men sat on benches on the main floor and the women were confined to a balcony above them. Maria Street, the synagogue, and the cheder constituted an environment quite different from Oak Ridges where our family was the only Jewish family. I imagine that Gringorten's cheder was not unlike my paternal grandfather's cheder in Uman. He taught religious practices and ritual, the significance of the Jewish holidays, and a smattering of Hebrew and Yiddish, drilled and enforced with the assistance of his belt and a wooden pointer, which he applied freely to the backs of the students. Needless to say, he was a strict disciplinarian and there were numerous cases of revolt. In one incident, an altercation ended with a student making his escape through an open window. On the whole, I received little benefit from this religious training and have considered that my father was shortchanged in his endeavour to provide me with a good Jewish education.

However, attendance at cheder gave me the opportunity of meeting the Jewish children of Maria Street as well as the children of merchants who operated shops on Dundas Street. Of course, I also became acquainted with Gentile children of the area, such as Tony Amodeo with whom I got into a fist fight and who gave me a bloody nose. When I came home and the shrieking subsided, I was asked rather unsympathetically: "And what did you give back to the other boy?" I could only reply, weakly, "He was bigger than me!" It was at about this time that I discovered that little girls were an integral part of the population. I was invited to a birthday party for a little girl who was a neighbour of ours. For this important occasion my mother made sure I dressed in my new suit with the short pants and a bellshaped black straw hat tied with a bow under the chin. It was my first party with girls and I found it quite interesting. We played games and I won the first prize. It was a beautiful grand kewpie doll. I was thrilled. A little girl who had won a tin whistle approached me with an offer. She said, playing on my sense of masculine superiority, "I'll trade you my whistle for your doll." Now, really, in the circumstances, what could I do? I could hardly afford to let the impression get round that, as a male, I preferred a doll, even a doll so large and gorgeous. So I made the trade — and regretted it afterwards because I so wanted to keep the kewpie doll. This was not the only instance, however, in which I have been outmanoeuvred and outwitted by an artful member of the opposite sex.

In one instance I was outmanoeuvred by my mother. I certainly did not want to spend a summer attending the Forest School at High Park for undernourished and underprivileged children of parents who could not afford to send them to a summer camp in the country. However, Ma decided that I was sickly and needed the sunshine and special care and attention of this unique facility that was available close by in High Park. Each day I would be sent off to the Forest School and would return home in the late afternoon. The school provided some light instruction, play, exploration of the wooded park, a healthy lunch, and a period of rest. Our teachers used the "buddy" system to ensure the safe conduct of their students to and from the summer school. Small as I was, I was responsible for an even younger lad, a tiny little fellow, and shepherded him to and from the school. My main regret about attending the Forest School was that I missed the opportunity of joining other children on the free streetcar service to the bathing beach and amusement park at Sunnyside, where most children were enjoying the pleasant and lazy days of summer. In addition, I took distaste for the lunches that were considered an important part of the program at the Forest School, especially the bread pudding that was an invariable part of the meal, and I looked for ways to avoid eating without being noticed. It took my mother the longest time when washing my clothing to realize what was the gluey substance she was finding in the pockets of my trousers!

Not long after we moved to Toronto a young man, newly arrived from the Old Country, appeared at our premises at 3134 Dundas Street

West; to me, he seemed to have come from outer space. The young man was Norman, about nineteen or twenty years of age, my cousin to whom I have already referred. He was the son of my mother's brother, Shalom. My parents took Norman into our home and he became, to all intents and purposes, a member of our family. Of course, our new immigrant spoke no English. Until he painstakingly acquired a facility in English, my only communication with him was in Yiddish, a language in which I never felt fully comfortable. My parents generally spoke to the children in Yiddish, especially in the early years, and we replied in English. Between themselves, they would occasionally carry on a conversation in Russian.

Norman brought with him an aura of mystery and adventure. Over time, I acquired some knowledge of the Russian Revolution; the condition of the Jewish population; the pogroms directed against them; and the turbulence in the period following the execution of the Czar and his family until the Bolsheviks finally established their supremacy over other political parties and took control of the country. The Bolsheviks established their own reign of terror that included a continuation of the Czarist regime's policy of enforced longterm military service. All youths, upon attaining seventeen or eighteen years of age, were required to join the army; for a Jewish boy this was regarded as akin to a sentence of death. Years after his arrival in Canada, Norman shared with me some of his recollections concerning his escape from Russia and the odyssey that brought him at length to his closest relatives in Canada. He told me that elaborate preparations were made for his departure.

"There were seven or eight of us who made our way to a certain farm from which we were transported a long distance. Finally, we came to a river, I believe it was the Dniester River, which marked the border between Russian and Bessarabia, later Romania . It was dark. We were told that on the opposite side of the river was a high mountain; that we should hike to the top where there were houses with lights in the windows; and that we should go to the first house, open the door, lie down and go to sleep. That is what I did."

"Tell me," I ventured to enquire, "what did you do for money?"

"Money!" he laughed. "Russian money was just paper; we had better than money, we had yard goods!"

"I remained in this last location a solid month," he continued "until at last I got a passport, and then I resumed my journey until I finally reached Bucharest. There I stayed with Grandma's brother Senzkofsky, who was a celebrated cantor in Bucharest." By Grandma, he meant the relative we shared in common — my maternal grandmother.

"Once in Bucharest," said Norman, "I remained six months. I almost stayed for good, because they really wanted me to marry one of their daughters."

"How did you finally manage to find our family in Canada?" I asked.

"After my arrival in Bucharest I wrote several letters to your parents at Cedar Valley, which was the last address I knew, and the letters finally reached them at Dundas Street."

I could not help remarking, "I must say I'm glad you didn't marry that girl in Bucharest."

Norman laughed, "I am too because, as you know, upon my arrival in Toronto your sister Faye and I were attracted to one another." Of course this I knew very well. Indeed, the attraction ripened into fullscale love and affection. They married, and that is how my cousin became my brotherinlaw.

Soon after joining our family, Norman had to be put to work in the serious matter of earning a livelihood. I assume it was my father who got him a horse and wagon — a broken down wagon and a rather decrepit horse. Norman embarked upon the usual occupation of an immigrant from Russia and became a peddler of dry goods. Later, he established his dry goods business in a shop that he rented next to Tom's store, where he struggled to make ends meet, let alone prosper. Norman never attended a secular school, not even a grade school; yet it did not take him long to become passably proficient in the English language. He clearly had received a very good training in Yiddish and religious subjects, but in non-religious matters, with the exception of a correspondence course in bookkeeping, he was wholly self-educated. He told me that he acquired an aptitude and fondness for bookkeeping and dealing with figures that never left him. In about 1927, Norman brought to Canada from Uman his mother, father, brother and three sisters, probably with some financial assistance from my parents and Tom, and installed them in a rented house on Borden Street in Toronto. He progressed from peddler to retailer, later to dealer in grocery products in bulk, and ultimately to buildercontractor.

No one, not even Norman Oster, displaced my brother Tom as the idol of our family. One day my mother asked me to do a special service as a favour to her. Since it affected Tom, I was bound to comply. It happened on a Friday before the commencement of the Sabbath. "Davelle," she said. She always addressed me with this endearing diminutive when she wanted to wheedle me into doing something she felt I might be disinclined to do. "Davelle," she said in her most coaxing manner, "poor Tommy has been alone in his store all day with nothing in his mouth to eat. He must be starving. I have made him a good dinner. Here is money for the streetcar. Please, Davelle, take the dinner to poor Tommy. It will be a mitzvah (an act of mercy; a blessing)." As she spoke she produced a full course Sabbath dinner — soup, kneidlich, chicken, potatoes, strudel, dishes, silverware. So, what could I do? I took up the parcel and set off on my journey. As the streetcar approached Runnymede Road and I rose to my feet, suddenly the whole dinner slipped through the soupmoistened newspaper and crashed to the floor of the car. Dumbfounded, I stared in shocked disbelief at the mess on the floor and the amused expression on the faces of the other passengers. Then I fled, leaving behind the soup, the kneidlich, chicken, potatoes, strudel, the broken dishes and silverware, and I ran all the way home. Poor Tommy; he had to forgo his Sabbath dinner! But this was one of the most embarrassing experiences of my life.

I was about ten years old when the peace and tranquillity of our household was shattered by The Great Matrimonial Dispute of 1925. My father announced that he was giving up his shoe store and taking the family back to live in Oak Ridges. My mother was outraged. She treated this pronouncement as equivalent to an act of war. She flatly refused to move to the country. She rallied her children round her and prepared to give battle on this issue. For sheer obstinacy and stubbornness, only her husband, who was adamant, outmatched her. She stormed, ranted, raved, pleaded, and shed bitter tears. Nothing availed her. Finally, she summoned her favourite son to her cause. Her eldest, Tom, the light of her life dutifully attended upon her and listened attentively to all her arguments, "Where can we find a good Jewish boy in the country for Laura, who is of marriageable age? What about the bar mitzvah for Morris and Davey? And you, poor Tommy, who will look after you and cook your meals in the city? And Norman too? And how can I keep a kosher house in a gentile community in the country? And the family has grown used to the life and comforts of the city. And why should we give up all our friends for a dull life in the country?" All these arguments, and more, she emphasized by a variety of emotional outbursts. Tom listened in silence. He assumed the function of arbitrator. At length, he delivered his verdict, which my mother felt bound to accept as an irreversible judgement. She must submit. Sadly, with the help of her children, she packed her belongings — the oval photographs of her revered parents, the samovar, the candlesticks, and her karzihnka with the downfilled blankets and cushions — and we moved back to the same store and house we had left only a few years earlier. An armistice, followed by an uneasy peace, settled over her relations with her husband, my father, who again undertook the operation of the business of a general store at this location in Oak Ridges.

Three
Growing Up at Oak Ridges and Lake Wilcox

Nothing seemed to have changed in Oak Ridges except, to my astonishment, I found that a second storey had been added to the oneroom school. One half of the grades were now accommodated on the first floor and one half on the second floor. I joined the older children on the second floor in a row of seats and desks reserved for the students in the grade then known as senior second. Separate rows of seats were also assigned to junior third, senior third, and junior fourth, and a final row by the windows served the few students who survived to senior fourth, the equivalent of the present eighth grade. My brother Morris was two classes ahead of me in senior third. My little sister Mary was assigned to the ground floor with the younger children. A teacher was in charge of each floor and taught all of the classes on that floor. Mary's teacher was Miss Malloy, a pretty young woman of whom I formed a very favourable impression. However, more important to me was Miss Spencer, who was my teacher for several years and to whom I am greatly indebted.

Miss Spencer came to exert a considerable influence over me and was my favourite teacher of all time. She was no doubt oldfashioned in her teaching methods. Perhaps she did not teach by rote but she certainly believed in learning by drill. That is how she taught the basic subjects of reading, writing, spelling and arithmetic, and other subjects such as history. We learned, for instance, the "times" tables, and it never seemed to occur to any of us to ask why six times nine was fiftyfour. She was also a dedicated teacher who was intensely involved in the improvement of the children under her charge. She must have sensed some potential in me that might be developed or a latent ability that might bring honour to her class and school. Thus, I was given a solo in the Christmas play. I was also assigned the responsibility of representing our school in a public speaking contest with students of other schools of our general area. I chose as my subject "Winter Sports in Canada." I wrote the speech myself; then I had to commit the speech to memory. Miss Spencer was nothing, if not a perfectionist. The nominee of her choice had to be perfect. Every morning, as a first priority, all grades were required to fold hands on desktop and act as audience while I recited my speech. By the time of the contest, I had quite mastered the content and even the delivery. I could have given the speech backwards. It was no doubt greatly to the credit of Miss Spencer, but rather little to my credit, that I won the contest!

When I finally reached Junior fourth, I was seated, of course, in the row immediately adjoining the senior fourth students. I could hardly avoid listening to Miss Spencer when she was teaching senior fourth grade. Gradually she began to include me in the instruction for this grade as well as the work for junior fourth. In this manner, almost incidentally, I undertook the studies for both grades in a single year and, ultimately, went along with Miss Spencer and the few senior fourth students to the Town of Aurora to write the Departmental examinations for admission to high school, a requirement of those times.

Although I was apparently making satisfactory progress intellectually, I cannot claim as much respecting development of a moral character. Thus, for instance, there was an episode at about this period when I feloniously acquired a plug of chewing tobacco to determine why it was such a favourite of the farmers. I took it by stealth from a shelf in my father's general store located not far from the spittoons that were available for the convenience of the customers. I chewed the tobacco and confess that I became violently ill and never chewed tobacco again. Even more blameworthy is an altercation I had with my father's Model T Ford, which seemed to exude an irresistible attraction. One day I even made an attempt to start the motor by operating the iron crank that had to be engaged in an opening near the radiator and given a strong pull in a clockwise direction. The problem was, however, that when I pulled with all my strength in a clockwise direction the mechanism suddenly pulled the crank violently in a counterclockwise direction striking me a blow to my right forearm that set me howling with pain for several minutes. Necessarily, I ceased trying to start the car.

I was far too apprehensive of my parent's reaction to this misbehaviour to disclose the incident to them. It was only two or three weeks later that my mother noticed that I appeared to be dragging my right arm and favouring my left. There was no use trying to conceal that I had a physical problem and the cause of it. I was dispatched to the doctor and then to the hospital in Aurora for x-rays, where it was determined that I had sustained a fracture in two places. These fractures had begun to knit and had be reset. This is how it came about that when Miss Spencer took me to Aurora with the other students to try the departmental exams, I wrote the exams with my right arm in a cast. It did not seem to adversely affect my ability to write the tests because I passed. What has always lingered in my recollection, however, is not this success, but rather the kindness of Miss Spencer who, after we had finished writing the exams, took all her matriculants to the ice cream parlour in Aurora and treated them to a sundae or soda of their choice. Miss Spencer was a fine, dedicated teacher. She gave me a gift of inestimable value. She imbued in me a sense of motivation and ambition. While I can not claim that these notions have invariably governed my conduct, they have in general been of use to me. After leaving public school, I never saw Miss Spencer again, but much later in life, years after her retirement, I was given her number by Jack Blyth, a younger schoolmate. I called her on the telephone. She said, "Dave who?" And I told her. She said, "How is your brother Morris?"

It did not take long for me to adjust again to life in the country. Our immediate neighbours were the Malloys who lived in the once popular hotel and coaching station across the road from us, the Carlisles who occupied a cottage on the opposite side of Lake Wilcox Road at a distance of about one hundred yards, and the Murphys who dwelt in the first house to the rear of our premises, just beyond a creek that drained into Lake Wilcox and the single track railway that led to the Ice House. I became a best friend with Billie Carlisle, now plain Bill to me, and John Murphy. I tolerated Bill's sisters, the Malloy girls of varying ages, and John's much older sisters. Bill was the acknowledged leader of the children of my age in the community and John was well established as a long time resident. With two such sponsors, I became well accepted and perfectly comfortable among my peers. My good relations were only marred once in each year when, at Easter, the local clergyman was accustomed to visit our school and show slides of the crucifixion of Christ. Then it would occur to my erstwhile comrades that I was a Jew and hence somehow responsible for what happened to Jesus centuries ago. I was called upon to answer to a variety of unsavoury epithets. In the climate created by this visit, it seems to me now, I became obliged to fight every youngster in my class, including my closest friends. However, this unfortunate interlude would soon pass and good relations would resume with only marginal ill effects. Through close association, I was generally on friendly terms with my classmates, became well integrated into a peer group, and was one of the gang.

I am reminded of an incident many years after the move to Toronto. I had become a professional man and was walking along Yonge Street in downtown Toronto carrying my briefcase. I came upon Jim Woods, an old friend from Oak Ridges, whom I had not seen in years. After we exchanged greetings, Jim asked: "Say, Dave, do you remember your big fight with the tall chap we met at the old railway station in Oak Ridges?" Of course I remembered and we reminisced about the affair. It was in the summer of my thirteenth or fourteenth year that I came to the Highway from Lake Wilcox and was chatting with Jim in front of the frame structure that formerly served passengers changing trains to travel to the town of Schomberg. A tall, gangling youth approached me and, without any preliminaries whatsoever, stated: "I'm ready to fight now." I could not understand why he was picking upon me for a demonstration of fisticuffs, but the moment did not appear opportune for polite discussion. As Falstaff might have observed, "Honour pricked me on." So I put up my fists and we fought. We fought to a standstill and until all honour on both sides had been vindicated. Jim assured me the contest was a draw. Only later did I learn that a short year or two previously, this lanky youth had been a small boy that my gang had bullied or tormented. Apparently he had complained to his father, whose response was to purchase boxing gloves and give him lessons in the manly art. Nature had helped as well by assisting in his rapid growth and the result was this altercation with me. I kept pondering the event: "Why Me?" Apparently I had become so integrated with my peer group that this chap regarded me as a prime participant upon whom he sought revenge concerning a matter about which I had no recollection whatever.

If I had been sickly during my sojourn in the city, as my mother apparently thought, my general acceptance in this rural community, good relations with my peers, and the fresh air, sunshine and open fields of the country restored me to good health, bursting with vigour and high spirits. Adjustment among peers produced a nickname. It was assigned and acquired intuitively without any deliberative act on the part of anyone, as far as I can determine, and adopted by common consent of my peers.

The derivation of nicknames could be the subject of a very interesting study. I believe they generally owe their origin to excessive endearments of fond and indulgent parents, or some physical abnormality or lack of it, or a mental quirk. In the first category, I have known several "Sonny"s. I remember one Sonny whom I came upon one day, years after full maturity; indeed, he had not only become a doctor but also a well-reputed paediatrician. Of course, I addressed him as "Sonny" as usual. To this, finally, he exploded, "For heaven sakes, how long am I to be Sonny? Long ago I have outgrown it. My name is ....," His voice was rising. "..Sydney!" He was right. Never again did I call him Sonny. But compare Curly Posen, who falls within category number two. He became "Curly" because of a complete lack of hair except for a bare fringe of curly hair at the side of his head. Curly is now far beyond his middle years and he is still addressed as "Curly" by everyone. I have never known him by any other name.

My nickname also comes within the second category. I attribute it to my somewhat diminutive stature at this stage of my existence. Accordingly, it was not uncommon in these days for Bill or John to appear outside a window of my dwelling and call up, "Hey Shrimp! C'mon out 'n play ball!" So to my boyhood friends and acquaintances in the Oak Ridges community, my name became "Shrimp" and "Shrimp" it remained for several years. I did not mind at all. I bore it as a badge of acceptance by my peers, and as an honour of distinction.

Whatever name by which I was called was really quite irrelevant. What was material was that I was enjoying life in the country; it was fun and games. In the summer, we played baseball in an open field on the opposite side of the road from our premises on Yonge Street, as well as a variety of games known to the children of those times. Nothing was structured or taught; we played according to our natural abilities. In the warm weather, of course, there was swimming at Lake Wilcox. In the winter, the countryside was generally covered with a blanket of white, crunchy snow, often to a considerable depth. Despite the advent of the automobile, much of the wintertime transportation in the area was still by sleigh or cutter drawn by a horse. What a delight it was to run after a sleigh, jump on the runner, and allow oneself to be pulled for miles through the snow! There was skating and hockey on natural ice wherever found: on ponds, creeks, or the frozen water of Lake Wilcox. The lake would freeze to a substantial depth, sufficient to justify the cutting and storage of ice for commercial purposes, and solid enough to permit its use for exhilarating recreational activities. In the early spring, there was an element of risk that added a degree of excitement to our skating. On one occasion, when skating on the creek near our house, I fell through the ice and was lucky to be pulled out, wet and shivering with the cold. In the fall, we could look forward to Halloween when quite adult persons suddenly transformed themselves once again into youths engaged in harmless sport. They would leave no outhouse unturned and I would be running after the gang and participating in the fun.

There were certain activities that I only tried once. I have already alluded to the chewing of tobacco and the cranking of the Ford. Farming, riding and caddying may be added to the list. My father once responded to my yen for farming on a day in autumn by taking me to a farm where I was put to work with a fork to pitch hay. Ultimately, I got to the top of a hayloft and was hard at work pitching hay when I slipped and fell off the loft. It was a considerable distance to the ground and I fell with a thud. I waited for my father to pick me up and never went farming again. As for the riding, there was an occasion in the summer when my cousin from Buffalo was paying us a visit. This was a reciprocal arrangement for I would sometimes visit him in Buffalo where I would be put to work at the fruit stand operated by his parents at the Polish fruit market. Somehow we managed to obtain the use of two full-grown horses, which we took for a ride to Lake Wilcox. Unfortunately, there were no saddles and we rode the horses bareback. Afterwards, we had difficulty dismounting and walking and, speaking for myself, I never rode a horse again. The caddying was another affair that ended disastrously. I went to the Summit Golf and Country Club to offer my services as a caddy and sat on a long bench with a number of other volunteers. The members came and, one by one, pointed to my left and to my right, "I'll take this one; I'll take that one," but never me. At last I was alone on the bench. No doubt I was the smallest of the boys, but I was disconsolate; sadly, I left and never returned.

I had much better success selling newspapers. Actually, I was a substitute for my brother Morris, who was the regular newspaper boy. Morris was twelve years old and now was being dispatched to Toronto on weekends to study for his impending bar mitzvah. I took his place at the Schomberg Junction station where all the action took place. I used to come home with much more money than the sales warranted and the family would jointly roll with laughter when they realized that I was deficient in giving proper change and that whatever the patrons tendered, I accepted as my due. Even this occupation was not without misadventure; once, I boarded a train and was so busy selling newspapers that I failed to notice that the train was in motion. What was I to do as the train gathered speed? Schomberg seemed to me to be a long distance away from home. So I jumped — and twisted my leg in the fall.

One day there was huge excitement among the gathered members of my family. A huge box had arrived by the radial train and was standing on the freight platform at the train stop opposite our premises. It was a piano! Somehow the huge parcel was brought into our house and unpacked. The piano was placed in a location in our living room near the pictures of my mother's revered parents, most appropriate to show it to best advantage. It was then decided that my sister Mary should be given lessons on the piano and arrangements were made with a piano teacher who was an elderly spinster of perhaps forty-five years. Unfortunately, Miss Morton lived about half way to Richmond Hill. Since Mary was just a little girl, she needed someone to accompany her on these lessons for protection and I was chosen. On this mission, Mary and I would travel along Yonge Street by the radial train. At first I sat and watched as the lessons proceeded. Then my parents accepted the obvious; I might as well receive lessons too. This is how I began to acquire an interest in the piano and in music generally. However, the lessons were a problem in that they interfered with baseball, and my friends could not accept my explanation that I had to practise. In the result, I became an indifferent pianist.

At about this time, the members of our family were somewhat

dispersed in various activities and occupations. My brother Tom and cousin Norman were in Toronto. Tom, of course, was operating the store at Runnymede and St. Clair in an everexpanding business that grew from candies and stationary to tobacco and cigarettes, phonographs and records and, ultimately, to almost anything that would turn a profit. Tom also occupied the living quarters over the store. My sister Faye was on loan to look after "poor Tommy"; that is, to do the cooking and housekeeping and also to help in the store. Laura substituted on occasion. My brother Abe was attending high school in Richmond Hill. On weekends, everyone came home, often bringing friends. Through Tom, we had acquired a phonograph and on each visit he would bring some of the latest records: Caruso, Chaliapin, various light classics, Al Jolson, Eddie Cantor, and many other popular pieces. The family was reunited; these were the best of times!

In about 1927, this idyllic existence came to an end and an entirely new chapter in my life commenced due to the coalescence of a number of different factors. First, I matriculated from public school and entered high school in Richmond Hill. This coincided with a decision of my parents to send me to Toronto on weekends in order for me take the religious training leading to my bar mitzvah. Then, for no reason anyone in our family has been able to comprehend, my father suddenly purchased, for a small down payment, a substantial lakeshore property in a strategic location at Lake Wilcox. This investment in an unproductive property, while characteristic, appeared to be quite lacking in practicality in the circumstances because, as we discovered later, our business of a general store in Oak Ridges had badly degenerated and, at the time, my father was headed for still another bankruptcy.

The year 1927 should have been a year of considerable educational and moral development. Unfortunately, circumstances seemed to contrive a different result, mainly because of two factors: my distance from high school and my freedom in Toronto.

My high school in Richmond Hill was located about five miles from home. I had to travel by the radial car, which passed our premises daily just before eight o'clock in the morning. This was just too early for me. Ever a late riser, I generally found it impossible to meet the train on time. Tardiness in the morning was an affliction that haunted me all the days of my schooling and a defect that I had to combat even in later life. Occasionally, even if I was ready in due time, I would deliberately allow the train to pass and rely on picking up a ride by car. Of course, hitchhiking was an unreliable means of keeping any fixed appointment. So, chronically, I would be late for the first class, pass the rest of the first period alone in the gymnasium practising with the basketball, and then present myself for the next period with a second teacher as if nothing untoward had happened. Thus it came about that I passed what we called first form with misleading ease, second form with rather more difficulty, and third form, almost not at all.

What should have been a time of great moral enlightenment, sad to say, turned out to be a period of ethical backsliding; if not actual degeneration. It was now my turn to receive the usual religious training that would equip me on my thirteenth birthday to lead a congregation in prayer, chant a portion of text in Hebrew from the Torah and another portion from the Haftorah, and hence to be accepted as a responsible adult member of the Jewish community. For this purpose, I was dispatched on weekends to Toronto for lessons with my teacher on Maria Street. We used to call him "Napoleon," because of his rigorous discipline. On Fridays, with high hopes for my spiritual advancement, my mother would provide me with a substantial sum of money, for carfare, lunch, allowance, and perhaps something extra for contingencies. It was intended that I spend the weekend in the apartment above the store under the supervision of Tom or one or other of my older sisters. Thus provided, after school I would take the radial car to Toronto, and then the streetcars to the West Toronto Junction and my brother Tom's store. However, my first priority was to protect my wealth. A favourite method was to avoid paying the fare on the train not by deceit, according to my view, but on the theory that it was the obligation of the conductor to ask for the fare, and if he did not demand, there was no obligation to deliver. Accordingly, I would take a seat at a window, hopefully with another person alongside so that, small as I was, I might virtually sink from view. As the conductor passed by, making a general call "tickets please," I would be looking out the window in contemplation of the landscape. Usually, I managed to reach Toronto with my financial resources intact.

Once arrived at Tom's store and apartment, I found Tom far too busy, and my sisters too soft and pliable, to provide meaningful supervision. Here I was — a twelve-year-old boy in the Big City. I was not lacking for food and accommodation, or for candy and other treats, all of which were available at the store or apartment above. I was footloose and fancy-free. My only substantial obligation was to attend upon Napoleon on Saturday for a oneonone session of bar mitzvah training. I managed to arrange this for about 12:00 noon on Napoleon's day of rest, just when I expected he would be hungering for his lunch. As a result, the lesson would usually occupy an abbreviated hour. Then I would be free for the day to cavort with former friends in the Junction or, on my own, partake of the agreeable amenities to be found in the area, such as the movies. On Saturday, for five cents plus one cent tax, I had the choice of attending a matinee performance at the Crescent Palace or the Wonderland or, for vaudeville as well as films, the Crystal Theatre. For eleven cents, even the more prestigious Beaver Theatre was available.

It was even possible to gain admission at night if an adult could be induced to buy a ticket for me! Since I was not invariably loaded with money, I would be forced to make a difficult decision: a ticket to the movies or settle for a cream puff. At the Wonderland, it was an excruciating exercise to decide whether to sit through a second showing of the feature film or take up the management's offer of a free bag of popcorn if you left the theatre after the first performance.

I spent many delightful weekends in riotous living in Toronto. This period of moral decline finally passed because the great day finally dawned to mark my thirteenth birthday. On that day, my father, in effect, took me by the hand and together we travelled to the Zionist Building on Beverly Street. A congregation had gathered there for the Sabbath services. In due course, I was summoned to the open scroll of the Torah. My preceding days of depravity apparently came to an end and I felt myself drawn back from the abyss. I chanted my pieces in a good strong soprano voice, with accuracy and perfect diction, to the satisfaction of the assembly and, particularly, my proud and beaming parent. Indeed, I made a most favourable impression for competency, learning and probity. Finally, I was presented with a fountain pen and a book. My father and I returned to our home in the country, where I expected life to continue on the same even course as before the bar mitzvah lessons in Toronto.

I believe Heracleitus once remarked, "All is flux, nothing is stationary. You can never step into the same river twice; all is change." This was a time of dramatic change for my family. The course of our lives was profoundly altered in two ways. First, in 1928, my father suddenly purchased a property at Lake Wilcox then called "Cedarholm." Second, my father's business in Oak Ridges failed; this occurred just prior to the crash of the stock market in 1929 that ushered in the Great Depression of the Thirties.

We took possession of the property in the late fall. Thereafter, I lived in two different worlds: in the summer, the fantasy world of a summer resort; in the winter, the real world of Oak Ridges and Toronto. Cedarholm was composed of a parcel of land fronting on the lake and intersected by a road that followed the shoreline, a parcel of land on which stood an old farmhouse and an apple orchard. When I first encountered the property, the trees were loaded with apples and the grass had grown long, dry and wild. My father was heavily involved at the store, so it was left to my mother to attend to these matters. Accordingly, she marshalled her forces, composed of all available children, and, under her supervision, operation "cleanup" began. We spent most of the day up in the trees picking, and eating, apples — large, ripe, juicy MacIntosh reds — that we accumulated in barrels. Then came the task of disposing of the grass that had grown to weed. My mother put us to work on this project by the simple method of burning the grass. As a precaution, we drew water in pails from a pump located near the farmhouse. The burning proceeded satisfactorily, controlled by occasional dampening by water, until the fire reached the vicinity of a wooden shack full of hay. Suddenly the flames shot toward this hut. In the flash of an eye, there was a huge conflagration. It was a sensational fire that the children rather enjoyed. Not my mother! Wildly excited, shrieking and shouting directions, she kept running back and forth from pump to blaze in a futile effort to extinguish the fire. To no avail, the shack and its contents burned to the ground. Later we discovered, much to the astonishment of everyone, that the shack was well insured. This quite assuaged my mother's concerns and my mother's project, which seemed headed for disaster, resulted in a tidy profit.

The apples were delicious but, as it happened, worth little money. Unfortunately, there had been a bumper crop that year and apples were said to be a glut on the market. On a crisp day in early winter, my father obtained the use of a horse and wagon, and he and I took the apples to a cider press, where they were converted into apple cider. I drank cider pumped fresh and cold into a cup from the press. We brought home two or three barrels of cider that we stored in our cellar. It did not take long for the cider to ferment and acquire strength in alcohol that made it inappropriate for the children but an occasional treat for the neighbours.

Shortly after these events, workmen invaded the property at Lake Wilcox, erecting a number of structures on the land. They built a refreshment stand or booth, fronting on the lakeside of the road. It was attached to a sizeable pavilion for dancing and related activities. They improved the beach somewhat and constructed a wharf and boathouse. On the opposite side of the road, they erected several frame buildings, divided into bedrooms. Somewhat later, we extended the farmhouse by attaching a spacious dining hall to it. Thus, the property was converted into a summer resort that we called "Cedarholm Park." It was intended to serve the Jewish population of Toronto and other urban centres seeking a summer holiday in the country, nearby a small springfed lake about thirty-five miles from the heart of Toronto.

My father was still enmeshed in affairs at Oak Ridges. Accordingly, the daily management of the summer resort fell by default to my mother. My mother operated this new business, of course, with the assistance of her children, but under the guidance of her eldest son. My big brother Tom arranged for a number of cottages to be built on part of the land and rented them to vacationers for the duration of the summer. Otherwise, he made his contribution toward the management of the summer resort on weekends. It was my mother who booked and catered to the paying guests. It was she who hired and fired the cooks. When cooks were fired, which periodically occurred, it was she who personally did the cooking and the baking, complaining bitterly all the while. She was in charge and worked hard.

The work that I performed at Lake Wilcox was actually a pleasure. On weekends, I assisted other members of the family in parking the visitors' cars, a service for which we charged a substantial fee. During the week, life was very much relaxed. Occasionally, I was left in charge of the refreshment booth. This was like leaving the fox in charge of the hen house. I was always able to relieve periods of monotony by playing records on a phonograph from a full stock of records supplied courtesy of Brother Tom. From constant practice, I acquired the ability to perform an excellent imitation of Al Jolson singing "Mammy" and other wellknown songs associated with him. My voice could often be heard in a duet with the recorded voice of Jolson as together we sang,

"I'd walk a million miles for one of your smiles." At other times I would be in charge of the boathouse and beach, in which case I would have free use of the boats for my own pleasure.

Generally, however, without any particular duties or cares, I was free to associate with the rich kids from Toronto. This I did on at least a level of equality, and perhaps even a notch higher, because I was considered to be part of the management. Our favourite sport was baseball, which we played on a rough diamond at a far corner of the property. For added excitement, we would challenge, or receive a challenge from, a team from the "other place" — residents of a much older colony of summer cottages in the vicinity of the original public bathing beach at Lake Wilcox. Sadly, according to the times, Jews were not welcome at this beach, to say the least. In consequence, these games were played in an atmosphere of considerable rivalry, tension and excitement. I believe it was fortunate that we usually lost the game because we were generally heavily outnumbered, not just by the pool from which the players were drawn, but the spectators in attendance for each side. When occasionally we won, the victory was sweet. Thus, with baseball, swimming, boating and generally cavorting with cronies, I managed to pass the lazy days of summer.

One summer day, when we were living at Lake Wilcox my father's business finally succumbed to adversity. He had to surrender the store and premises at Oak Ridges. This turn of events came as a shock to me. I had been quite oblivious of any difficulty that he had in business. I discovered that my father had purchased a large truck and had embarked upon an entirely different business of selling sugar at wholesale to shopkeepers in the towns and hamlets scattered along the Yonge Street Highway and environs. No longer a young man, for he was then about fifty years of age, he was unaccustomed to heavy physical labour. Still, in his new employment, under the necessity of earning a livelihood, he would customarily drive the truck to the Terminal Warehouse at the waterfront in Toronto, pick up a load of sugar in one hundred-pound bags, then sell and deliver the sugar to an increasing list of customers. My heart would ache to observe him lift and carry these heavy bags of sugar. However, it did not take long for my father to heed his own limitations, and employ a young, strong man to assist him in the heavy work.

My father was by no means handsome. At this time, he was of medium height, slightly stooped and yet surprisingly strong. He had a rather large head but only a thin crop of hair. His face was creased with wrinkles and disfigured by a prominent nose and a large mole. Finally, he tended to walk with feet turned outward so as to present somewhat of a likeness to Charlie Chaplin when in motion. I regret to concede that I have inherited some of these physical characteristics. I am afraid he suffered from various defects emotionally. By temperament and disposition, he tended to be inflexible, stubborn and obstinate. He was often shorttempered and quick to anger and tended also to be a hard taskmaster. Consequently, he found it difficult to keep employees and maintain good relations with people. Yet, he was an excellent salesman with a technique that was unique to him alone. He could importune, urge, woo, press, insist, demand and implore, all in the same interview. Often, after heated discussion leading a bystander to fear actual violence, the tense atmosphere would subside and he would leave the shop with an order for merchandise, and on the best of terms with the customer.

Regardless of his various defects of character, I was fond of my father. Despite all my own defects, I believe he was also fond of me — his youngest and only nativeborn son for whose success in life he entertained great hopes. He enjoyed a good sense of humour. He relished a good story and often could be found entertaining himself with humming a tune, usually a liturgical melody. At the end of the Passover dinners, he would lead the whole family in the singing of the traditional songs peculiar to this festival. My father could exercise considerable charm. He was an intelligent man, well versed in Hebrew, completely literate in Yiddish, which was his principal language, and in Russian, which he rarely used. However, in English, he could barely scratch out his signature and make a primitive record of his business transactions. His ability to communicate in English was limited; he spoke with a heavy accent and mispronounced many words. He would say, for instance, that something was "simspossible." I have already mentioned that, to him, "bananas" was properly to be pronounced "pananas." As a result, my poor father had great difficulty getting ahead in the New World. Still, for all his faults one had to admire him, at least for his fortitude, resilience and resourcefulness. Yet one grave fault that we, as members of his family, found hard to forgive, was that he tended to be impulsive, unrealistic and impractical in his decisions affecting his family. At times he was downright neglectful of his duty, as witness his delay in providing alternate accommodation for his family.

Four

Toronto "The Good"

"Do you remember, Davey, when your family lived in the unheated house on the Highway in Oak Ridges?"

My interrogator was Mima Sonya, my father's sister. She dwelt in St. Catharines, an urban centre about eighty miles from Toronto, all her days in Canada. She was then well over ninety years of age. Did I remember? How could I ever forget? The wonder is that she could remember because it was an insignificant event in her life. In those days, it was a long journey to Oak Ridges from St. Catharines and she visited infrequently. We only occupied those premises over one winter and partially into a second.

When my father was obliged to give up his general store in Oak Ridges because the business had failed, we had to vacate our dwelling that was contained within the same building as the store. The year was 1929, but nobody told me there had been a stock market crash and that we were now in a depression. Unfortunately, Pa failed to make timely arrangements for alternative residential accommodation for his family. So, as the glorious days of summer came to an end and all paying guests at our summer resort had departed, we continued to reside in the summer cottages at Lake Wilcox. Autumn arrived. Our summer residence became quite cold and uncomfortable, but still we remained. On the day after the Labour Day holiday, normally the first Monday in September, the schools re-opened. I was in second form at Richmond Hill High School. To attend classes I had to hike about a mile and quarter to Yonge Street to catch the radial car. It passed by at 8:00 a.m. and took me to Richmond Hill, a further five miles away. I had to arrive at school by 9:00 a.m. and, almost invariably, was late.

At last, in late fall, my father made temporary arrangements for his family in a frame cottage, lightly covered with stucco, adjacent to the north of the Oak Ridges Public School. There was no basement, no furnace, and no heat, except for a wood-burning stove in the kitchen around which we constantly huddled for warmth. I believe Pa made an exchange with a Mr. Monkman, who took over our spacious and comfortable residence in exchange for this stuccoed icebox. Here we remained over the winter and into late fall of the next year. I was well into third form of high school, when relief finally came and the family moved to the big city, Toronto.

We took up residence in a house at 637 Shaw Street that featured a wide private driveway and a lot of substantial depth. It had a two-storey garage at the rear that was unique in the neighbourhood. My mother, still smarting from the discomfort of the cold winter in unsuitable quarters, claimed that Pa got his priorities mixed up; that he first sought out a garage and driveway and only afterwards looked for a house. Still, she was quite pleased with the house, which she considered acceptable, and was gratified, at last, to be living near Jewish people. The house was not too far from Kensington Avenue, a congested market of stores where she could shop for kosher foods. I found the house adequate as well, except as to the restraints imposed by a single bathroom, despite the advantages of indoor plumbing. By the custom of the household and the rule of seniority, as the youngest male child, I was last in line following my brother Morris in entitlement to the use of the bathroom. As a result, I was often late for school in Toronto, just as I had been at Richmond Hill.

Although my father discovered the house on Shaw Street, and no doubt negotiated the purchase, he did not buy the house himself. This he left to Tom, who was on the way to becoming the only affluent member of the family. Tom put up the $500 cash payment and, for the balance, assumed a mortgage. Due to a moratorium on repayment of principal, by way of legislated relief under a wartime statute, the mortgage obliged him to pay interest charges only, for a number of years. Tom was now thirty years of age. His business at the corner of Runnymede and St. Clair was thriving and expanding, despite the soot and dirt from the cleaning of trains in the roundhouse across the road and the stench from the abattoirs about a half-mile away at Keele Street.

Our family was temporarily re-united by the acquisition of the house. We all moved in, Tom included; Laura and Faye as well. Even cousin Norman moved in. Soon after, he married Faye and helped produce my first niece, June. Then Tom married Anna and took up residence elsewhere, thereby depriving me of the use of his expensive ties. Faye and Norman also created their own household and gave me my first nephew, Raymond, but deprived me of the services of my niece.

At a wild guess, I would estimate the population of the City of Toronto of the thirties at approximately 700,000, composed overwhelmingly of people of English or British stock. There were a considerable number of Italians and a sprinkling of people of other ethnic origins, including a Jewish community of perhaps 50,000 people. The main section of the Jewish community was an area west of Yonge Street. Its focal point was at the corner of College Street and Spadina Avenue. Yonge Street still divides the City into east and west sections and Spadina is located a few blocks west of Yonge. In the thirties, the main east-west thoroughfares, north from the waterfront and spaced at intervals of 1 1/4 miles were Front Street, King, Adelaide, Dundas, College, Bloor, and St. Clair. There the city ended, except for an extension further along Yonge Street to the city limits at Hogs Hollow, at the top of a deep ravine. Our dwelling on Shaw Street still stands and is located between College and Bloor Streets, on the fringes of the main area of Jewish population at that time.

In those years, Toronto was commonly referred to with some sarcasm as "Toronto the Good." That was because of an aura of virtuousness attributed to the city because of its "Blue Laws" and the solidity of its people with the British Empire. These were the years of laws enforcing temperance regarding the sale and consumption of intoxicating beverages; forbidding retail trade and sporting events on Sundays and legal holidays; and enforcing early closings. The Loyal True Blue Order of Orange Lodges annually marched in a grand parade in honour of William of Orange and the Battle of the Boyne. It was also an era throughout Canada of rampant anti-Semitism, more intensive, virulent, and pervasive in large congested urban centres, such as Toronto, than in less densely populated rural districts. Generally, Jews were excluded from employment in banks and large business corporations and were subject to quotas restricting entrance to universities in some courses, particularly in medical schools. As well, attempts were made to keep Jews from buying property in select areas, for example by restrictive covenants running with the land.

There were other less subtle and more express ways of demonstrating that Jews were not wanted. Kew Beach was an area in east-end Toronto increasingly frequented by poor Jews from the congested central core, seeking relief from the heat of summer, relaxation and a swim in the cool waters of Lake Ontario. Large signs began to appear there, bearing the legend "Gentiles Only." In the summer of 1933, the worst race riot in Canadian history occurred. It took place in and around a park in a saucer-like depression, known as "Christie Pitts," located on the north side of Bloor Street, a short walk from our house on Shaw Street. The episode was, in part, an outgrowth of a baseball rivalry between a home team composed of young men from working class English families of the area and a Jewish team from the playground of Harbord Collegiate. Winning or losing both brought forth epithets, racial slurs, and an occasional, more physical reaction. At the conclusion of one game, some Gentile spectators ran onto the field exhibiting a huge banner with a Nazi swastika. Extremely provoked, a Jewish contingent tried to seize and tear up this notorious emblem. Numerous fights broke out. The Jewish fellows sent cars to College and Spadina for reinforcements; the Gentiles countered with reinforcements of their own. The rioting went on all night, spilled over onto Bloor Street and continued into the next day. It was a black day for "Toronto the Good."

I was not unfamiliar with anti-Semitism and its manifestations. We also had a rivalry in baseball between Jewish vacationers at Cedarholm Park at Lake Wilcox and a Gentile team from a summer cottage community of longer vintage about a half mile along Lake Shore Road. Similar tensions and emotions accompanied the rivalry. At the Gentile beach, I recall seeing signs with the caption "Gentiles Only" and an even more opprobrious and insulting statement "Jews and dogs not welcome." Indeed, from my youngest days in Oak Ridges I was conscious of the distaste for Jews. I was subjected to racial and anti-Semitic epithets and the attitude of others towards my parents and siblings was apparent.

Since I had been so well adjusted to living amongst Gentiles in a rural area, it might have been expected that I would have no trouble at all getting along with my contemporaries in an urban Jewish setting. To the contrary, it took me a very long time to become acclimatized to the change. Upon moving to Toronto in mid-term, I was assigned to Harbord Collegiate Institute while my sister Mary was enrolled at Bloor Collegiate. Apparently 637 Shaw Street was located between the two school districts. Both schools were public schools. The overwhelming majority of students at Harbord Collegiate were drawn from the adjoining Jewish district. Only a sprinkling of Jewish students attended Bloor Collegiate, a school located well outside the Jewish area. Harbord Collegiate was a huge school, with a student population of at least a thousand persons, housed in an old building that was then undergoing extensive renovations. In contrast, Richmond Hill High was a modern, much smaller school with perhaps two hundred students. Mr. Glassey, the principal at Harbord, was a short, bald, bespectacled man. He was a strong disciplinarian who, despite his physical stature, was generally feared by the students. He had a discomfiting habit of suddenly appearing in the hallway behind an unsuspecting student who had attracted his displeasure, grabbing and shaking him, or delivering a stiff cuff to the ear. At Richmond Hill, the atmosphere was much more easy-going. We regarded Mr. Stewart, the principal, who often played basketball with the boys, as a friend, and we called him "Jimmy." Many of the students at Harbord seemed to have acquired the ways, mannerisms, and even the inflections of their immigrant parents. Some others appeared to be rough, wild, unruly, and not in awe of anyone, including Mr. Glassey. Nobody welcomed me to Harbord Collegiate and my classmates, and even the teachers, seemed oblivious of my presence. The students already had their coterie of friends, their teams and extra-curricular activities. I was dying to participate but received no invitations. In consequence, from being a happy-go-lucky extrovert — my mother sometimes called me *"gringe leiberlich"* that literally translates as "easy livers" — I was friendless and lonely and became rather shy and withdrawn. I so remained during all my days at Harbord Collegiate Institute.

It did not help that I failed or barely scraped through the Christmas examinations in every subject. However, most of my classmates fared not much better. The teachers had set a tough set of exams, no doubt as a wake-up call. I proceeded to apply myself more diligently to my studies and, ultimately, passed all the final examinations in the third, fourth and fifth forms with creditable marks, sufficient for admission to any course of my choosing at university. At the same time, I was astonished at how well my fellow students were performing. I discovered that many of them were by no means dull and ordinary, as I had been inclined to believe, but were bright, intelligent and, in some cases, even brilliant. In later life, for example, Wayman became a scientist, Weinzweig a composer, and Leibel a physician of repute.

Meanwhile, I was put to work in a completely different capacity. In his new business, my father urgently required a bookkeeping service to keep his day-to-day records. Accordingly, I received some lessons from Mr. Goldenberg, whom my father had hired as an accountant, and I became my father's bookkeeper. As such, after each day of business, it was my job to enter the sales into a sales ledger, tally the receipts by cash or cheque, make up the bank deposit, and, as time went on, make up the general ledger. Not only did my father entertain difficulty speaking and making himself understood in the English language, he had virtually no ability expressing himself in English in writing. He could barely scribble what passed for a likeness of his name. So, incidental to the bookkeeping, I had the task of deciphering his peculiar hieroglyphics and learning the correct names of all his customers. In due course I became familiar with all of them, many of whom still linger in my mind. They included Dempsey Bothers (Lansing), Scanlon Bakery (Aurora), Bruntons (Newmarket), Dave Pivnick (Sutton), L.A. Ostrander (Woodbridge), W.E. Cornish (Pinegrove), and, in Toronto, Fauman of the Orange Dandy Company and Joe Caplan. My father was a hard and difficult taskmaster, but it was his credo that everyone should work and those who worked should be paid for their labour; so, despite the chronic need for money to finance his business, I was paid a weekly stipend.

In the summertime, I took on an expanded role. In addition to the bookkeeping, which was a daily exercise, I would, on an occasional or regular basis, be sent out on the road with a truck to pick up and deliver a load of sugar. I recall an instance when my father made a special purchase of semi-granulated sugar that came in sacks of 160 lb. All alone, I loaded the sugar onto a truck at the Terminal Warehouse and then unloaded it in deliveries to customers along a specified route. I revelled in the physical exercise. I became robust, sinuous, tough and rather strong for my size. On occasion, I accompanied my father to the bank for his daily ordeal with Mr. Duck, the manager. My father carried on his business as though he was teetering on the edge of a volcano that could erupt at any time. He was on a cash basis with the refineries, relaxed only to the extent that they would accept his cheque each day for the purchases of that day. I would cringe in humiliation for Pa as he would squirm and plead with the manager, and exercise all his guile and not inconsiderable charm, to ensure the bank honoured each cheque upon which depended the continuation of supplies. An NSF cheque would have been fatal to the business. So, attending to my studies at school, working for my father as bookkeeper, with extended physical duties in the summer, and assisting at the lake on weekends, friendless or not, I was kept fully occupied until the time came for decision about attending university.

Five
College Days

In about September of 1931, at sixteen years of age, I presented myself at the Registrar's Office of the University of Toronto and applied for admission to the Honour Law course in Arts. I really do not know whether my parents individually or jointly made a conscious decision to allow their youngest son the benefit of a college education. It was simply assumed, I believe, that if I qualified and it was at all financially possible, I should be allowed to continue my education. Happily, a very well-reputed university was available in Toronto within walking distance from home. I could even travel, on occasion, by a streetcar that passed along Harbord Street and turned at Spadina quite near the campus. It was out of the question, of course, in our financial circumstances to even dream of attending a university away from home. As for Honour Law at Toronto, I virtually blundered into that course. It was an Honour Arts course, requiring four years of study for a Bachelor of Arts degree, in contrast to a Pass Arts course requiring only three years. Only gradually, moreover, did I come to a full appreciation that graduation from Honour Law did not automatically confer the privilege of engaging in the practice of law. In the Province of Ontario the legal profession was, and still is, officially governed and regulated by the Law Society of Upper Canada. It controlled the admission to the Bar and the right to practise law in Ontario.

The Benchers of the Law Society, in effect its board of directors, operated the official law school. The Osgoode Hall Law School was contained within an extension to Osgoode Hall. Osgoode Hall is one of Toronto's most ancient edifices, enclosed by a high wrought iron fence that, according to local legend, was built to keep out cows from its spacious grounds. Osgoode Hall contained the main offices and courtrooms of the Supreme Court of Ontario. The Osgoode Hall course in law required three years of attendance at lectures and concurrent service under articles with a legal practitioner. If I had taken a less demanding University course, I could have qualified in as little as five years. In the path I had selected, qualification for the Bar and the right to practise law in Ontario required seven years of post-secondary education.

Why did I choose law? One or other of a variety of factors possibly determined the decision. My parents, like other Jewish parents, opted for medicine or law. I had no inclination towards medicine; I used to say I could not stand the sight of blood. Lawyers, especially lawyer-politicians, heavily impressed my father. He would often speak with great admiration of Colonel T. Herbert Lennox, his favoured federal election candidate in our former riding of North York. He also strongly approved of the young Norman Borins of the Borinsky family, centred in nearby Stouffville, who campaigned for other candidates and became the first Jewish Crown Attorney in Ontario. I fear I let down my poor father for I never became a celebrated politician. However, I took the seven years of study and was ultimately called to the Bar of Ontario in 1939 just as World War II was breaking out in Europe.

I never regretted taking Honour Law at the University even though, inevitably, there was some duplication with subjects I had to take at Osgoode Hall Law School. The curriculum at Honour Law was designed primarily to provide an academic and intellectual background to future lawyers. The Osgoode course was supposed to serve the practical purpose of training students for the actual practice of law as a profession. The University course was therefore much more theoretical in approach. In addition to basic legal subjects taught at Osgoode, such as contracts and torts, Honour Law included classes in jurisprudence, Roman and civil law, public international law, and subjects in newly developing areas, such as administrative law and labour law. Furthermore, Honour Law provided tuition in a number of non-legal subjects: philosophy, psychology, history religious knowledge, and economics. These non-legal subjects were brought into the Honour Law Course in co-operation with the Arts Colleges affiliated with the University. I well remember, for instance, second year philosophy with Professor Anderson. He was a huge man who carried into class a small red book, entitled Plato's Republic, for our first lecture. We studied that book for an entire academic year. I also have a vivid memory of Professor Taylor, who dealt with the life of Jesus Christ from a purely historical perspective.

There were four Arts Colleges: Trinity, an Anglican College; Victoria, a United Church College, St. Michaels, a Catholic College; and University College, an inter-denominational institution. Of course I registered at University College. It is still the most architecturally impressive edifice of the buildings of the University of Toronto and commands the best location on the campus. Immediately adjacent to it stands Hart House, the building most used by the student body of the University. Hart House offered to all students of the University meeting places, dining halls and lunchrooms, and an extensive variety of athletic and recreational facilities. The Massey family built it in honour of Hart Massey who was killed in World War I. The best-known members of the Massey family are Vincent, the family diplomat, and Raymond, the actor.

The Law Department occupied an ancient three-storey house on St. George Street, then the western perimeter of the University campus. It was in this building that I spent most of my time. There were approximately twenty to twenty-five students in my first year class. This resulted in more opportunity for individual attention and a closer association with staff than in larger classes. The teaching staff was also very small in number, composed of merely four full-time professors. The Dean of the Law Department was Dr. W.P.M. Kennedy. Clyde Auld, an Oxford graduate, taught jurisprudence and Roman and civil law. Norman Mackenzie taught public international law. The youngest member of the faculty was Jacob Finkelman, himself a recent graduate from the University. In addition to teaching basic subjects, he developed the course in administrative law. Later, he drafted the first labour code.

The pre-eminent personality and guiding spirit of the University course in law was Dean William Paul McClure Kennedy, although he himself was not even a lawyer. Essentially, Kennedy was an historian. He was an expatriate Irishman and graduate of Trinity College, Dublin, where he earned a doctorate. He never quite lost his brogue and, with a rather high pitched voice, his speech had a lilt that was pleasing to the ear. Both his speech and written works were precise, grammatically correct, clear and impressive. He was masterful in the invention and application of unusual and graphically descriptive expressions that caught the imagination and lingered in memory. Physically, he was about five feet eight inches in height, bald, and had an ascetic appearance, prominent nose, and thin, wiry build. He leaned toward wool tweed suits and bow ties. His personality was charismatic. He was eccentric in various respects, whether by nature or design. His students, who greatly admired him and enjoyed his eccentricities, considered him to be a "character." I once heard him describe himself in his later days as the "last remaining character" at the University. He used to deliver a well-attended lecture on the difference between the obscene and the beautiful. In small classes held in his office, he had the habit of lying on his back and lecturing from a reclining position. Kennedy was the author of several books, the most notable of which was a work on the Constitution of Canada. He lectured mainly on the history of English law and constitutional law and would let his students know that Ministers of the Crown often consulted him on constitutional issues. He was an inspirational teacher.

It did not take long for me to adjust to the daily routine of university life: travel to and from the University, attendance at lectures and seminars, and study at the University library. In my first year at the University, while I fraternized on equal terms with my classmates, I nevertheless felt unaccepted, friendless and lonely, all of which exacerbated my shyness. Three Jewish students in my class, outgoing and popular, came from out-of-town. They lived in residence and were able to socialize in the residence, a socialization from which I, as a Torontonian, was effectively excluded. My gentile classmates were good companions during incidental contacts at school, but otherwise extended no association on a social basis. The social side of College life was substantially governed and left to international fraternities and sororities, notoriously selective and restrictive as to membership. I was left out.

In common with other students of the University, I made use of the facilities of Hart House. Full course meals were available in the

Great Hall. The price was right. For twenty cents, one could sit down to a reasonable luncheon and, for only thirty-five cents, a quite superior repast. However, I normally brought my lunch that I consumed in a lunchroom or while witnessing a game of billiards. I took relatively little advantage of the athletic facilities. Certain extra-curricular activities were organized and conducted by students of the Arts Colleges or on a University basis with committees centred in Hart House. I regret that I participated very little in these programs in my first year at the University. I nearly failed to continue law for a second, third and fourth year.

In late summer or early fall I received an unprecedented phone call from Professor Finkelman. He wanted to know why I had not yet paid the fees to allow for my continuation into the second year of the law course:

"You won the Carswell Prize for the best paper on English constitutional law, Dean Kennedy's favourite subject, but you can't pick up the prize until the tuition fees have been paid."

This information created a great stir in the Vanek household. Where do we find the money? It was my brother Morris, now engaged in the sugar business with my father, who became my benefactor; he surrendered to my use what amounted to his entire savings of about $100.00 so I could pay the fees. In this selfless act, Morris earned my eternal gratitude. On my part, I earned the goodwill of Dean Kennedy but the prize itself, however, was disappointing: I was given two huge volumes of law published by the Carswell Book Publishing Company, but no money.

My second year at the University continued in much the same vein as the first, until a dramatic event occurred that led to a profound change in my mental and emotional well being. I was invited to join a fraternity. It was not a prestigious gentile fraternity, nor even one of the well established three Jewish fraternities, two of which were general fraternities and the third, a medical fraternity. I was approached by Abby Muter, someone I had not previously met. He was the chancellor (president, leader) of a Jewish fraternity very recently established in Toronto. It was part of an international fraternity known in customary fashion under Greek letters as Beta

Sigma Rho or BSR. The small membership included some acquaintances of my former days in the West Toronto Junction. Jack Culiner and Sidney Lipman lived in apartments above clothing shops on Dundas Street. Gilbert Seltzer lived on Laws Street in a more affluent area near High Park. I was delighted. I pledged to BSR and, after a short period of probation, initiation and just good fun, I was taken into membership. In the process I met fellow members Harry Bowman, Milton Shulman, Bill Shub, Sam Speigel and Iz King. Later, we added Saul Wolfe to the list. We all became lifelong friends. In succeeding years, we attracted a number of new members. Amongst ourselves, we were known as "fellows," either the "older fellows" or "younger fellows."

About a year or two after I joined, the fraternity acquired two new members who came to the University from Harbord Collegiate, Lou Weingarten and Frank Shuster. They were already known as actors who had established a reputation as a comedy team. After I became a lawyer, I had the privilege of changing Lou Weingarten's name under the Ontario Change of Name Act, to John Wayne, thereby creating the comedy team of Wayne and Shuster. That, however, was the only professional work I ever did for either of them. I was always somewhat ambivalent about Lou Weingarten's new name; I would sometimes call him Lou or Weingarten, but could never bring myself to address him directly as Johnnie or Wayne. "The boys," as we fraternity brothers referred to Wayne and Shuster, became immensely popular as the top comedy team in Canada, with a considerable following as well in the United States. For many years they starred in their own show, coast to coast for the Canadian Broadcasting Corporation. First they performed on radio and then, on television in Canada and on the Ed Sullivan Show in the United States.

Many others of my brethren enjoyed illustrious careers. We used to laugh about Morton Applebaum. He appeared somewhat socially unpolished, but was an excellent basketball player. In a sudden change, he majored in Hebrew and religious studies, went down to the United States for post-graduate studies, became a rabbi and, in our version, married a string of gasoline stations. Harry Bowman became a physician. Unfortunately, he could not obtain an internship in Canada and we lost him, as well, to the United States. Gilbert Seltzer graduated in architecture and also located in the United States. Lou Applebaum became a composer, gained prominence as well in public organizations related to the arts, and was recently awarded membership in the Order of Canada. Bill Shub practised law in the northern town of Timmins. Later in his career, he was given a quasi-judicial appointment as a member of a powerful governmental agency known as the Ontario Municipal Board, a Board on which he ultimately served as chairman.

Sam Speigel qualified as a chartered accountant. He used to be a frequent visitor at my home. I thought that, as my good friend, he was there to see me, but I was quite wrong. He actually was courting my young sister, Mary. They married and he took her off to Sudbury, another northern town, where he built up a considerable practice and became a fellow of the Institute of Chartered Accountants. Later, they moved to Toronto and Sam joined Bill Shub as a member of the OMB. Upon graduation, Jack Culiner went into partnership with Abby Muter in the advertising business, a business in which they enjoyed considerable success. Upon his retirement, to my astonishment, Jack developed an artistic aptitude I never dreamed he possessed. He became a professional sculptor of repute, with numerous exhibitions of his work, both in Canada and the United States. Milton Shulman became an officer in the Canadian Intelligence Corps. Overseas, he had the privilege of interrogating many of the top Nazis charged with war crimes and chronicled the results in a book that received acclaim. He remained in England and joined Lord Beaverbrook's *Daily Express*. For years, he was the drama critic for this influential newspaper.

In our fraternity days, we enjoyed the company of one another and had a great deal of fun together. None of us older fellows enjoyed the benefits of affluence. We spoke of BSR as the "poor" fraternity, in contrast to the three established Jewish fraternities that were the "rich" fraternities. We could rarely afford to take a girl to a dance, or out for dinner, or even to a movie. So we made our own good times at the fraternity house and, on weekends, would sometimes bring our girl friends along. We rented our first fraternity house on Wilcox Street, not far from the campus. How we managed to financially defray the cost of operation of a fraternity house is difficult to recall or explain. There must have been initiation fees and some provision for membership dues, but I have no memory of having paid either. Some fellows lived at the house and made contribution to the upkeep. Altogether, we barely managed to scrape through. Unfortunately, we were not overly punctilious about the payment of debts. Poor

Zoberman, the cleaner. We made jokes about his repeated entreaties for payment of his modest cleaning bill. When this item came up at meetings, there would be general astonishment: "What, hasn't it been paid yet?" I do not recollect it ever being paid. In other respects, we exhibited great moral strength. We established rules prohibiting alcoholic beverages, gambling and active displays of sex in the fraternity house. I never knew any of these rules to have been broken. In those days, we had no rules concerning drugs, because we were not even aware of any social problem regarding them.

We ran an occasional party at the fraternity house, but on weekends there was usually a huge gathering anyway. We indulged in a great deal of play-acting in the manner portrayed in Puccini's opera "La Boheme." We were a bunch of iconoclasts and poked fun at everybody and everything. Each of the fellows had his own speciality or act. Harry Bowman, for instance, played the part of a corpse that would fall out of a closet when by prearrangement the door was suddenly opened. Milton Shulman was Zinzindorff who had just come down from the far north, entered the saloon, pounded on the bar, and announced: "I am Zinzindorff, spelled z-i-n-z-i-n-d-o-r-ff, double f; I just got my man!" These antics would invariably produce peals of laughter. My speciality was to mimic Reginald Stewart as he made his athletic entrance to the stage, mounted the podium, and bowed to the audience before conducting the symphony orchestra. On occasion I would perform my take-off on the movie version of "Michael Strogoff," special courier of the Czar, sent on a secret mission to warn the Grand Duke of a conspiracy against him. Our fraternity house got the reputation of the place to be on weekends.

The tempo increased with the advent of Wayne and Shuster. They came from a series of starring roles in Gilbert and Sullivan plays at Harbord Collegiate and were already established comedians. Weingarten or Wayne, as the case may be, loved to do comedy for the sheer joy of performing. He would literally stand for hours on end regaling all and sundry with an unending stream of jokes and amusing anecdotes.

It was Milton Shulman who thought up the idea of a fraternity show. With all the talent in our fraternity, we could produce a full-scale show as a public attraction and entertainment. The idea caught fire and received the approval of two of our members with the special ability to produce such a show — Wayne and Shuster of course. The boys wrote the script; composed the skits, sketches and songs; produced and directed the show; and played most of the principal parts themselves. Lou Applebaum was in charge of the music. Frank's sister provided the piano accompaniment. All the fellows of the fraternity participated, if nothing else as part of a male chorus. I took a part in a short skit and also in the male chorus. The fraternity rented a sizeable theatre in Hart House and the fraternity put on the Beta Sigma Rho show for three performances. It attracted full houses and was a smashing success. It became a legend in the folklore of Beta Sigma Rho fraternity.

Meanwhile, as a fraternity man, it was necessary for me to adjust to the company of members of the opposite sex. Unfortunately, I continued to be shy and awkward with women. On one occasion, I made a date to take a girl for a drive. She was an exceptionally pretty and sexy young woman. With difficulty, because of my lack of priority in the family, I managed to obtain the use of the family car. On a lovely summer day, I drove to High Park and the waterfront. As evening began to close in, I began to receive suggestions to park here or there, in this lane or that, all of which I pretended to misunderstand and ignore. I felt that my companion was becoming disappointed and irritated with me. I did not know what to do about what I most wanted to do. I never had a date with that girl again, which bothered me until I decided that it really did not matter. I rather fancied another girl anyway, but she was all of four years my junior and I considered her to be too young. Moreover, she was my sister's best friend and classmate from Bloor Collegiate and often visited at our house. Still, I managed to tease her a great deal and took her to the fraternity house on occasion. I hardly realized I was falling in love and that Joyce Lester was my girl.

I started to enjoy a social life that often kept me up late at night. In consequence, I gave myself good training in breaking and entering. I practised on my own home, invariably because I never carried a key to the front entrance and often was locked out, either by accident or design. In these circumstances, I developed a strategy. First I would test the doors and ring the doorbell, then test all windows on the ground floor. If all were locked, I would ascend to the second floor at rear of the house, because access could sometimes be gained through the bathroom window. If all else failed, I would sleep in one of the trucks or the family car or, as a last resort, would return to the fraternity house and sleep there overnight.

On one occasion, I barely managed to open a window in the basement and, inserting myself, fell onto a pile of coal. I brushed myself off and ascended the steps leading to the kitchen. Unfortunately, the door was locked. Baffled, I accepted the inevitable and drowsed off in a crouched position on the landing. In the early morning, I heard a rustling in the kitchen. I tried to think how I could attract attention without causing alarm. I did the wrong thing: I knocked on the door and the answering scream told me I had almost frightened my sister Faye out of her wits.

This was not the only time I made a bad decision. After I arrived home late on the previous night, I slept in on a warm summer morning. The rest of the family was at Lake Wilcox and the only other occupant of the house was my father. He was sleeping in another bedroom off the second floor corridor. The ringing of the alarm clock in his room awakened me. The clock would ring loudly, then stop for an interval, and then ring again. It occurred to me that my father was deliberately allowing the clock to ring in order to annoy me. I shouted to him to turn off the alarm. The intermittent ringing continued. Finally, exasperated, I shouted, "Turn off that damn alarm or I'll throw the clock out the window." No response; continued ringing. In a white heat of anger, I strode down the hall and into my father's room. He was sitting on the side of the bed in his underclothes; the clock was directly in front of him on a side table. Without further ado I picked up the clock and threw it out the open window. There was a loud crash as the clock struck the ground. I then turned on my heels and went back to bed. About an hour later, I got up and went downstairs. My father was seated at the kitchen table drinking from a glass of tea with lemon. The clock in all its dismemberment was assembled in front of him in a neat pile on the table. My father gazed upon me with an utterly mournful expression in his eyes. Not a word passed between us as I too helped myself to some tea and sat at the table with him.

All was not fun and games, by any means, during this period of my life. There were numerous occasions for discussion of serious subjects with my friends; democracy, communism, and fascism were topics of general concern. These were the times of the Italian conquest of Abyssinia, the Spanish Civil War, the rise of Hitler in Germany and the German occupation of the Rhineland. I argued or debated on these subjects constantly with my friends, particularly Milton Shulman who was very interested in international affairs. Sometimes, for the sheer intellectual exercise, we would change sides and argue against a formerly expressed position. I also continued my interest in music and became a member of the Hart House music committee. It was supposed to be an elective office, but I believe I became a member of the committee by default of other student interest. The committee arranged for a series of musicales, mainly of string instruments. It was not a particularly rewarding experience, except that I got the opportunity of meeting Sir Ernest MacMillan, the conductor of the Toronto Symphony Orchestra. He took an interest in the committee and acted as a sponsor. He sometimes left with the committee some tickets for a concert at Massey Hall. I took advantage of one of these free tickets and attended my first symphony concert. The orchestra played the Beethoven Pastoral Symphony. It enthralled me then and it still remains my first love in music.

One year, I also became chancellor of the Toronto chapter of Beta Sigma Rho and accepted the responsibility of conducting its affairs. However, this accession to power also carried with it the privilege of attending the expenses-paid international conference of the fraternity in New York. It happened that Abby Muter and Eve Jordan had just married and travelled to New York on their honeymoon. We met in New York and I spent part of their honeymoon with them, celebrating the new year at Times Square. It was my first visit to New York. I shocked my Brooklyn relatives by telling them that, unaccompanied, I wandered through Harlem, attended a service at Father Divine's Church, and sat through part of a Chinese musical in a Chinese cinema.

Generally, I kept very busy during my years as an undergraduate at the University. In addition to my studies, I did my father's bookkeeping or assisted in the sugar business. During the summer, I helped at the lake, mainly on weekends. I participated enthusiastically in the programs and social life of Beta Sigma Rho fraternity. I still managed to get good marks on all of my law course subjects. In 1936, I graduated with a BA in Honour Law and went on to the official law school at Osgoode Hall.

Six
Qualifying for the Bar. Then What?

At or about the time I was completing my course of study as an undergraduate at the University, I received an offer of gainful employment I could not possibly have refused. I felt very flattered; as well, I needed the money. The offer came from Professor Auld. He had just been appointed assistant editor of an ambitious legal work undertaken by the Carswell Law Publishing Company that became well known to the legal profession as the Canadian Law Abridgement. The editor-in-chief was Mr. Justice Riddell who was then a member of the Ontario Court of Appeal. The project was to publish a comprehensive digest, or summary, of all Canadian case law from earliest times to current date. It was to be arranged under subject and topic, referenced and cross-referenced, in order to make the decisions or judgements of all levels of courts readily accessible to the legal profession. It took several years to complete, was augmented by annual supplements, and became a useful, perhaps indispensable, tool in the practice of law by lawyers.

I joined the editorial staff of the Abridgement as a full-time member and, with other staff, worked in a library containing all the law reports and reference books needed for the work. Carswell established the library especially for this project. The subject assigned to me was the law of contracts. In this assignment, I read every reported contract-related judgement of every court in every province of Canada. In each case, I prepared a concise summary setting out the pith and substance of the case as I understood it, and arranged like cases together, according to the particular topic or aspect of the cases. After contracts was completed, I was assigned marine law and likewise read and abridged all the Canadian cases on that subject. I became rather expert in that specialized branch of the law. Unfortunately, later as barrister and solicitor, never was I called upon to deal with a case even remotely dealing with marine law.

I was the youngest member of the editorial staff of the Abridgement. My work was scrutinized by one or other of more experienced members of the staff. Before the material was sent for printing, it was then turned over to Professor Auld, as assistant editor, for whatever revision he deemed appropriate. Sections of page-proof were periodically sent to Mr. Justice Riddell by messenger for final approval. On occasion, when no material was yet available for him, he would request that we send over a detective book or mystery story, because he had completed his judicial work and time was hanging heavily on his hands. I had no similar problem, because I had no time to spare. For my part, I was engaged in piecework, the mental equivalent of labour in the garment trade. I was paid at the rate of fifty cents for each abridgement I prepared. Naturally I pushed myself to work as quickly as my mental capacity could accommodate. However, due to inexperience, I was slow and deliberate, albeit conscientious; in the result, my weekly remuneration was usually within a relatively modest range. I continued in this employment from the spring prior to graduation from the University, until the commencement of my second year at Osgoode Hall Law School.

The program set up by the Benchers of the Law Society for admission to the legal profession was composed of lectures at Osgoode Hall and contemporaneous practical training in a law office. The course at Osgoode consisted of two one-hour lectures each day, the first at nine o'clock in the morning and the second at four o'clock in the afternoon. The intervening hours were intended for service under articles to a lawyer. The teaching staff was comprised of some full-time lecturers and a number of lawyers brought in on a part-time basis to lecture on their particular speciality. As anticipated, graduates from

Honour Law found that there was duplication with some subjects that had been taught at the University. Despite changes in presentation and emphasis, this duplication substantially reduced our interest in the lectures. Other lectures, particularly those delivered by part-time staff, tended merely to be a recital of the lawyers' practice notes. Even worse, some lectures were no more than a recital of statutory provisions, read to the class at dictation speed. Consequently, many of the lectures at Osgoode were tedious, if not outright boring.

There were exceptions, of course. The Dean of Osgoode, Dean Falconbridge, was learned in every subject he taught and his lectures, while not exciting, were nevertheless very worthwhile. John Robinette, then still a young barrister, had already established a reputation as counsel and also acted as editor of the Ontario Law Reports. He still found time to lecture on a part-time basis on first year torts. He was always articulate and clear and his lectures attracted good attention and interest.

Then there was Cecil Wright who, even in those early days, was called "Caesar" by everyone. Possessed of a formidable intellect and a doctorate from prestigious Harvard Law School, his teaching method was designed to help students to think, rather then to be fed solutions to problems in the law. He tended to present so many possible solutions to each problem, however, that students could end up uncertain as to the actual state of the law on each issue. Still, his was an accepted teaching method at the time and Wright was a master in the art. Moreover, Wright's lectures at Osgoode were virtually the only lectures to stress the theoretical side of the law. The main fault of the Osgoode program was the emphasis on practicality. The practical lectures and the practical service in a law office, simply accentuated the dull, monotonous and humdrum character of the program.

As a student-at-law I was articled to a very busy sole practitioner, to whom I will refer as HSR. In my first year at Osgoode, he and I were a perfect match; I provided no services to him and he paid me no remuneration. I was far too occupied working full-time for Carswell on the Canadian Law Abridgement, when not attending classes at Osgoode. Upon commencing the second year, however, strict compliance with the requirement of the Law Society appeared not only necessary, but desirable. Accordingly, I regretfully gave up my job on the Abridgement and went to work for HSR on a daily basis.

However, just as I received no practical training in a law office in

Fulfilment

my first year, neither did I receive any substantial training in my second year. I was faced with the insuperable problem that HSR already was served by an articled student a year ahead of me at Osgoode. He held a monopoly on the legal work available for a student at this law office. I regarded the senior articled student with envy. He was familiar with the documentation in an action under the Mechanics' Lien Act and, in addition to his other responsibilities, he dealt with the collection of accounts in the Division Court. Nothing of substance seemed to be left for me. Instead, under the domination of a young, efficient, and aggressive secretary, I was dispatched hither and yon, to file papers at court offices, serve writs of summons, and deliver other documents and messages. I considered myself overpaid at a stipend of three dollars per week. That amount was subsequently raised to five dollars in my third year.

HSR was very decisive; he worked hard, spoke quickly, and even walked quickly. Unfortunately, HSR was far too overloaded with legal work to have time to teach any law to students, unless incidentally and occasionally. One of my first lessons in legal practicality learned at HSR's side occurred when I was allowed to trot beside him, carrying his briefcase on the way to attend on a motion before a County Court judge in the judge's chambers on the second floor of the City Hall. J.L. Cohen, a combative little man with a big reputation as a tough labour counsel, opposed HSR on this motion. The judge's chambers contained a long table with chairs set at the sides and a chair at the front. On arrival at the chambers, I failed to comprehend the antics of the two lawyers. They kept circling the table until the judge, a somewhat eccentric individual who appeared to have a fixation to a tattered legal gown, made his entrance. After the hearing, as I ran alongside HSR on our return to the office, he explained that the manoeuvring was to determine which of the two counsel would gain the advantage of speaking into the poor deaf judge's good ear. While I learned nothing about the law, I received a substantial lesson in legal tactics.

On another occasion, I also received a good lesson in the practice of law although the lesson was unanticipated. I was pleased to be approached by Tom about a legal problem. He brought to me a document with which he had been served as registered owner of our home on Shaw Street. As a result of wartime legislation, the mortgage of the property was subject to a moratorium on the repayment of principal. However, the statute allowed a court to relax this restriction.

The document that had been served on Tom was an application for an order requiring the owners of the property to make periodic repayments of the principal secured by the mortgage. I realized that Tom was really seeking my help to persuade my boss to handle the case. With some diffidence, I approached HSR who readily agreed to act for Tom at the forthcoming hearing. However, when the date for hearing arrived, HSR was too busy with other matters and sent me instead merely for the purpose of requesting an adjournment. He assured me that a first adjournment was invariably granted. So I appeared in this matter flanked by my brother Tom, both of us rather flustered and worried. The motion came on before a Master of the Supreme Court of Ontario, a powerful court official who shortly afterwards was appointed a judge of that Court. When the case was called, I rose and informed the Court that I was merely a student-at-law and that HSR, who was counsel, was unavoidably unable to attend and I respectfully requested an adjournment of the hearing. Without calling upon opposing counsel, likewise later elevated to the judiciary, the learned Master exploded: "Adjournment? Not at all; no adjournment. You are quite capable of handling the matter yourself. We shall proceed." So, I rolled up my sleeves, produced paper and pencil, and presented the best defence to the motion that I could in the circumstances. The Master made an order for periodic repayments of principal in a relatively modest amount. I was rather gratified that the Master, normally an intimidating judicial officer, added, in a not unkindly fashion, his opinion that I had done quite well and that he was satisfied that nobody could have achieved a more favourable result. Tom as well appeared to be satisfied with my performance and, more importantly, the result.

Since lectures at Osgoode were dull and tedious and service in a law office unrewarding, this young man's fancy turned to thoughts of light entertainment. In this regard, I fell under the influence of Milton Shulman. He was a year ahead of me at Osgoode. He had graduated from the three year Pass Arts Course at the University, whereas I came from four year Honour Law. I became acquainted with Milton in my first year at the University. He wrote a periodic column for the *Varsity*, the students' newspaper, that he entitled "Krazy Kat" and that I felt was hugely amusing. Milton loved the movies. Osgoode Hall fronted on Queen Street at University Avenue and there were three theatres in its immediate vicinity. Just to the east, on the south side of Queen Street, were two dilapidated burlesque houses, the Roxy and the Casino, within whose walls no self- respecting student-at-law should ever have been found. However, on Bay Street, just north of Queen stood the Sheas Hippodrome Theatre. It was a large, luxurious theatre in the style of the lavish entertainment palaces of New York. For the price of admission, the patron was given a concert on the great organ of the theatre; was shown the news of the day, a cartoon, and a full length feature film; and presented with a live performance of vaudeville on the stage. All too often, Milton and I would deliberately miss the four o'clock lecture to take in the show at the Sheas, particularly when the RKO Circuit brought the comedy team of Olson and Johnson or one of the great bands of the day. For different reasons, I was frequently late for the nine o'clock lecture as well. I had the embarrassing necessity on those occasions of passing directly in front of the lecturer in order to take a seat in the classroom. I was told by fellow classmates that, on one occasion, it appeared that the lecturer was about to seize me by the throat as I passed by but resisted the temptation at the last moment and with difficulty.

My behaviour may have improved in my third year at Osgoode, but that would have been because I obtained remunerative employment. For this too, I was indebted to Milton Shulman. In his third year at Osgoode, Milton was the editor of *Obiter Dicta*, the official students' publication of Osgoode Hall Law School. The publication was "official" only in the sense that it was permitted or tolerated by Osgoode and the Benchers without any intrusive supervision. Actually, it was a private enterprise operated by a business manager and an editor who were third year students. I used to write an occasional article at Milton's request, because he was always in need of material.

When Milton graduated from Osgoode and I moved up to third year, he transferred the editorship to me. Bill Sutton, my classmate, became the business manager. He looked after the financial side of the enterprise, brought in the advertising, received the revenue, paid the bills, and turned over part of the profits to me. As editor, I solicited and obtained articles on legal subjects and other material of interest to law students; wrote additional pieces myself; sent the material to the printer; checked the galley proof; did the make-up; and checked the page-proof. We produced issues of *Obiter Dicta* monthly during the school terms and distributed copies free of charge to students and anyone else who wanted it.

Although *Obiter Dicta* was an unpretentious undertaking, occasionally quite learned articles on the law graced its pages. Decades after my days as editor, I was looking through some back issues still in my possession and came across an interesting article. It dealt with the admissibility into evidence of a statement or confession by a person accused of a crime to a police officer or other person in authority. It was then, and is still today, a troublesome issue in the criminal law. G. Arthur Martin who, for years, had been Canada's leading criminal lawyer and authority on the criminal law wrote the article. Martin was a year ahead of me in Honour Law and later at Osgoode Hall, where he led his graduating class in the final examinations and won the coveted gold medal.

The task of producing the "official" students' publication, as well as other extra curricular activities of a less intellectual character, appreciably distracted from the time and effort available to me in the more official program at Osgoode. In previous years, I had achieved good grades in the examinations. In first year, Caesar Wright assigned the highest mark in the class to my paper on contracts. I hardly regarded this as a particular accomplishment in light of all the work I had done on this subject for the Abridgement. Late in my third year, suddenly, I was struck with the realization that the days of reckoning were fast approaching. The final examinations for admission to the Bar of Ontario were looming and I was ill prepared for them. Chastened, I took to my tiny room in the third floor attic of the Shaw Street house. I donned my lucky sweater, worn out at the elbows; produced my law books; read my lecture notes and the borrowed notes of lectures I had missed; and engaged myself in serious protracted study. Periodically, I called downstairs for nourishment to little June and grown Mary, each of whom I expected to be on stand by. After two or three weeks of intensive study, I attended at the designated place and wrote the examinations and the period of stress and strain came to an end.

There followed a party at a downtown hotel. It was the wildest party in which I have ever been involved, the graduation party of the Osgoode Class of 1939. The conduct of the participants reflected not only the general release of the tensions built up in the preceding weeks, but in several instances a complete relaxation of inhibition as well. At Osgoode, there had been little occasion for any socialization among the students. In appearance, dress, and conduct, my classmates appeared to me to be junior replicas of the conservative members of the profession to which they aspired. It was, therefore, with some astonishment that I witnessed the extreme hilarity and antics at the graduation party, antics that preceded a particularly memorable event. One of the invited guests, an elderly member of the judiciary, call him Mr. Justice John Doe, had joined in the celebration with enthusiasm and perhaps an over-indulgence in an alcoholic beverage. The word passed like wildfire that he had locked himself in a closet with one of the dancing girls who had been brought in for the entertainment of the assembly. This likelihood produced a profound sobering effect, at least among the students who had organized and felt responsible for the affair. A group of concerned students gathered about the closet repeatedly pleading for the learned judge to come out: "Mr. Justice Doe, come out! Please, Mr. Justice. Your Lordship, won't you please come out of the closet!" The incident became a sensation. So large a group gathered about the closet that my own view became completely blocked. I do not know if he ever emerged. For all I know, he may still be inside. What I do know is that the party concluded only in late morning of the next day.

After the graduation party, I waited two or three months for the results of the final examinations. Ultimately, they were published in the newspapers. I passed with grades that fell within the top segment of the class. My showing did not particularly impress me. I felt I could have done better if I had only applied myself more diligently to my studies. Still, having qualified, I now waited to become a lawyer. The magical transformation occurred without particular fanfare. One day, I simply attended in court dressed in the traditional black cotton gown and the other accoutrements of a Canadian barrister. The presiding judge of the Supreme Court of Ontario took note of my presence and remarked on my newly acquired status as a barrister and solicitor duly qualified to practise law in the Province of Ontario. In due course, I received a confirming certificate from the Law Society of Upper Canada, but no academic degree, and was left to consider: "So I have been called to the Bar and am a full-fledged lawyer. Now what?"

Any feeling of elation or accomplishment I entertained, upon reaching my ultimate goal of admission to the Bar, was merely transitory. It gave way to sober considerations about the reality of my situation.

Although I was now a lawyer, I was a practitioner with no connection to any law office. If no gentile firm would accept me as a student-at-law, there was even less likelihood of acceptance as a practitioner. Certainly, there was no possibility of eventually joining a firm as a partner. Moreover, these were difficult times. The Canadian economy had still not recovered from the great depression precipitated by the 1929 crash of the stock market and legal practice was in the same doldrums as other business enterprises. In this climate, the few Jewish firms were reluctant to increase their overhead by taking on additional young lawyers and most sole practitioners were hard pressed to earn a living themselves. So I was a barrister and solicitor without affiliation to a law firm, without clients, without financial resources and, it seemed, without any prospects either. I could not expect help from my father; he needed help himself.

My father's business had been incorporated under the name Merchants Trading Company Limited. The company was now trading at wholesale in a variety of grocery products, in addition to sugar, and was being operated out of leased premises with substantial warehouse space. My father had acquired the services of a full-time bookkeeper. I believe it was at this time that Norman Oster, now my brother-in-law, struggling to earn a livelihood, was taken into the company. He joined Morris and my father in the arduous task of producing the sales essential to keep the company afloat. Although the business had expanded considerably, the underlying problems remained the same and the business continued to flounder. Profit margins were very low and overhead was high; the company could not avoid carrying heavy receivables; and, as ever, there was a lack of adequate financing. Twisting and turning to keep the business operative, my father managed to get my brother Tom financially involved. Now a married man with his own burden of supporting a wife and children, Tom worried about the failure of his father's business causing his own financial ruin.

Tom suggested that I should consider joining Merchants Trading in the hope that I might exert a salutary influence over my father and help keep the operation of the company on a sound footing. Undecided on my own future, I too joined Merchants Trading, ostensibly in its management, but without any specific responsibilities. I should have known, however, that I had little skill in business or ability to control or even influence my father in the operation of the company; nor could I resolve the problem of inadequate financing. So my father, with his personal limitations and subjected to constant pressure and frustrations, continued to run the company and dominate everyone in it.

Meanwhile, in the international arena, events were moving swiftly to a culmination of catastrophe. On a beautiful Sunday in late summer, I was bicycling at the Toronto waterfront with Saul Wolfe and Jack Culiner when we learned the news: Britain had declared war on Germany. It was Sunday, September 3, 1939. Canada quickly followed suit and declared war. Thus began World War II. Although we were shocked, it was, after all, no surprise. Chamberlain thought he had achieved "peace in our times" at Munich, but that did not prevent Czechoslovakia from being absorbed by Germany. Only a few months later and contrary to all assurances, Hitler let loose the full might of his armed forces against Poland and sent his Luftwaffe to carry out an intensive bombing of Warsaw. The conquest of Poland occupied a matter of only a few days. After the subjugation of Poland, there followed an eerie period of calm that lasted about a year. At the end of the "phony war," the armed conflict between nations was joined in full force.

I contemplated, but deferred, enlisting in the Canadian army. Instead, I tested my aptitude in military matters by joining a newly formed contingent of the COTC, a unit of militia composed of graduates of the Osgoode Hall Law School. I attended a few sessions of training at the Armouries in Toronto. One day, with a troop of trainees, I was taken for rifle practice to an indoor rifle range at Hart House. I had never previously held a rifle in my hands. Each member of the troop was handed a heavy rifle and a dozen rounds of ammunition. When my turn came, I put the rifle to my shoulder and, as instructed, gently squeezed the trigger. I heard the sound of the discharge and a sharp "ping." On each attempt, not only did I miss the bulls-eye; I missed the target altogether. The bullet merely struck the tin border against which the target had been placed. With restrained contempt, the sergeant in charge said, "Here's another twelve rounds; try again." I did and, with each additional shot, heard the same "ping." Again, I missed the target completely with all twelve rounds. I came away from the rifle range entirely crestfallen. I fared not much better at a two-week training session at Niagara-on-the-Lake. I decided I had little liking for, nor any qualities conducive to, military service.

Instead of enlisting in the armed forces, I procrastinated. I was adrift in a sea of uncertainty. On the one hand, I felt useless at Merchants Trading. It was a vain hope that I could either control my father or contribute to the management of the business. On the other hand, I was not quite ready to embark upon military service. To the contrary, having undergone years of study to qualify as a lawyer, I had a hankering first to acquire some experience in actual legal practice. Accordingly, after a futile period of employment with Merchants Trading, I took the plunge into the realm of practice as barrister and solicitor. Actually, it was a mild dip into very cold waters.

Arthur Cole, a chartered accountant, was a good friend of Sam Speigel; they had graduated from university and qualified as accountants together. Arthur opened a tiny office in Manning Chambers. It was an ancient office building about seven floors high on Queen Street, just west of Bay. It stood opposite the Roxy and Casino theatres in an area that, in those days, was in need of redevelopment. Arthur acquired the space by sublease from Lou Davidson, a lawyer who, in his capacity as entrepreneur, had taken a lease of a substantial area in the building. Davidson subdivided the space to yield a law office for himself, another office for his brother Philip, also a lawyer, and a minimal amount of space for sublease to Arthur. The space barely accommodated a desk and chair for the accountant in his inner sanctum and a desk and chair in the adjoining anteroom for his secretary. Into these confined quarters entered lawyer Vanek. The result was reminiscent of a scene from a Marx Brothers film. I shared with Arthur Cole his minuscule office and untrained secretary on the premise that Arthur's accountancy business required his absence more often than his presence at his office. However, if he happened to be present, I necessarily had to be absent. In this fashion, I commenced my legal career. It was an inauspicious beginning; the facilities were discouraging and the clients few and far between.

Nevertheless, I managed to financially support myself according to my new station in life, particularly since I was still living with my parents on Shaw Street without contributing toward any of the upkeep. I was even able to purchase a second-hand automobile. I required the car for my secondary employment. A group of people, including two lawyers of my acquaintance, had acquired a tract of land on Bathurst Street, just north of Toronto, for a private golf club to serve the Jewish community. They called it the Fairmount Golf and

Country Club. It was the second Jewish golf club. Oakdale, a well-established, prestigious club, already served the more prominent and affluent members of the Jewish community. These members could afford the high initiation fee, and the annual dues and charges, and safeguarded their interests with strict rules governing further admissions into their club. I joined the new Fairmount Club. Sam Ciglen, who was then the president of the club offered me a job, which I readily accepted, as secretary of the club. As secretary, I was paid a stipend that was a welcome supplement to my income and gave me the opportunity to play golf at a minimum of expense.

My second-hand car was not lacking in mechanical defects. One day I was driving north on McCaul Street and stopped at a red light. A streetcar and a line of vehicular traffic were stopped behind me. When the light turned to green, I pressed my foot hard on the gas pedal. Instead of shooting forward, as anticipated, the wheels simply fell off! The car disassembled. What was I to do? The traffic behind me was at a halt. Ultimately, a group of the disgruntled drivers lifted my car, including the wheels, and placed the wreckage at the side of the road. I was most embarrassed. However, I nevertheless purchased another well-worn second-hand car shortly afterwards. This car served me fairly well.

Two of my first clients in the practice of law were Joyce's parents: Sam and Lily Lester. They must have waited for me to be called to the Bar before they sold their large, old, detached house on Gladstone Avenue, north of Bloor, and purchased a small, new bungalow, under construction in a newly developed area south of Eglinton Avenue. This transaction gave me the opportunity not only to enhance my knowledge of the law of real property, but also to scrutinize the people who later were to become my in-laws. They were a handsome couple. Sam Lester operated a motion picture theatre called the "Doric" located on Bloor Street at Gladstone, east of Dufferin Street. The Lester family had settled in England after leaving Poland. Sam married Leah, better known as Lily, in England and they emigrated to Canada in 1905. Sam then helped two brothers to come to Canada from England. Both brothers became motion picture exhibitors in Toronto. Anchel, the elder brother, was called "Angel" by some people, generally members of the family, and, strangely, addressed as "George" by others. He operated the "King Theatre" on College Street, west of Bathurst. The younger brother, handsome Harry, operated a theatre in the east end, a part of Toronto east of Yonge Street well outside the main centre of Jewish population. Joyce has told me many times that her father was the first exhibitor of motion pictures in Toronto. Other anecdotal evidence, photographs, and the occasional nostalgic story in the press have confirmed this fact.

I have told Joyce many times of my after-acquired theory that, in choosing a wife, a man should pay careful regard to her mother. In all likelihood the mother is what the wife will approximate in later years. Joyce's mother, Lily, was endowed with a fair complexion; fine chiselled features; prematurely white hair; good bearing; and reserved English speech and manners. She was born and raised in England as part of a large family, the Alexanders. The patriarch of the family, Grandpa David Alexander, was to Joyce a tall, dignified, and strict but kindly man. He had come to England from Poland. In contrast, Grandma Blume Franks was a tiny, undemonstrative, submissive woman. She came to England from Hungary. They married and ultimately settled in Bristol, where Lily was born. Despite her diminutive size, Grandma Blume gave birth to children numbered in double digits of whom no less than thirteen survived. Grandpa David carried on a tailoring business in a building behind their Montague Street residence. According to one of his children: "Our father was a stern taskmaster. He believed in hard work. All thirteen of us kids worked in the factory."

The Lesters, also a substantial family, but of more reasonable size, came to England from a small town in Poland. There were a series of intermarriages between these families that rivals the inter-relationships amongst royalty. Another family, the Kings, complicates the story. The mind-boggling facts about this saga go something like this:

Two Alexander sisters married two Lester brothers; (Lily and Sam; Janie and Anchel);
Two Alexander brothers married two King sisters;
Another Alexander sister married a brother of the two King sisters;
One Alexander sister married an Alexander cousin;
Still another Alexander sister married the uncle of her two Lester brothers-in-law;
The Alexanders had a set of twins: each of the twins married gentiles and thereupon was virtually turned out of the family;

> Two Alexander brothers also married gentile girls; in one case
> the girl died; in the other case, the parties divorced. Both
> brothers remarried into the faith.

I acquired this awesome collection of relatives by my subsequent
marriage to Joyce. Most of the progeny emigrated to Canada, where
they added to their numbers and settled in or about the City of
Toronto. Some Lesters remained in London; one Lester went to South
Africa; and two Alexanders settled in California. The delicate exercise
of discerning all these relationships was further complicated because
some of the parties adopted names different from their given names. I
have already referred to Anchel. Then there was Isaac, whom the
family called "our Ike," but others generally knew as "Jack." And what
about Jack, who was really Jack? Imagine my discomfiture when, after
our marriage, Joyce introduced me to a grandchild of Jack. I could not
determine whether the cousin was a grandchild of "our Ike," who
divorced a gentile and married Minnie King, or a grandchild of Jack,
who was really Jack and went to live in California!

Of course I knew nothing about this family history at the time I
acted for Sam and Lily Lester in the sale and purchase of their
dwellings. In automotive terms, my romance was then still in low gear.
I took Joyce out on an occasional basis. One afternoon in early spring,
I needed to attend at the Fairmount Golf Club. Joyce kept me
company as I drove my second-hand car along the gravel road that was
the extension of Bathurst Street, northerly from Eglinton Avenue to
the Club. The Club had been closed for the winter. Upon arrival, I
unlocked the front door of the clubhouse and built a fire in the
fireplace. We were alone in very comfortable circumstances. We
passed a pleasant couple of hours. Our romance might then have
heated up considerably in consonance with the warmth of the fire.
However, with a start, Joyce reminded herself and, necessarily,
confided to me, that she had a pre-arranged date with another
undisclosed male later that day. I had to take her home immediately.
However, when we looked out the window, we found it had been
snowing heavily during all the time we had been warming ourselves by
the fire. Indeed, so deep was the snowfall that my car was stuck in the
snow and could not be moved. We had to make our way through the
generally undeveloped area to a place where we could arrange for
transportation. At first I regarded our situation and Joyce's predicament

with her date as a huge joke, but my attitude changed when she cried plaintively that she had left her galoshes at home and had to trudge through the snow in feet covered only by thin stockings and flimsy shoes. I recall ultimately resting at a farmhouse, but have no recollection of how we finally managed to reach our respective homes. I have never been told, but suspect that Joyce was not able to honour her date and believe that in this adventure, unwittingly, I succeeded in eliminating one of my rivals for her affection.

Later, still in automotive terms, our romance went into high gear. Unbeknownst to each other, Joyce and I were both invited to visit Mary and Sam, now married and living in Sudbury, a nickel mining town about 250 miles north of Toronto. It was the Victoria Day weekend holiday. Upon arrival in Sudbury, we found that Mary, Sam and a group of their friends had decided to spend the weekend on a fishing trip to French River, about fifty miles from Sudbury. Naturally, we were included in the party. All arrangements had been made: boats, rods, tackle, bait, and the services of a guide. It was a very enjoyable outing. We were fishing for pickerel. The fish were bountiful, hungry and biting at the bait. I made the biggest catch of the group, which I proudly exhibited for photographs. Our guide fried the fish in butter over an open fire and made a delicious repast. In this happy group, bubbling with good humour, it was assumed that Joyce and I were a couple. This was a relationship much more intimate than mere boyfriend and girlfriend, and we too made the same assumption.

Without any words between us about engagement or marriage, our romance blossomed. We found more occasions to seek out the company of one another. As well, I heard no more about another rival of undisclosed identity who dwelt in Rochester. He also fell by the wayside as a competitor. However, as has often been noted, the course of true love rarely runs smoothly. An inner call to wartime service was becoming increasingly insistent.

PARENTS

Jessie Vanek

Jacob Vanek

My mother when still in Russia (standing to the right), with my grandmother (seated) and her sisters and brother.

THE FAMILY

Joyce and David

The children (Peter, Howard, Nancy)

OAK RIDGES
&
LAKE WILCOX

Our house and store at Oak Ridges just prior to their having been torn down in about 1983, to provide a parking lot for a hamburger stand.

Dedication of the Vanek property on October 3, 1993, as a public park in memory of our mother. I am present with brother Morris, sister Mary, and Mayor and Councillors of the Town of Richmond Hill

LAW STUDENT

The graduating class of 1936 in Honour Law at the University of Toronto. Seated in the centre is Dr. William Paul McClure Kennedy, the Dean, flanked by professors F.C. Auld (left) and Jacob Finkelman (right).

University of Toronto Moot Court, 1935–36
Front row: W.D. MacDonald, Chief Justice, Fourth Division; S.C.
Biggs, Chief Justice, Second Division; W.G.C. Howland, Chief Justice of
the Moot Court; D. Vanek, Chief Justice, Third Division; C.M. Milton,
Magistrate. Back row: W.R. Chamberlain, Deputy Registrar; E.M.
Shortt, Secretary-Treasurer; W.G. Gray, Bailiff; P.E. Band, Registrar.

With former colleagues on the staff of the School of Law, U of T (in 1998). Sylvan (Van) Sommerfeld and J.E. (Gene) La Brie.

Dean Kennedy in 1949, at leisure at "Narrow Waters," his summer home.

OBITER DICTA

OFFICIAL PUBLICATION OF OSGOODE HALL LAW STUDENTS

VOLUME XII.   TORONTO, FRIDAY, JANUARY 20, 1939   NO. 3

STUDENTS DEBATE SECESSION TOPIC

Osgoode-Laval Debaters To Consider
Canada's Foreign Policy In
Event of War

Justice Chevrier to Attend

OBITER DICTA

Published at Osgoode Hall Law School.

EDITORIAL BOARD

Editor .... DAVID C. VANEK, B.A.
Business Manager .... WILLIAM R. R. SUTTON, B.A.
Assistant Business Manager .... R. G. BURROWS, B.A.
Editorial Staff .... JAMES I. STEWART, B.A.
WILLIAM A. SUTHERLAND, B.A.
B. BARRY SHAPIRO, B.A.

TORONTO, WEDNESDAY, APRIL 19, 1939

Ashley & Crippen

Called to the Bar of Ontario

Seven
You're in the Army Now!

The story of "my" war is a tale full of sound and fury signifying nothing. I freely acknowledge that nothing I did altered the course of events shaking the world or even made a significant contribution to the general war effort. By the time I took positive steps towards enlisting in the armed forces, the calendar had turned to the year 1942. I acted in concert with my best friend, Saul Wolfe. Saul opted for a role in combat with the Canadian Armoured Corps (CAC) and I went along with him. It was my first mistake.

I was now twenty-seven years old, relatively cautious, and beyond the years of reckless and foolhardy deeds of heroism. I decided that if I were to volunteer for military service at least I should serve as an officer, and not as a mere ordinary soldier. With this objective, I wrote to the headquarters of the CAC and, on the strength of their response, I drove to Camp Borden for an interview with a high-ranking administrative officer. The officer informed me that, with my credentials, I would be accepted as a POM, Potential Officer Material. More importantly, he said that I would have no difficulty obtaining a commission, upon passing the normal tests and examinations of basic training and the course for officers' training. With this assurance, I accompanied Saul and we both enlisted in the Canadian Armoured Corps and were immediately noted as POMs. It was June 3, 1942.

Our induction into the army took place at Exhibition Park, a tract of several hundred acres of land and the site of the Canadian National Exhibition. We were assigned to quarters in a huge structure known as the Horse Palace. Prior to the war it was used to store the horses shown at the CNE and other special events. During our initial orientation into the army, we slept in the stalls formerly occupied by the horses. Although the building had been cleaned up for the troops, the odour of the horses, and their droppings, continued to permeate the building. This period of orientation took two or three weeks. Then, with practically no advance notice, we were taken by train, first to Union Station and then to the outskirts of Camp Borden. From there, we marched with full pack to our ultimate destination, a section of the Camp assigned to the CAC designated as A8 and A9. It was often misleadingly referred to as the "Wireless Section." We were brought there for basic training as wireless/gunners, to handle the communications and operate the guns of the tanks.

Camp Borden is located about fifty miles from Toronto and fifteen miles west of Barrie, a resort town on Lake Simcoe. Camp Borden was then, and no doubt still is, the largest military camp in Canada. I found it to be a man-made desert of deep sand on a treeless expanse of land studded with uniformly monotonous drab huts of various sizes and configurations.

Saul and I were directed to barracks in A9 where we first met the other POMs with whom we were to be associated. We soon became friends with the other POMs. We also applied ourselves earnestly, diligently, even enthusiastically, to the course for the training of wireless/gunners. One of the subjects, wireless telegraphy, was monotonous and very outdated. It was an attempt to teach the Morse code even though, in practice and even in training, the CAC. used radio for communication generally and between tanks. With this exception, the course included a variety of subjects, lectures, and drills, of a practical and utilitarian nature. It led ultimately to schemes and exercises simulating the manoeuvring of tanks in combat, and even some actual experience with the tanks themselves.

Shortly after my arrival at A9, I was feeling rather lonely and sent the following note to Joyce:

Dear Joyce:

Much as I hate writing, or, at least to the same extent, I like receiving letters. Particularly, here, one feels like a lost orphan if his name is not called out when mail arrives for the Company. Therefore, please send a letter with a blank piece of paper enclosed, just to save me this embarrassment.

This little note drew an immediate response that led to an extensive and intensive correspondence and an accumulation of letters that we have retained to this day. There was no doubt now that Joyce was my girl. With the ever-increasing intimacy between us came a heightened need for passes — day passes, weekend passes, any kind of passes — to enable me to get away from Camp and spend time with Joyce. Obtaining leave, even for a day or an hour, became an obsession. Often, therefore, one way or another, I managed to get home. I had to be awakened in the middle of the night to get a ride or catch the troop train to return to Camp in time for early morning roll call and the first parade. Although this endless commute between Camp and home was tiring and distracting, nevertheless I continued to energetically apply myself and felt that I was making good progress in basic training. I passed all the tests and examinations and was on friendly terms with my fellow POMs. On the whole, I enjoyed this introductory taste of army life.

We were nearing the end of our basic training when, one day in October, I was dispatched with other POMs to take an aptitude test, designated as the "M Test." It was an examination, to be completed within a fixed time frame, requiring "yes" or "no" answers to a series of questions. The questions concerned the identification, knowledge and use of tools and mechanical devices and the solution of a number of simple arithmetic problems. I encountered some difficulty with the test and was unable to finish the paper on time.

Somewhat later, I was given the bad news: I had failed the "M Test." Much later I learned that the failure was marginal — a matter of two or three marks. It came as a severe shock to me. It was not a particularly difficult test. Many a farm boy could have passed it with ease. Despite the difficulty I encountered with the questions, I could hardly believe that with my background of education and experience, I actually failed to pass the test. I offer, at least in partial explanation, that I have never had any particular knowledge of tools, instruments or matters mechanical. Further, I had had little call upon my expertise in solving problems in arithmetic since leaving high school where, oddly enough, I had always achieved good grades in mathematics.

My letters to Joyce describe in some detail what happened in consequence of the failure. In particular, in a letter of October 19, I wrote about being on parade preparing for a march in Barrie to be headed by the POMs representing the CAC:

> We were standing in line on parade wearing our webbing and tin hats, and a slow drizzling rain was falling. The Sergeant Major and our O.C were giving us instructions concerning the coming march, when another officer appeared and spoke briefly to the O.C. who turned and said: 'Is Vanek here? .... You're to report to Corps Headquarters.'

Later I attended at Corps Headquarters before Captain Morrison. The letter gives the following description:

> Captain Morrison was very nice to me — and frank — for which I was grateful.... There is no question of me staying in the Armoured Corps, unless I am going to be content with stripes alone. Oh I have several choices, even in the C.A.C. except they do not lead to a commission, save by what Captains Morrison, Smythe and Tait universally term the 'hard way' — up through the ranks, from trooper and corporal to sergeant, the hard way. 'Meanwhile, Just carry on as usual, Vanek.'

I was devastated. This was a blow from which I never fully recovered. What I could not accept was that the failure to pass the "M Test" was a complete bar to obtaining a commission in the CAC. This bar was despite my academic and professional background and experience, my ability to perform all physical requirements, and the competence already displayed by passing all basic training exams and tests.

After my interview with Captain Morrison, events moved with relentless speed in regular military fashion. I returned to the POM. barracks to find that word of my debacle had preceded me. Life was going on in the hut as usual — but not for me! There was a general atmosphere of excitement and merrymaking amongst the POMs. Word had passed amongst them that they were to be interviewed by the Camp Commandant preparatory to transfer to Officers Training School in Brockville. Several of the POMs were engaged in polishing shoes, pressing uniforms and the like for their appearance before the Camp Commandant. It may have been that my personal disaster was regarded as an object lesson of what might befall the other POMs if there was any deviation from the perfection expected of potential officers. Nevertheless, I felt isolated and abandoned, and very hurt.

Next morning a corporal entered the barracks and, not having seen me immediately, called out in a loud voice: "Is Vanek here? Vanek — We might as well get your stuff and move you over to Wireless now." The move did not occur at that time, because I was awaiting a further interview that I had been seeking. Later the same day, however, my fate was sealed when Daily Orders appeared that included this succinct item:

> The following personnel have been posted to Wireless from T.S.S.Wing....Tpr D.C. Vanek....to take effect as from 19/10/42.

My further interview simply confirmed what I had already been told. There was now no possibility of securing a commission in the Armoured Corps. This officer extolled my "obvious administrative ability," just as the other officers who had dealt with me previously. I requested to be transferred to some other branch of the armed forces in which I could make a contribution in accordance with my capabilities. The officer may or may not have noted this request.

My eviction from my quarters with the POMs occurred the following day. After dinner, I packed my belongings. A radio in the hut was tuned to a station playing martial music. A band struck up "Three Cheers for the Red White and Blue" as I made my way, melodramatically, past the POMs and out of their barracks. I took my few possessions to the hut in the wireless wing to which I had been assigned and selected a bunk. The next day I joined another class, designated R16, in order to complete my basic training as a wireless/gunner. Thus my separation from the POMs was complete.

It took some time for me to accommodate to my new situation. Ultimately, I pulled myself together. I decided that if I could not be an officer, at least I could be a man, and would try to perform any duties required of me to the best of my ability.

There was one person who was my staunch supporter during the trials and tribulations that I have related. My correspondence with her continued unabated. A letter of November 11 makes reference to all sorts of interesting happenings: finding Joyce at my home for dinner when I arrived from Camp, taking her to a dance at the Royal York Hotel, seeking entrance to the City Hall to obtain a marriage licence, and being frustrated because we arrived after the City Hall closed at 11:30 a.m.

When I returned the next weekend, we successfully obtained the marriage licence. We still had to implement it. In this regard, my sole responsibilities were to obtain leave to marry from my commanding officer and present myself at the Lester bungalow on the pre-determined wedding date. All the other arrangements, I left to Joyce and her parents.

We encountered some problems. My father was in the hospital recovering from a heart attack and therefore could not attend the wedding. Mary could not attend either because she was in the later stages of pregnancy and ailing. My mother, in her most autocratic manner, instructed Joyce to postpone the wedding, because she had to travel to Sudbury to look after Mary. Joyce refused point-blank. She informed my mother in no uncertain terms that the wedding would proceed as scheduled. It did not.

I was to have been married on a Sunday, provided I could obtain a leave that would allow for it. I surprised everyone, however, by arriving home on Friday on a weekend leave lasting until the following Tuesday morning. Accordingly, all arrangements were immediately changed and Joyce and I were married instead on the intervening Saturday after sundown and the termination of the Sabbath. Rabbi Monson officiated. He was the Rabbi of Sharei Shomayim Synagogue, the synagogue attended by my father-in-law, and also the Jewish Padre at Camp Borden. Bernice Saxe was present, with her husband Percy, and acted as bridesmaid instead of Mary. My sister Laura produced the wedding ring. Two of my friends, Abby Muter and Iz King, arrived uninvited and unexpected, saying that they would not countenance my getting married without their attendance. They signed the marriage certificate as the official witnesses. Otherwise, only the members of our immediate families were present. It was November 28, 1942.

After the wedding, Joyce and I borrowed my father-in-law's automobile. First, we visited my father at the hospital. Then we drove to Hamilton, about thirty miles from Toronto, and checked into the Royal Connaught Hotel. It was just after 10:00 o'clock at night; the restaurant and all the shops in the neighbourhood were closed. We had to retire without even a light repast. Bernice and Percy awakened us the next morning. There had been a heavy snowfall overnight and they brought Joyce her galoshes.

Joyce and I decided to return to Toronto that day because her parents were holding a dinner party for the wedding guests. We were not expected. Much to everyone's delight, we walked in just as dinner was being served and found the guests seated at trestle tables set in the recreation room. My mother made a simple and touching speech: "What can I tell you? I am the mother of seven children and this is my youngest boy ...." We stayed overnight at the Royal York Hotel and on the following Monday evening, I returned to Camp Borden.

The rest of the week at Camp Borden was a time of feverish activity for me. My efforts were ultimately crowned with success. I managed to obtain twenty-two days of leave.

I arrived home that Friday. My father was out of the hospital but still convalescing. Joyce and I stayed in Toronto a few days and then visited friends and relatives in Buffalo. Then we took the train for New York City where we passed an exciting and memorable holiday. We saw several radio shows and plays, attended the Metropolitan Opera, and visited a number of nightclubs. Finally, surfeited with entertainment, we returned to Toronto late at night on December 23 and went to bed in the recreation room of the Lester bungalow. It thereafter became our married quarters whenever I could get home from Camp.

Joyce awakened me early the next morning. She had been unable to sleep, because she was so disturbed by the information imparted to her by her mother the previous evening, information that she had withheld from me. Still somewhat groggy from lack of sleep, I was told that while we were away a telegram had arrived from the military authorities. In it, I was instructed to return to Camp by December 18, now well past. My in-laws decided, in their wisdom, not to disturb our holiday. My mother-in-law wired back that I was travelling in the United States on my honeymoon and that she did not know how to contact me. I was shocked to the core! Gradually I summoned sufficient nerve to phone Camp Borden. I learned that I had been put on draft for overseas with my Wireless Class of R16 and that the draft had already departed. Nevertheless, according to my informant, since it seemed pointless for me to return to Camp during the Christmas holidays, I could wait until my leave had fully expired and then return on December 26.

My return to Camp, after this brief taste of married life, the honeymoon and extended holiday, was like being recalled to reality by diving into ice cold water. I expected punishment of the worst order: to be shot, slapped in the jug, or at least put on charge. Fortunately, none of these unhappy consequences occurred. Instead, I was put on fatigues — just about every dirty job that required doing in a military camp. Of course, I could expect no more passes or leaves of any kind in the near future.

In low spirits, discouraged, and disconsolate, I went about the menial tasks assigned to me. During this period of desolation, I kept receiving urgent and insistent letters and phone calls from my stubborn wife about my coming home for the New Year holiday. I tried to explain to Joyce that I could not possibly obtain a weekend pass. Finally, she compromised: she would come to Barrie so we could spend New Year's eve together. Worn down by her insistence, recklessly I told Joyce that I would meet her at 5:00 p.m. on December 31 at the Queens Hotel in Barrie. Then I went about the delicate task of making good on this commitment. To my surprise, I managed to accomplish the impossible and obtain an overnight pass from after duty, normally about 7:30 p.m. Somehow, I met Joyce at 5:00 p.m. in front of the Queens Hotel as arranged. In the busy holiday season there was no accommodation for us there, but luckily Joyce had been able to obtain a room at another hotel. Joyce and I spent a quiet, but pleasant, New Year's Eve together. I was due back in Camp the next morning by reveille, at 6:00 in the morning. I had to be awakened by 4:30 a.m. and arrived very tired, but in time to resume my duties. Joyce had a cold and I expected her to return to Toronto.

I was on kitchen fatigue. I went back to the kitchen and found that preparations were under way for dinner that, it being New Year's Day, was to be a special event. The troopers were to be given a turkey dinner with all the trimmings, and the officers and the non-commissioned officers (NCOs) were to wait on the tables. This was all very well except, when the dinner was over, I had the unenviable task of washing the dishes. Since there were extra courses, I had many more dishes to wash than usual. After dinner, I donned my coveralls and set to work with another soldier who shared the duty with me. Everyone had departed from the large mess hall. I was standing beside a huge pile of dishes, laden with the refuse of this extravagant turkey dinner, when I heard my partner cry: "Pipe the dame!"

I turned about and observed my pretty young wife approaching in considerable excitement.

In complete astonishment, I exclaimed: "What are you doing here?"

"Never mind, come with me, come with me to the orderly room; we've got a pass."

"Don't be silly," I responded in disbelief. "I have all these dishes to do. It's impossible."

"No, it's really true; Captain Vance says if you will come to the orderly room, a weekend pass will be there for you."

And so, tugging, pushing and shoving, and with many words of explanation I could barely understand, Joyce got me to follow her, leaving my partner in stunned amazement and in sole charge of the dirty dishes.

Miraculously, at the orderly room there was indeed a weekend pass for me. We snatched it and fled. On the way to Toronto, Joyce told me her story, full of coincidences. An officer riding on the same bus that she took to the Camp struck up a conversation with her. He turned out to be my former OC. Upon her arrival in Camp, she became lost and was assisted by a person who happened to be the messing officer in charge of the kitchen where I had been working. He took her to his office and, while she was seated there, another officer entered and introduced himself. Of all people, he was my present OC, Captain Vance. I must have been notorious; I was well known to all three officers. My OC and the messing officer had been engaged in waiting on the tables for the troopers' New Year's dinner. Captain Vance was delighted to meet my lovely wife. He knew all about my recent marriage and recall from my honeymoon. To my surprise, I learned that he was very supportive of us. He took Joyce for a drink to the officers' mess and, after some preliminary conversation, asked: "Are you kids getting a little time together?" As one might anticipate, Joyce responded appropriately. Captain Vance considered for a brief moment and then posed a question to which there could only have been one answer: "How would you like some leave?" We passed a delightful, quasi-illicit weekend, certainly unanticipated and unearned by me. This is how my wife rescued her husband from battle with a huge pile of greasy dishes and spirited him away for a few days to replenish his vigour, restore his soul, and prepare him for battle on another day.

Hello Joyce:-   January 9th, 1943

I now enclose the result of my cogitation with respect to my inglorious experiences as assistant dishwasher men's mess A9 Training Centre:

Isn't It Swill!

We join the army to fight the foe,
But there's many an odd job in the army, you know,
So if on kitchen fatigue we languish.
Our spirit is keen, no sign of anguish,
Washing dishes for victory!

And isn't it great, to work in the kitchen,
Isn't it fine to begin,
Clearing the dishes of beans and bacon,
And all the remains the lads haven't eaten?
Isn't it swill!

Residue of ham on plates of tin,
What if it <u>was</u> sliced a little too thin?
Lubricated by carrots and peas,
Into the garbage it glides with ease,
Isn't it swill!

The Colonel, the Adjutant, and Sergeant too.
Say we each have our respective jobs to do,
To win the war all out we go;
What a thrill, to work in the kitchen,

Isn't it swill!!

DCV

Any resemblance to Keats and Shelley is purely coincidental.

Sorry, I was unable to get a weekend pass; neither am I able to get a pass for Sunday.

Have to leave now for dinner. So long.

Love,
David

Eight
From P.O.M. to F.S.P.

Despite my low aptitude for service in the Canadian Armoured Corps, I must have had a respectable aptitude for teaching. After my return to Camp following my rescue from kitchen fatigue and after a brief period of vacillation as to my future role, I was put to work in the Wireless Wing as an instructor. Initially, I assisted another instructor who was in charge of a class of recruits in training as wireless (operator)/gunners. Soon afterwards, I shared the burden with another instructor, each of us taking responsibility for teaching one-half of the subjects of the course. Eventually, I was given full charge of a class on my own with sole responsibility for all subjects, gunnery excepted. This included supervision of the exercises in truck convoys during the course's final stages. The subjects, such as R/T procedure and electricity, were remote from my field of expertise. Still, I felt that I acquitted myself creditably as instructor, at least in the theoretical aspects and regardless of my own ability in the practical applications of my lectures. When I took out a convoy on a scheme, for example, I did not trust myself to install and hook up the batteries to facilitate communication between vehicles. This task I left to the trainees.

My new role as instructor brought me increasingly into contact with the Orderly Room, the nerve centre of the Wireless Wing. It therefore brought me into association with the NCOs who, as instructors or administrators, operated the Wireless Wing under the direction, of course, of the OC and higher echelons of the military establishment. Soon I enjoyed good, friendly, and even cordial relations with the NCOs of all ranks, although within the limits of authority attributable to rank, even as amongst NCOs. My altered status as instructor did not detract from my penchant for getting into trouble.

I was unable to obtain a pass, but Joyce came to Barrie to take a room I had booked at the Queen's Hotel. I left Camp after duty on a Saturday, with the intention of returning on Sunday morning in time for reveille at 6:00 a.m. I awoke very early and was walking on the main street toward the bus stop to catch the bus for Borden, groggy from lack of sleep, when I happened to glance toward the Town clock. It was at least an hour later than I expected. I had made a serious mistake and could not possibly return to Camp on time. I gave the matter consideration and decided that, on a quiet Sunday, I probably would not be missed. If I were missed, I would be in no more trouble than I was already in now. On this reasoning, I decided to stay in Barrie until Monday, retraced my steps, and climbed into bed again.

On Monday morning I returned to Camp without incident, checked in at the Guard House and made my way to the barracks. There, I found that everyone knew Vanek had been AWOL, including the students of his class. Corporal Beswick, in charge of the hut, was waiting for me.

"You had better see Sergeant Briggs right away."

Before I had a chance to seek him out, Sergeant Briggs came to me in haste to warn of impending disaster. Just as classes were about to begin, I went to the Orderly Room to pick up my syllabus. Nothing was said. As I was leaving, in the over-optimistic belief the whole incident had blown over, Sergeant-Major Boorman casually inquired:

"Where were you yesterday?"

Flustered, I began to stammer, uncertain how much of the episode he knew, and finally decided honesty was the best policy:

"Barrie, Sir."

"What were you doing in Barrie? Weren't you on church parade?"

To give him his due, the Sergeant Major was a good cross-examiner. Little by little, he drew from me the whole story. I was somewhat nonplussed, because all he actually knew in the first instance was that I had missed the church parade. When he was through with me, he turned to the Orderly Sergeant:

"Did Trooper Vanek phone the Orderly Room on Sunday?"

"Yes."

"Why wasn't I told about it?"

"I haven't had a chance to tell you about it yet."

Then the radio communication system connecting with one of the classrooms was turned on:

"Corporal Beswick!"

"Sir."

"Was Vanek on hand at roll call Sunday?"

"Yes sir."

And so all the detail was exposed. What a morning!

I had managed to get at least four NCOs into deep trouble. This is what happened. The first casualty was the Sergeant who took the church parade on Sunday. When my name was called during roll call, another person answered. The Sergeant Major happened to be passing by. He knew my voice very well. He wanted to know who answered to my name. Then there was the soldier who drew a pass for me for Sunday and turned it in at the Guard House. Then poor Beswick, the hut Corporal, had marked me present on roll call Sunday morning. Then there was the Orderly Sergeant who had also tried to cover for me. Finally, I had to make my peace with personnel at the Guard House. When the escapade, and its aftermath, was over my popularity with the NCOs suffered a sudden and decided reverse.

In the evening, shortly before "lights out," Corporal Beswick was calling the roll and, approaching my bunk, called:

"Lance Corporal Vanek."

I thought he was joking and thanked him for the promotion,

"Why," he asked, with a show of surprise, "don't you know about it? It's coming out in Orders tomorrow."

It was, in fact, official. The next day, Daily Orders, under the heading "Promotions," contained this item: "B 62876- Tpr. D.C.Vanek, promoted to rank of L/Cpl, with pay."

I was inordinately pleased with the military's expression of appreciation of my services to the Armoured Corps. Moreover, the timing could not have been better. How could the Army justify promotion and punishment at the same time? Thus, despite all previous indications, my most recent escapade passed without punishment. Not a further word was said on the subject, except for Sergeant Briggs. He could not resist an expression of disbelief, albeit in humorous vein, that the entire debacle was due to the fact that I had forgotten to wind my watch. Soon, I even recovered my good reputation and relations with the NCOs. Much later, when I was again promoted, this time to full Corporal, the promotion occurred again on an occasion when I was in trouble. This time I was given a good lesson on the doctrine that the punishment should fit the crime.

On a Monday after a long weekend away from Camp, I was, naturally, very tired. After lunch, I fell asleep in my bunk and did not awaken until well after I was due to instruct in the afternoon. In a panic, I raced to my classroom adjoining the Orderly Room to find that my unsupervised students were making an unearthly uproar. As I entered, the loud speaker summoned me:

"Lance Corporal Vanek!"

"Sir," I responded weakly.

"Come into the Orderly Room."

My punishment was swift, appropriate, and embarrassing. My class was assigned the task, after duty in the evening, of washing and scrubbing the floors of the classroom and the Orderly Room — and I was designated to supervise the work. For the record, the men of this class were a bunch of good sports. They fell to the work with vigour and enthusiasm. Mops, brushes, pails, soap, and all other necessary utensils were produced. There was much joking and calls to pass the soap and utensils. Meanwhile, I sat at a table and wrote a "scrub-by-scrub" description of this activity as if I was reporting a game of hockey. When the job was done, I read my account to the class. My students seemed to enjoy my version of the event and I suffered no adverse effects in my relations with them.

These awkward predicaments into which I fell were usually a consequence, directly or obliquely, of my conduct as a newlywed weekend husband. Not only would I come home for weekends whenever I could, but I would occasionally arrive mid-week to stay overnight and return to Camp next morning in time for reveille.

Often I would make the trip to and from Toronto with Corporal Beswick. He was the proud owner of a car with numerous ailments. Of course, he never had any difficulty getting a load of passengers. Beswick had an easy-going manner and a sensitive understanding of the illnesses of his vehicle. When it stalled, which was often the case, the hood would be raised; calmly, Beswick would putter and poke here and there; miraculously the vehicle would be restored to life; the passengers would board the car; and the journey would resume.

For the return to Camp, we had a regular meeting place: Fran's Restaurant. It still stands on St. Clair at Yonge Street. My problem was to awaken in the middle of the night in time to be at Fran's by the stated hour. Invariably, I was indebted to my father-in-law. Dad, as I now addressed him, watched over me with care. At about 3:30 a.m., he would virtually pull me from bed, load me into his car, and drive me to meet Beswick by about 4:15 a.m. The rest would be left to Beswick and his broken-down vehicle that, after several hiccups and stops, would eventually bring us to Borden in time for 6:00 a.m. reveille. Thus, between my duties in the Army and my duties to my wife, and the transition from military to civilian life, I passed the winter and spring of 1943.

In about July 1943, a distinct change occurred in my circumstances. Once again, I was unable to obtain any leave one weekend owing to some previous misbehaviour. I was assigned the duty of Orderly Sergeant for the Sunday solely, in my opinion, to make very certain that I would not leave Camp. In these circumstances, Joyce not only came to Barrie but into the Camp and was with me in the Orderly Room. We were both looking after the Orderly Room and one another, when I happened to notice Daily Orders on the desk on which we had been resting. One item attracted my particular attention. It directed Corporal Vanek to proceed forthwith to Three Rivers in the Province of Quebec to take an officers' training course. This development was not entirely unexpected.

About two months previously, I had been given an interview with an army examiner. He told me that when I tried the "M Test" the required score was 160 and I had scored 157. He also told me that, since then, the minimum score had been lowered to 150. This made me eligible for a commission. He told me he was going to recommend me for further consideration. I had almost given up hope that anything would come as a result of this interview. It was with gratification and pride, therefore, that I read and re-read this item in the Daily Orders. It appeared that I was being given a second opportunity to become a commissioned officer — this time coming up through the ranks, the "hard way." I had been told months ago that, in my case, this was nearly an impossibility.

A day or two later, I was on a train to Montreal, where I transferred to another train to Three Rivers and the Training Camp. I found Three Rivers to be a picturesque city of about 40,000 inhabitants, situated on the banks of the St. Lawrence River at the bottom of a steep hill. The Camp was located at the far end of the city. I was assigned to a platoon of newly arrived personnel. On the day after my arrival, the platoon was given an orientation tour of the Camp. I acquired a much clearer understanding of the nature and purpose of the training and the possible disposition of the trainees. The facility at Three Rivers was not an officers training centre in the full sense. Rather, it was a testing ground to determine which of the trainees, considered as candidates, should be sent to an officers' training centre (OTC). The object of the training, therefore, was to determine the physical and mental suitability of the candidates to attend an OTC and become commissioned officers. At the end of the course at Three Rivers, candidates would either be sent to an OTC or returned to unit (RTU). An appraisal board, whose decision was final, determined success, or failure, at the end of the three-week training period.

I found the course to be extremely rigorous. The candidates were told, and made to feel, that they were under constant appraisal. They were criticized for the slightest deviation from perfection of performance. There was a constant threat of RTU hanging over their heads. The candidates were kept in a psychological state of tension throughout the course. A typical day began with morning parade, then hard drill in battle order, and a half mile run followed immediately by an onslaught upon a difficult obstacle course. In the afternoon, there was a route march through brush, swamp and a creek. A highlight of the training was an exercise that began with a high speed march of twenty miles. On two nights, we slept under the stars on ground sheets, and, on occasion, were subjected to sudden attack with tear gas. My endurance was tested to the extreme on several occasions.

As the course was coming to a close, I had little doubt that I was headed for another disappointment. A letter to Joyce, written on a Sunday preceding the Monday on which the decision of the Appraisal Board was to be announced, amply reveals my state of mind. My pessimism is reflected in the candid self-evaluation contained in the following passages:

I feel quite certain as to my fate and think I should prepare you for it. I do not expect to pass. I believe I shall be R.T.U.ed. I have tried my best, but I can't seem to make myself the kind of soldier they care to give commissions to. Perhaps I am being premature in expressing these statements — there is perhaps some hope — but to be honest, with you and myself, very little, I do believe....

The chief trouble has been, I think, that I have been over anxious; far too tense and strained at all times during the appraisal period to show myself off to best advantage.

Then too, there's no denying that there are certain eccentricities and oddities about me that do not help matters. It would require a thorough stock-taking to set down accurately the long list of articles I have lost, at one time or another, and some permanently. Not improbably I have spent more time than anyone else looking after my kit and equipment, yet these probably have been in the worst condition. I never could make up my webbing properly and neatly, like a good soldier. On parade I march in an awkward and unorthodox manner, so everyone says. Invariably, to quote Mr. Selkirk, I complete a drill movement either slightly behind or ahead of anyone else in the platoon. In addition I lack basic training, and that shows. In shorts, battle order, bowed legs, sun helmet that covers my face as well as head, holding a rifle that is never quite spotless, I guess I must cut a somewhat ridiculous figure.

(At current date I retract my comment about the bowed legs.)

The next day I was standing on parade with the rest of the Company when a list of names was announced of candidates who had failed and were to be RTU. I listened for my name to be called. What a surprise! It did not happen; I had passed! I was included amongst those candidates who had been designated by the appraisal board as "Approved Officer Material." Once again, I was a POM. Later I learned that out of seventy-two men in my Company, about twenty-six were RTU. They were paraded together, given a brief address, and summarily sent back to their units.

The good news was that I had been approved. Then came the bad news. It was a partial corroboration of rumours that the training centres were being closed. The candidates who had been approved as officer material were also paraded together and addressed by a high ranking officer. We were informed that, for the present, there appeared to be a sufficiency of officers, or a reduced need for additional officers; that there was to be no draft of personnel from Three Rivers to any of the OTCs for the current month; and that, accordingly, the approved candidates would also be returned to their units, or sent for further training elsewhere, to await an opening at an OTC. A few days later, therefore, I was back at Camp Borden, as a POM. I was assigned to barracks with other POMs in GMT Squadron. During the next several months, I was occupied in basic military training. I also experienced a stiff drill course for NCOs. Time passed, and still there was no word of an opening for me at an OTC. It seemed to me that I had exhausted all benefit of any basic training that was available to me at Camp Borden.

By this time, I had given up all hope of a summons to an OTC, or of becoming a commissioned officer in the Armoured Corps. Early in December 1993, I learned that applications were being considered from personnel wishing to attend a security course offered under the auspices of the Canadian Intelligence Corps. I was immediately interested. I arranged for and attended an interview with an Army examiner, who gave me a sympathetic hearing. I asked to be transferred from the Armoured Corps to the Canadian Intelligence Corps and the opportunity to attend this course in security. The Army examiner stated that he would recommend the transfer. Nevertheless, I was surprised, but immensely pleased, when, several weeks later, the transfer went through Orders. Officially, I became a member of the Canadian Intelligence Corps and a few days later was on my way to Kingston, Ontario to attend the security course.

The city of Kingston, Ontario, is a substantial urban centre and was one of the first European settlements in Canada. Kingston, like Three Rivers, is located on the bank of the St. Lawrence River, but much lower down river. It is situated at about the confluence of the St. Lawrence with Lake Ontario and opposite a myriad of islands, known as the Thousand Islands.

The security course was given at the Royal Military College (RMC). It was located somewhere across the St. Lawrence, because I remember trudging back and forth across the frozen river waters in the dead of winter. The object of the course at RMC was to train personnel of the Canadian Intelligence Corps for service in Field Security Units attached to various military formations. Each member of a Field Security Unit, regardless of rank, was supposed to be clothed with the authority to instruct officers of the highest rank, even a colonel in command of a regiment, in security matters. This lofty view of the role of Field Security Units was reflected in the amenities, the teaching, and the treatment of the trainees. The staff dealt with the trainees with the courtesy and respect due to personnel destined for special duties of particular importance.

The course was unlike any training I had hitherto experienced in the Army. It was concerned with the possible infiltration of enemy agents. The curriculum included lessons on the German hierarchy and military establishment; how to follow a suspect without being noticed; how to evade a person when being followed; field studies of essential utilities and the danger of sabotage; and the proper method of making an intensive search of premises. The lectures were interesting and the exercises, some of which were reminiscent of games played as children, were also enjoyable. Altogether the course was to my liking.

When my dear wife learned that I was to be sent to Kingston, she insisted upon joining me for the duration of the course. I strenuously resisted this. What would the military authorities say? Nevertheless, Joyce won the argument. Somehow she discovered that there was an elderly Jewish woman who owned an ancient dwelling in Kingston and who was prepared to provide lodging for us. Although the quarters for the field security personnel (FSP) were the comfortable rooms at RMC occupied pre-war by cadets enrolled at the College, I spent my days at RMC absorbing the knowledge essential for service in the Intelligence Corps and my nights with my wife in this lodgement.

Our landlady allowed us the use of the kitchen. She did so with obvious misgivings, because she was constantly in a flutter for fear we might breach the kosher environment of her home by mixing her dishes for milk and meat foods. However, our use of the kitchen was dictated by both compassion and necessity, because the only source of heat in a very cold winter was a stove located in the kitchen. Joyce complained of the cold and we spent our evenings huddled around the stove for warmth. Nevertheless, my sojourn in Kingston was an idyllic interlude in an otherwise unrewarding existence as a Canadian soldier.

All too soon, I completed the course and this dreamlike episode came to an end. Thereupon my group of FSP were put on draft for overseas and dispatched to the east coast of Canada. Joyce returned home to Toronto. After a long and tedious journey by train, we arrived at a military camp in Windsor, Nova Scotia. Our draft seemed to bog down there. We remained in Windsor for what seemed to be an indeterminate sentence, with nothing to do except fatigues of one sort or another. With the know-how acquired from previous experience, and an alleged skill in typing, I was given some work in the Orderly Room. Time weighed heavily on my hands. Joyce kept calling and writing about coming to Windsor. This time, however, I had the good sense to firmly reject this suggestion.

One day, I was seated in the Orderly Room at the large desk of the Sergeant-Major, quietly engaged in reading, when I was disturbed by an unusual commotion. I looked up to find that a group of officers wearing battle order had just entered. The group included former POMs, now all lieutenants, with whom I had been associated when I first came to Camp Borden: amongst others, Stan Brereton, Bud Gendron, Ken Ramsden, and my particular friend, Saul Wolfe. Seated as I was in a position of apparent authority, and one of the first to greet them on their arrival at Camp, they beheld me with amazement bordering on incredulity. There was a great deal of laughter and expressions of goodwill. It would be difficult to say who welcomed whom. They ultimately left the Orderly Room to take up their accommodation, separate and apart from other ranks. I rarely saw any of them again while at Windsor, and never afterwards during my time in service.

At long last, the order came for the movement of troops from Windsor to Halifax. With my group of FSP and others, I embarked on the New Amsterdam for the voyage, in convoy, to Britain. The New Amsterdam had allegedly been a relatively new luxury liner, but it was no longer recognizable as such. It had been reconstructed by eliminating all traces of excess and luxury and converted, to the limit of its capacity, into a wartime transport ship for troops. The troops were packed like sardines into the hold of the vessel, where there were insufficient toilets and related facilities to service their needs. The sleeping arrangements consisted of rows of bunks, three or four bunks high. There was a constant line of soldiers waiting to use the toilets. It was in these conditions that, in the last week of March, the troops endured the Atlantic voyage in the still-rough winter weather. I could only imagine the much different conditions for the officers who occupied the decks above. I knew then, or learned afterwards, that my former associates as POMs were on board the same vessel in a draft over which my friend Saul had charge.

An incident occurred when I was trying to fall asleep in a lower bunk assigned to me. Without warning, Jim Woods, an FSO in a bunk above mine, turned on his side with a groan and gave up the contents of his stomach. Some splattered on me. I was furious with the offender. I admonished him harshly.

"Jim Woods," I said, waving my outstretched index finger at him for emphasis, "You SOB. Look what you've done! As long as you live I won't let you forget what you've done to me!"

There is a sequel to this story. At the time, Jim was a very young soldier, perhaps eighteen or nineteen years old. When the war was over, he returned to his home in Toronto and became a lawyer. I became a judge. Years after this incident, he would occasionally come into my court. It was usually merely to request an adjournment or other administrative disposition, for I never tried a case in which he was involved. Whenever I noticed him in court, I would call a recess at a convenient juncture and wait for him in the hall. When I met with him I would remind him that he befouled me many years ago in the hold of the New Amsterdam. I would make it a point to address him in the very words I used on that previous occasion. Poor Jim! He could never verbalize any adequate defence. It was a great joke amongst comrades-at-arms.

As we were approaching the end of the voyage, the weather turned stormy; it rained and the wind blew in steady violence. Then, early in the morning, just as dawn was breaking, someone spotted land. Everyone appeared on deck peering out into the horizon. As land came more distinctly into view, the storm abated and it became a lovely day in spring. As we sailed up the calm waters of the Clyde River to our anchorage, I feasted my eyes on the green grass and fresh sown fields on both sides of the river. It was one of the loveliest spectacles I have ever seen. In musical terms, the termination of our voyage was like the concluding passages of Gotterdammerung, or better still, the fifth movement of the Beethoven Pastoral Symphony.

As we disembarked, we were greeted by a group of women who offered the comforts of tea, coffee and biscuits. We had landed at Greenock, Scotland, en route to Aldershot in the south of England. It was April 3, 1944.

I was posted to a wartime military camp, located somewhere in the south of England between Aldershot and Farnborough. Upon arrival, there were two distressing incidents. The first was the failure of the carrier to transport my kit that, amongst other items, contained a list of addresses of my Lester relatives; I had promised Joyce to visit them as soon as possible. The second matter was more serious. I was required forthwith to remove the stripes signifying my rank as full corporal. I protested this to the authorities most strenuously, all to no avail. I was firmly informed that no record could be found confirming that I was a corporal, and nothing further could be done about it. Once again, I became a plain soldier without rank of any kind.

Basically, the Camp was a holding unit or staging area for troops pending their transfer to specific military units. In general, therefore, no special training was provided for the FSP. While awaiting transfer, however, the FSP were subject to the prevailing discipline and activities of the Camp, including drills, parades, inspections, and route marches. They were also required to maintain themselves in a neat and orderly fashion, with shoes well polished, uniforms ironed, rifles cleaned and oiled, and badges well shined. The aversion of the troops to the "spit and polish" of the army, as it was termed by soldiers, was reflected in a little rhyme we created about "blanco," the accepted product in the military for cleaning and shining brass buttons and badges. It was sung to the strains of a Strauss waltz, and included the lines: "We are FS NCOs; we even blanco our clothes."

This period of waiting was tedious and time hung heavily on my hands. Fortunately I was assigned to barracks with the other FSP who had come overseas with me and I got along very well with them, especially several who became very good friends of mine.

A few days after my arrival in Camp, while my kit was still missing, I met a soldier who gave me the address in London of Uncle Herschel, father Lester's eldest brother. I also encountered Leo Lichtenberg, an acquaintance who was familiar with London. The Jewish festival of

Passover was approaching. For this occasion I was able to obtain leave and I accompanied Leo. A friend had invited Leo to spend the "seder" on the first evening of Passover with the friend's family in London.

The day after the seder, Leo and his friend led me to Hanbury Street in the London east end, a district known as Whitechapel. I walked along a bleak, dirty, desolate road searching for number 60, horrified by what I beheld. On both sides of the street were rows of houses and shops that were mere shells, without an interior; occasional empty lots where structures had once stood; and brick and rubble everywhere. Then I came upon 60 Hanbury Street — miraculously, a structure still standing, the first in a row of buildings not demolished by the German bombing raids of the early forties. My friends went to the door before me and explained to the occupants that a young man wanted to see them.

What a welcome! Uncle Hershel, Aunt Sarah, and Cousin Esther swooned with delight. They rushed to produce a photograph depicting me standing with my father-in-law. Cousin Ida who, with her husband, operated a grocery shop a few doors along the street, was sent for, and she put in a breathless appearance. Then, I was seated at a table and fed. I passed the rest of the day with these new-found relatives. I fully established my credentials and was accepted as an honoured member of the Lester family. In the evening, Leo and I returned to camp.

About a month or two later, I attended the wedding of a young Lester relative. It took place at Golders Green Synagogue, with a dinner-dance afterwards a short distance away at the Regal Ballrooms. On this occasion, I met the rest of clan Lester. It was a very substantial extended family living in London and environs. It included the family of a deceased Lester brother, who dwelt in north London on Winchmore Hill, and Aunt Esther, father Lester's only sister and the youngest of his family. She lived in High Wycombe, north of London.

Back at camp, life continued to be dull, dreary and unrewarding. One day, however, an event occurred that considerably brightened an otherwise monotonous existence. The Canadian Army Show, and with it Wayne and Shuster, came to the camp.

To appreciate this story, it is necessary to know about a skit that they performed some years back as part of our fraternity show, the Beta Sigma Rho Review. In this skit, Johnnie played the part of the Swami, a magician clad in suitable attire, including a turban; Frank

Shuster was his faithful attendant. A large black box was in place on stage. After a humorous introduction and explanation of the trick that was to be performed, Johnnie called: "Will a brave young man come forward from the audience." An individual ascended the stage. He was placed inside the box and the lid was closed. Then Frank passed several swords through the box. When all was quiet, Johnnie opened the lid, peered inside, and looked toward the audience allowing an expression of amazement to appear on his countenance. Then came the "punch line." In a loud, clear voice, Johnnie proclaimed: "Give this man his money back!" I witnessed the rehearsal of this skit at the fraternity house on numerous occasions. Each time it was performed, with variations, we would laugh uproariously.

The Canadian Army Show was at camp for two performances, one at 6:00 p.m. and the other at 8:00 p.m. I arrived from a march much too late to attend the 6:00 p.m. performance but, naturally, I was eager to see the show. I set out about 7:00 p.m. to ensure that I had a good seat for the second performance. When I arrived at the theatre, however, I did not go to the line-up of soldiers seeking admission. Instead, I entered a hall to the side of the stage where I could hear, although not see, what was transpiring on stage during the 6:00 p.m. show. A new scene was beginning and, to my delight, I distinguished the voices of both Lou and Frank. Thrilled, I pushed past the attendant at the door explaining that I was a friend of the boys on the stage. I slipped along the wall and stood close to the front and side of the stage. To my utter amazement, I observed that the boys, clad in Yogi costumes complete with turbans, were in process of performing the "box trick" of the fraternity show. Lou, in the part of the Swami magician, was speaking in what passed for Hindustani. Frank, his faithful attendant, Haasan Ben Pull-Through, was interpreting his words for the benefit of the highly amused audience. I was transported with delight. Lou explained the nature of the powerful feat of magic to be performed: a volunteer from the audience will be confined in the box; Haasan Ben Pull-Through will thrust five swords through the box; and yet the volunteer will emerge safe and sound. Then came the call: "Will a brave young man step forward from the audience!" At this cue, Haasan Ben Pull-Through, with a devilish glint in his eyes and wagging a forefinger at the audience began to count: "Eenie, Meenie, Minee." When he reached "Moe," I strode up the steps and onto the stage.

What perfect timing! Ascending the stage was virtually involuntary. I could not possibly have resisted the temptation. What a joyous reunion then occurred on stage! Young veterans of the theatre as they already were, the boys displayed perfect stage presence and aplomb, although all three of us were nearly convulsed with laughter at this extraordinary meeting. The situation brought forth considerable improvisation — humorous exchanges well understood by the actors, if not entirely by the audience. Lou spoke words of welcome:

"Look who's here!" and a variety of quips. Then: "What is your name?"

"Vanek," I responded. There followed an elaborate introduction to Haasan Ben Pull-Through, and I shook hands with Frank.

"Is this the first time you have been on the stage?" asked Lou.

"Yes," I replied, untruthfully.

"That's all right," Lou continued, "This is the first time Haasan Ben Pull Through and I have done this trick!"

The audience was roaring with laughter and, on stage, we were laughing with the audience. After these lines, and others of like import, there was nothing left to do but put me into the box. Frank thrust the swords through the box to the accompaniment of blood-curdling screams and Lou delivered the punch line. But, I never got any money back!

Later, I was backstage with the boys and we were all still in laughter over this incident. Lou and Frank were somewhat concerned about the poor fellow they had planted in the audience who was to have come forward as their "volunteer." Ultimately, he too arrived backstage and was relieved to find that he was forgiven for missing his cue. I conversed with the boys while they changed for the next skit. I watched it alongside the curtain while, from the stage, they addressed a variety of remarks and smiles in my direction. Next day, Wayne and Shuster and the other members of the Canadian Army Show were gone and I resumed my normal activities at the Camp.

"Normal" for the FSP at our holding unit was equivalent to monotonous and dreary, except for the efforts of the FSP to amuse themselves. One incident involved "One-L" Wilson, so called to distinguish him from another member of our group who, for obvious reasons, we called "Two-L" Willson. Our FSP were part of a parade of the camp troops in full battle order and an inspection by a Colonel. I was standing in line directly behind One-L when the parade had been brought to attention in open order formation. The Colonel slowly passed behind each line and occasionally tapped the haversacks slung over the shoulder that were supposed to contain various items of personal equipment. When the Colonel came to One-L and inserted his hand into a partially open haversack, I observed his expression of sheer incredulity as he began to pull out a long sheet — of toilet paper! Apparently, to lighten his burden, One-L had stuffed the bag with toilet tissue instead of his equipment. How I managed to stifle my laughter, I shall never know. Nor do I recall what punishment this misadventure attracted. I know One-L was not shot at dawn, because I continued to enjoy the benefit of his company for many days thereafter.

As we waited for posting to another unit, time passed agonizingly slowly. Occasionally, it was possible to relieve the tedium by a brief excursion from camp. Thus I became somewhat acquainted with the towns of Aldershot and Guildford. On weekend leave, I also visited the Steins, cousins of my father-in-law who lived in Camberly.

At long last, however, the period of waiting came to an end, with the exciting events of June 5 and 6, 1944. On the 5th, the officer commanding No. 13 Canadian Field Security Section, which was administered directly out of Canadian Central Military Headquarters in London, came to the camp to interview and select reinforcements. I was pleased to learn that I was his first choice of two FSP he had selected. Leo Begley was the other. Later, when I found that most of the other FSP had been posted to Sections serving on the continent, I was dubious about my good fortune at being transferred to London.

The next day, June 6, 1944, was invasion day. I need hardly dwell on the excitement that news of this event engendered. Early in the morning, the rumour began to circulate that the "big show" was on. Shortly afterwards, the rumour was confirmed as fact: allied forces had landed on the coast of France. Towards evening, gazing skyward with mixed emotions, I stood transfixed at the sight of countless airplanes. Some were towing gliders or carrying airborne troops, and all were headed for the English Channel and the coast of France as part of the invasion force. The planes kept coming in a seemingly endless stream and ultimately disappearing into the horizon. It was a sight destined to dwell forever in my memory.

My transfer to No. 13 Field Security Section was not effective immediately. First, there was the matter of an additional course the

FSP had to undergo, which for some unaccountable reason had been deferred to this late date. We had to learn to drive a motorcycle. In the field, a motorcycle was regular army issue to FSP, and the motorcycle of choice was the huge Harley-Davidson. It must have weighed at least 1000 lb. This was the motorcycle I drove for the duration of the course.

I found the motorcycle course exhilarating. It provided the opportunity to get out of the encampment and to view and appreciate the pleasant English countryside. On one trip, we drove to Windsor and, on another occasion, we travelled as far as Reading. I encountered no substantial difficulty learning to drive a motorcycle. After all, I was well experienced in driving an automobile and a truck, and I had even driven the huge army tank. A motorcycle was just another motor vehicle. Of course, there were increased hazards associated with the operation of a motorcycle. Moreover, I had never driven a vehicle in the conditions prevailing in wartime England. I was not used to narrow winding roads, driving on the left side of the road or driving in a blackout. I well remember one exercise in which, in extreme tension, I drove a motorcycle in a long convoy at night and in a blackout. According to a piece of propaganda attributed to the Germans, if enough motorcycles were issued to Canadian troops the army would suffer more casualties through gross recklessness than could be inflicted by the German armed forces in combat. There may have been a kernel of truth in this claim.

One climactic episode of our training in the driving of a motorcycle was the attempted conquest of the Devil's Punchbowl, somewhat akin to the climbing of Mt. Everest. The physical feature called, by some, the Devil's Punchbowl, to which we were brought by our Sergeant-instructor, was a deep valley with very steep slopes of deep sand. Our project was to drive the motorcycle from the base of the valley to the top of the slope. The exercise required us to accelerate to a maximum and attempt to overcome the effects of the sliding and shifting sand. I tried at least three times and, upon each attempt, my cycle came to a stop partially up the hill and fell over. The Sergeant, a man of great strength, had to lift the vehicle and set it upright on each occasion. At a mere 135 lb., I could not possibly lift the 1000 lb. cycle myself. On the last occasion, the Sergeant roundly dressed me down, not just because I failed to reach the top of the hill. My unforgivable transgression was that I had allowed the vehicle to fall in a way that caused it to lose its petrol. This single default, however, did not prevent my approval as a qualified driver. A few days later I was officially transferred to No. 13 Canadian Field Security Section (13 Cdn FSS) in London.

Nine
My War

I arrived in London to join 13 Cdn FSS on June 19, 1944, almost contemporaneously with the advent of the guided missile, described by Churchill as the "Flying Bomb." It has been variously referred to as the "V1," "buzz-bomb," "doodle-bug," or "robot bomb." This was the Germans' secret weapon that, by indiscriminate bombing of British cities, was intended to accomplish what the huge blitz by airplanes in the early days of the war failed to do, to bring the British people to their knees and make them sue for peace.

My first experience with the missile occurred when the sirens sounded the alarm and the officer whom I was accompanying donned a steel helmet. I followed him as he ran to a shelter. Shortly afterwards, someone told me that the odds against a direct strike were some astronomical figure like ten million to one. Although not renowned for personal courage, I decided these were odds that allowed me to accept the risk. I never ran for cover again, with one painful exception. As a member of 13 Cdn FSS, I was billeted with Jack Milnes in a room in a private home on Nottinghill Gate near Oxford Street. It was late at night and I was lying awake in bed nervously listening to the sound of a series of buzz bombs as they passed overhead. I sensed that Jack was also awake and listening in his bed. The bombs emitted a sound of buzzing that increased in intensity the closer they came. If the sound gradually decreased, one would know it was safe and that the bomb had passed by. However, if the buzzing increased to a maximum of intensity and then stopped, it was likely the bomb was directly overhead and falling and one could be in grave danger. That is exactly what appeared to happen. One of the flying bombs emitted a low drone that gradually, as it approached nearer to us, became louder and louder. When the sound became a roar, the motor stopped. We did not wait to hear the explosion. Both Jack and I leaped from our respective beds in unison, rushed to the stairwell leading to the basement, collided, and fell down the steps together. It was not our finest hour!

When I joined 13 Cdn FSS, the Section HQ was located at 25 Kensington Palace Gardens in central London west of Hyde Park, occasionally referred to as Millionaires Row. The street took its name from Kensington Palace, the birthplace, I am told, of Queen Victoria. Several other buildings on the street were occupied by foreign embassies. Our Section shared the building with an equivalent British field security section. About two months later, however, we separated from the British and moved our headquarters to 150 Victoria Street. It was located in an office building directly opposite the Victoria Railway Station, a landmark of London and a very busy terminal. Our Section took over most of the fourth floor of the 8-storey building. Windows enclosed the offices. As a result, there was an increased danger from shattered glass caused by a flying bomb, direct hit or no. Years later, upon a visit to London with Joyce, I was eager to show her the location of Section HQ. Although I knew she was not particularly interested, I led her by subway (the "Tube") to Victoria Station. To my dismay and embarrassment, I could not find the building. Gradually I realized that the structure had been demolished to make way for a realignment of the roads serving this busy hub of London.

Thirteen Cdn FSS was a very small military unit. It was composed of thirteen members: the OC, the sergeant major (CSM or SSM), two sergeants, four corporals, and the remainder lance corporals (L/Cpls). Upon joining the unit, once again I was elevated to the exalted heights of L/Cpl, but this time merely as an "acting" rank. Ruefully, I recalled being told by the staff at Kingston that, in the field, FSP were given rank as sergeants. This provided external indicia of authority enabling FSP to exercise their functions to the point even of instructing colonels in security matters. This assurance may have applied to service in a field security section on the continent, but apparently did not apply to FSP serving in Britain.

The personnel of 13 Cdn FSS were much older and more experienced in life than the average Canadian soldier on active wartime service. CSM Black, for instance, was over forty years of age. He told us that he had spent about twenty-four years with the RCMP in Canada, much of this in undercover activity; had risen to the rank of Sergeant; and had left the RCMP because of some trouble to which he made vague references. According to general knowledge in the unit, Sergeant Flemming had worked as a miner, was married, and had a wife and several children in Canada. Both sergeants had the bad habit of borrowing money from me, a habit that I found embarrassing and hard to resist. One of our FSP was a high school teacher and another was an experienced journalist.

We were required to make our own arrangements for living quarters and were given a regular subsistence allowance to cover the cost. I shared a room with Jack Milnes. Initially, we lived in a dwelling on Nottinghill Gate near Hyde Park and Marble Arch, the Mecca of soapbox orators with a message for their British compatriots. After our HQ was moved to Victoria Street, Jack found a dwelling closer to the office. In early January of the new year, we moved to this location, 24 Oakley Street, about three hundred metres from the Thames River and the Embankment. Our new accommodation was located in Chelsea, a district of London to which people who engaged or professed involvement in the arts or other cultural activities tended to gravitate. It was also close to the Peer Hotel, a public house that attracted a curious, eclectic group of habitués from this neighbourhood. I enjoyed my brief residence on Oakley Street. I met a variety of interesting people who frequented the Peer Hotel and attended, on occasion, the Chelsea Palace Theatre, which still operated as a typical old-fashioned English music hall.

More satisfying than the promotion to the rank of L/Cpl was the issue to me in due course of a Harley-Davidson motorcycle. I believe, however, that I spent more time in the required cleaning and maintenance of the machine, than in its actual use and operation. It was more practical and convenient, generally, to make my way about London by subway than by motorcycle. Apart from riding the motorcycle on specific military assignments, including initial exercises to familiarize myself with driving in the heavy traffic of London, I took the vehicle on the road infrequently.

On one occasion, I drove to the east-end to visit my newfound relatives on Hanbury Street. Clad in my army-issue greatcoat, wearing helmet and goggles, and mounted on my immense Harley-Davidson, I must have created a sensation as I thundered to my destination. Esther's twelve-year-old boy, Peter, whom I regarded as my young "limey" or "cockney" relative, heralded my approach by running about in wild excitement, shouting: "Uncle Di..ivid is coming! Uncle Di..ivid is coming!" The peculiar accent and dialect of the cockney clung to little Peter as tenaciously as it did to most people residing near the markets of "Petticoat Lane" and "Dogs Row." According to legend, a cockney is anyone born within hearing distance of the bells of the church of St. Mary-Le-Bow. I found Uncle Herschel in his back yard amid scattered debris of lumber. Despite his advanced years, he was busily engaged in repairing pushcarts. He earned a livelihood by renting them to tradespeople for use at the adjoining markets.

The role of 13 Cdn FSS was to serve as a security patrol of London for the protection of the Canadian armed forces and the safeguarding of their operations. With this object, we routinely visited the numerous service clubs in London, the several railway stations, public houses, of course, and, generally, all places where the troops tended to congregate. At the service clubs, for instance, we checked on the integrity of staff who dealt with the troops, whether stationed in London, on leave, or passing through to other locations. We were concerned about loose or careless talk, divulging the nature or timing of operations, and even expressions of disillusionment with the war effort that could affect military morale. We regularly attended at the railway stations to observe the movement of troops through London. If we noted a breach of security, we could attempt to deal with the matter on the spot. Naturally, if we encountered a spy or enemy agent, we would have been expected to do our best to apprehend the malefactor. I confess, however, that just as I never instructed any colonels in matters of security, neither did I, as far as I am aware, come to grips with any spies or enemy agents.

Our function as FSP was to observe, listen, and report. At our HQ, we submitted daily reports, and a weekly report, together with an expense account. The OC held a weekly conference on Saturdays. Each member of the Section took a turn acting as Duty NCO. This duty included taking charge of the Section HQ overnight. One day of the week was reserved as an "off-day," a day of rest from regular duties. Occasionally, an official training program was scheduled, as on a day when Cpl. O'Sullivan and I were assigned a surveillance exercise.

The exercise required us to trail CSM Black, acting in the capacity of a suspect. The one flaw of the exercise, of course, was that the suspect knew, although he was to act as though he did not know, that he was being followed. Still the CSM led us on an elaborate, evasive tour of London while we grimly managed to follow and keep him under continuous observation. Finally, the CSM came full circle to Victoria Station, entered it, and descended a set of stairs to the basement. We decided that O'Sullivan would follow and I would remain on the landing to carry on when the CSM emerged. Shortly afterwards, O'Sullivan returned, crestfallen. He had lost the CSM. He explained what had happened. Both he and the CSM had entered a lavatory and were standing in adjacent cubicles with three-quarter partitions separating them. The CSM briefly passed from view, presumably as he crouched down to button his trousers. He never re-appeared. In distress, O'Sullivan wanted to know why I also failed to notice the CSM when he should have ascended the stairs. To our chagrin, we had not realized there was another stairway leading to and from the basement. Somewhat embarrassed, we had to telephone to learn where we could again pick up the CSM. Our failure was not disastrous, however. We followed the CSM for the rest of the exercise and, at its conclusion, joined him at his favourite pub for a beer or two.

I sometimes reported on the state of civilian morale, particularly as affected by the flying bombs. On this subject, it was instructive to visit the pubs to meet and converse with the patrons. The harm and destruction from these missiles was increasingly extensive. The bombs usually detonated over London at night. We would learn the extent of the damage the next morning. On one occasion, for instance, there was a direct hit on a subway station; on another, a subway line. On both occasions travel by subway was discontinued. Vehicular and pedestrian traffic in busy London was tied up until the debris could be cleared and repairs effected. In still another instance, a bomb landed adjacent to a cinema in the district of Clapham. About thirty people who had been standing in a queue to buy tickets were killed.

About a month after I joined the Section I decided to pay a visit to the Groships, the friends of Leo Lichtenberg with whom I had spent the Seder night of Passover. They lived behind their candy shop at 156 Peckham High Street, south of the Thames River. I had heard that South London had been hit particularly hard by the bombs, but I was still not prepared for what I saw. As I walked along High Street to their residence, I observed shops with windows smashed; the more I walked, the worse the damage appeared. I reached number 156 and found it had been bombed out. There was a gaping hole in the roof and nobody was home. Peckham High Street, the main thoroughfare of the district, was bomb-stricken, deserted, with hardly a store intact. I made inquiries about the Groships and, with great relief, learned that they were safe. Later, I visited with them. It was the second time the poor middle-aged couple had been bombed out of a home and business in London. I was amazed at the resilience of the Londoners. The civilian population withstood the shock, danger, hardships, uncertainties and inconveniences of this new form of indiscriminate bombing, with courage, fortitude, and even a touch of humour.

Civilian morale in London during the onslaught by buzz bombs was exceptional. Later, however, the Germans perfected a variation of the flying bomb by eliminating the mechanism that caused the buzzing. The silent bomb was called the V-2. It was an even more lethal weapon because it emitted no warning of its approach. There was no way to escape the danger of injury or destruction by the bombs that got through the network of defences protecting London. Civilian morale stiffened into a grim determination to withstand even this formidable type of attack to the end. This occurred only when the allied forces ultimately captured the launching pads on the continent.

Despite the nefarious effects of this new form of aerial bombardment by the flying bomb, blackouts, fog, influx of troops of all allied nations, food rationing, and other governmental restrictions, amazingly, life in London went on in a normal and usual course. The pubs were full of customers, restaurants were open and busy, people stood in line for the cinemas, and it was a bumper season for the theatre and all manner of cultural events. Laurence Olivier and Ralph Richardson headlined the Old Vic, a repertory company of worldwide acclaim. John Gielgud was performing in Hamlet. A fresh young ballet company featured Margot Fontanne and Robert Helpmann. Myra Hess, a noted pianist, gave noontime concerts at the National Gallery. Violinist, Yehudi Menuhin, played to a sell-out audience at Albert Hall.

I devoted my "off-days" to attending as many of these events as I could afford and time would allow. I also occasionally visited Joyce's relatives, particularly the branch of the Lester family at Winchmore Hill in north London. The elderly widow could barely make herself understood because of a recent stroke. Daughter Becky, a mother of infant twins, was ostensibly in charge of the household, supported by husband Sonny, brothers Jack and Barney, and teenaged sister Golda. The male members were disqualified from military service, but two younger brothers were on active service with the British army, one in Italy, and the other in the mid-east. Never did I arrive without receiving a warm welcome. Instantly I would be seated at the "Morrison" table, the frying pan would be produced and the potato chips and tea got under way. The table, incidentally, had a metal top and was intended for the dual purpose of protection as well as its customary use. In the event of an aerial attack, the babies, and adults as well, could huddle under the table. Shamelessly, I took full advantage of this hospitality, although I would give Becky any extra ration coupons I might have and share the contents of parcels I received from home. Fortunately I was the recipient of numerous boxes containing quantities of good and useful products — more than all other members of the Section except Ken Clarke, who must have left behind in Canada an exceptionally caring girlfriend. I also managed to travel extensively through England and Scotland on furlough or other leave and I spent a week with a fisherman and his wife in the coastal village of Mousehole in Cornwall. The quaint dialect and speech of the Cornish people, who habitually exchange subject and object in their sentence structure, captivated me.

I used to be intrigued by the wide variations of accent, dialect, custom and speech of British people. I made note, for instance, of a statement of opinion by cousin Barney concerning baseball. Barney was about thirty-five years of age, mild-mannered, and soft-spoken with a cultured English accent. He remarked that a few days previously he was walking through the park and noticed some soldiers playing that game — he fumbled for the word — "baseball". He said that he stopped to watch it.

"Do you know," he continued, "I cawnt see a thing in it." "To tell the truth," he added, "I got the greatest pleasure from watching the spectators — the way they shout and act."

Somewhat amused, I responded, "It's a little different from

cricket. There the batsman misses the ball, so they stop the game and have tea."

Then I added by way of encouragement, "but go on, tell me what you know about baseball."

"Well," said Barney, "the bowler throws the ball over the wicket; the batsman almost always misses it with the stick, and the wicket-keeper catches it."

This thorough application of the language of cricket to the great American national pastime, in the context of his mode of speech and accent, seemed to me indicative of the differences in custom, manners and outlook between British and American people. I recall another occasion when I was in the company of a young woman possessed of an impeccable Oxford accent. I failed to realize, until she broke into laughter, that she had been quietly making fun of *my* Canadian accent and quality of speech. After that, never again was I critical of the British with respect to accent, dialect, inflection or other kindred superficialities.

I was footloose and fancy-free and my sojourn in London was comfortable. London was one of the most exciting cities in the world. I was quartered in private lodgings in wartime, backed by military pay that was supplemented by a subsistence allowance and an expense account, and pampered by parcels from home and the generous hospitality of local relatives. Yet, despite these apparently providential circumstances, I was dispirited, discontented, unfulfilled and lonely. The main problem was my increasing disillusionment with 13 Cdn FSS and its role in London. No doubt the Section had an important function, prior to D-Day, to ensure the secrecy of the Allied plans, but, after the invasion of the continent, field security in London was a diminishing concern. My routine patrol was becoming meaningless and my career in the army wholly lacking in personal satisfaction. This disenchantment with 13 Cdn FSS extended to my relations with some of its personnel and culminated in a serious altercation with a fellow-member of the Section.

This episode began on October 30, 1944 when, at about 5:30 p.m., I was sitting at a table in the conference room of our HQ engrossed in writing a letter. Sergeant Flemming approached me and asked, "How would you like to make some money?"

I looked up, somewhat startled, and replied with the first foolish thought that popped into my head, "I'm always glad to earn some money."

Whereupon Flemming said, "I'll give you a pound if you take over my tour of duty as Duty NCO until 11:00 o'clock tonight."

"Okay," I responded, quite simply.

As I may have already mentioned, in our Section everyone was required to take his tour of duty as it appeared on the duty roster without distinction as to rank. Flemming immediately produced a pound note and I immediately accepted it. A moment or two passed and then Flemming added,

"You will see or hear nothing here tonight."

I was completely taken aback by this remark. While I was still somewhat in shock, Fleming hustled me out of the premises for an early dinner. I was to relieve the current Duty NCO who was ending his tour and wanted to get away early. In some consternation, I pondered the possible implications of Flemming's parting statement and decided to return his pound note and cancel my supposed agreement with him. When I got back to the HQ, however, he was gone and not to be found. Without recourse, therefore, I reluctantly relieved my fellow-FSP and took over as Duty NCO.

Soon, I was alone in the Section HQ 10:00 p.m. came and Flemming had not appeared. At 11:00 p.m. he had still not appeared. Finally, I went to sleep on a cot in the Duty NCO's office. The ringing of a telephone in another office awakened me. Still half asleep, I got out of bed and answered the call.

A voice at the other end of the wire directed, "Put on your clothes, get ready to leave, and come down and open the door."

"Who is that?" I asked.

"Flemming," was the response.

I said, "All right", then looked at my watch. It was almost exactly 1:00 a.m.. I returned to the Duty NCO's office, dressed, and went down the four flights of stairs to the ground floor and opened the front door. There stood Flemming, somewhat unsteady on his feet, and rather dishevelled in appearance; obviously he had been drinking hard.

"How do you expect me to get home at this hour in the morning?" I asked.

He answered in a single word, "Walk."

"Then you walk!" I responded in exasperation. I closed and locked the door leaving him outside. Very much upset, I returned to the fourth floor, locked an outer door leading to the Duty Office, left open an inner door, and again prepared for bed. Shortly afterwards, I heard footsteps in the hallway and loud pounding on the outer door.

"Who's there?" I called.

"Flemming. Let me in."

I unlocked the door. He entered, and I said, "What do you want?"

He swept by me wordlessly, went to a board on which were kept a number of keys, and selected one, as he mumbled: "What do you mean, what do I want? I don't tell you what I want." He then added in a menacing tone, "You would be well-advised, Corporal Vanek, not to exceed your authority."

Heavily provoked, I called after him, although in a low voice, as he was leaving the room, "You might be sure you do not exceed yours."

Instantly, Flemming turned on his heels, came back deliberately, stood directly in front of me, and, with his clenched fist, struck me an uppercut blow to the point of my chin.

I reeled back, stunned. It was at about this moment that "the woman" appeared. She must have been lurking in the corridor during our exchanges. Now she began pleading as Flemming closed on me: "Mike, don't Mike. Mike, for God's sake, don't make a scene. Please Mike, please!"

I was no match for Flemming, who was a physically powerful man of about thirty-five years. He was about six feet in height and 200 lb. in weight, compared to my meagre five feet, seven inches and 135 lb. I never struck back. The best I could do was try to fend him off, hold his arms, shove him away, and prevent him from inflicting further injury. By now, Flemming was a wild man. He got me onto my back on the cot. I was calling to the woman to fetch help. She was quite beside herself. Somehow, I was able to get to my feet and lurch to a table, where I noticed a small pliers.

I grabbed the pliers, and as Flemming sought to close with me again, I warned, melodramatically, "Take one more step toward me, Sergeant Flemming, and by God I'll brain you."

It was an empty threat. I could not bring myself to throw the instrument at him. He came at me again and I tried to get away. He caught me. I struggled briefly, but was too exhausted to put up further resistance. Again he had me flat on my back on the floor. He held me in this position, and I waited.

"You know, I could kill you now," he breathed into my face.

I believed it; a long moment passed while I expected the worst to happen. The thought ran through my mind: "What an ignominious ending to Vanek's war!"

The woman was in an extremely distressed condition. She kept pleading with Flemming to release me. Slowly, he relaxed his hold on me and allowed me to get to my feet. Surprisingly, I became quite cool at this juncture. I wiped the blood from my face, dressed and, amid a thousand apologies from the woman but none from Flemming, left the building. I walked to my billet that, at this time, was still at Nottinghill Gate, a distance of about three and a half miles. I arrived about 2:30 a.m.

I stayed up the rest of the night discussing this affair with Jack Milnes. What should I do? My situation was intolerable. Sergeant Flemming was a superior officer. I could not continue in 13 Cdn FSS under his domination. Should I complain to the Sergeant Major? It could do more harm than good. CSM Black and Sergeant Flemming were good friends, comrades; they went out drinking together. It was likely the CSM would be more supportive of Flemming than me. I agonized over my own conduct in accepting the pound note from Flemming. For what it was worth, my explanation is that I actually intended to teach the Sergeant a lesson. Amongst the members of the Section he was notorious for avoiding his turn as Duty NCO. When he offered me the pound, I believed he expected me to refuse the money and undertake to relieve him anyway. So I called his bluff. He had been routinely borrowing from me. I expected he would ask for it back as a loan. I handed the pound note to Milnes and asked him to give it to some needy person or to a charity of his choosing. We wondered how Flemming had managed to get into the building. Later, Jack discovered he had gained access through an adjoining building that fronted on a side street and connected with our building. He had awakened the caretaker of the adjoining building and bullied the caretaker into admitting him. After full consideration, I finally decided upon a course of action.

It was only a matter of an hour or two later that I arrived at Section HQ to report for duty. I made my way directly to the Sergeant Major's office. Flemming was in the office beside CSM Black. I approached the Sergeant Major and said "Sir, I should like to be paraded to my Officer Commanding." It was my right, and the CSM knew it.

The Sergeant Major acted with reasonable alacrity and soon I stood before my OC, Captain Brookhouse, in private in his office. I told him the entire story, omitting only at this stage, out of a mistaken notion of chivalry, all reference to the woman. I told the OC that I wished to bring up Sergeant Flemming on charges. Thus began a second phase of the affair that concerned the course of military justice with which I was unfamiliar.

In order to lay charges, I had to attend before authorities at CMHQ, where Military Intelligence was centred and, under whose direct control, 13 Cdn FSS was administered. I attended first upon a prosecuting officer to whom I again related the facts concerning my encounter with Sergeant Flemming.

Then there was a hearing before the Camp Commandant himself, Colonel Williams. At this stage, there was only a single charge against Flemming: "Striking a person of inferior rank." Flemming was asked how he pleaded to this charge. He pleaded not guilty. I was called to testify. After the Camp Commandant heard my evidence, at his instance a second charge was added: "Bringing an unauthorized person into military premises." At the conclusion of this hearing, Flemming was put under close arrest, from which he was released shortly afterwards, pending the taking of witness statements on which a court-martial might be founded. In common with others, I submitted a sworn statement. I was told Sergeant Flemming would be put on trial on the above charges by a field general court-martial.

From my initial attendance before the OC to the conclusion of the court-martial, I was in an almost constant state of tension. I was overwrought, nervous and apprehensive. I realized that the case depended on the acceptance by the tribunal of my evidence as against any version to which Flemming would testify. I anticipated that the woman would be called as a witness and corroborate his story. Thus it would come down to my word, as against both of theirs. Somehow, the woman managed to obtain the phone number of my billet and called me. In a conversation, more of a wheedling monologue on her part than a dialogue, she did her utmost to attract my sympathy with the obvious intent of getting me to drop the charges. I kept trying to terminate the call. At one point, she wanted to know, for instance, whether I was married, whether I had children.

"Sergeant Flemming, you know, has a wife and three children," she said.

If I were not so overwrought, I would have laughed. What circulated amongst the members of the Section was that he had a wife in Canada and seven children and was living openly with this woman in England.

Then she asked in a sugarcoated, coaxing voice: "Corporal Vanek, can I ask you to do something **really** big?"

That is when I finally terminated the call. "You are wasting your time," I said, as I hung up the receiver.

I was the innocent victim, but felt beset by intrigue and was apprehensive of a conspiracy against me. I had become extremely suspicious of the Sergeant Major and the part he was playing in this affair. I had grave doubts about his impartiality. I found too many incidents tending to show that he was acting in concert with Flemming and the woman and was bent on discrediting me. In one instance, in the hearing before the Camp Commandant, he flatly contradicted the OC, who stated that a senior NCO did not have the right to require a junior NCO to take over his tour as Duty NCO in our Section. I believed he was feeding information about the case to Flemming and was doing his best to discourage me from proceeding. Except for the OC, CSM Black was the most senior officer in 13 Cdn. FSS. With his considerable experience in the RCMP and in undercover activity, he was clever, wily, manipulative, and devious. He also had friends in high places. He could have been a most formidable adversary.

A day or two prior to the court-martial, I was on a tram on the way to my billet and brooding over the case against Flemming. I noticed an advertisement on the tram with a message that seemed to be singularly appropriate to my current circumstances:

WHAT THE SITUATION DEMANDS
1. WHEEL, for putting shoulder to
2. SOCKS, for pulling up
3. STONE, for not leaving unturned
4. BRASS TACKS, for getting down to
5. TRUMP CARD, for playing
6. BOLD FACE, for putting on
7. BELT, for tightening
8. GUINESS, for strength.

The trial of Sergeant Flemming by field general court-martial on the two charges already noted came before a tribunal composed of four officers: two majors and two captains. One of the officers acted as the president of the court. He was a member of the Judge Advocate General's Branch and the only trained lawyer of the four officers. The prosecuting officer and another officer who acted as defence counsel were also present. All the witnesses were assembled in an adjoining room: this complainant, the OC, the Sergeant Major, Jack Milnes, the caretaker of the building adjoining our HQ, and the woman. The atmosphere in the room was tense and strained.

Sergeant Flemming's defence was ingenious, even plausible, but with glaring defects and discrepancies that should readily have disclosed its true nature. Essentially, it was that the woman was lawfully in the premises and he only acted in self-defence. According to this fanciful version of the events, the woman was a "contact" from whom he received important information. He had been wining and dining this contact. He did not have to pay me a pound to take over his duties, but did so anyway. His contact decided to stay overnight at a nearby hotel. She wanted to phone relatives to tell them about her plans. Sergeant Flemming suggested she call them from the Section HQ. He called from a pay telephone to the office to instruct me to open the door. I was very rude and offensive to him. In the Duty NCO's office, I had threatened him with a wrench. He had used no more force than was necessary to take the wrench away from me. As I had anticipated, the woman corroborated his testimony.

After CSM Black testified, he returned to the witness room flushed, but smiling and very loquacious. In an expansive mood, he commented on the nature of his evidence in considerable detail.

"I had a hard time making 'them' understand that a Security Section is not like any other unit of the army. The OC had made quite an ass of himself, but the Court was not interested in what the standing orders of the Section were. However, I had explained everything to everyone's satisfaction now. Of course, they had to understand that FSP had to have contacts. That's how we work. They had asked me whether it was all right for an FSP to have a woman contact in the office, alone, at 1:00 a.m. I had answered that I did not want them to get the impression there were thousands of women running around Section HQ but, of course, there was nothing wrong with having a contact up there at any time."

Apparently, it was on the strength of this testimony that the defence counsel brought a motion to dismiss the charge of bringing an unauthorized person into military premises. To my astonishment, the motion was successful and this charge was dismissed. On the more serious charge, however, of striking an inferior officer, Sergeant Flemming was convicted. In due course, the sentence for this offence appeared in Orders. Sergeant Flemming was stripped of all rank, reduced to a simple private, and transferred back to the holding unit. He might also have been transferred out of the Intelligence Corps, but I lost track of him after that. I believe he was very fortunate in the result. In my opinion, the prosecuting officer made a grave tactical error in that he called both CSM Black and the woman as witnesses for the prosecution. He should have allowed them to be called by the defence and retained the very important right of cross-examining them on their evidence. However, with respect to the punishment meted out to Flemming, I was satisfied. My main concern was to rid the Section of Flemming and that object had been accomplished.

I was far from satisfied with regard to my continuing relationship with the Sergeant Major. I was more convinced than ever that I had good cause to fear him and that he was in a position to do me great harm. I went to Captain Brookhouse and requested to be transferred to another security section. Naturally, he asked me for my reasons. I listed a number of incidents giving concerns about the CSM's attitude toward me. The OC tried to calm my fears. He also stated the timing was not propitious to place the request before the authorities at CMHQ. He asked me to let the matter stand for a while. I had no alternative. Fortunately for me, my problem was resolved in a way I had not at all anticipated. Without any previous indications, an Order came through official channels transferring both the OC, Captain Brookhouse, and CSM Black to another field security section in a straight exchange for the OC and Sergeant Major of the other section. Accordingly, Captain MacMillan and CSM Schroeder joined 13 Cdn FSS as OC and Sergeant Major, respectively. I got along reasonably well with the new Sergeant Major, but could never form an attachment or easy relationship with Captain MacMillan. He was a friend of long-standing of CSM Black and I found him cool and correct in my contacts with him. I tried my best to give no offence whatever. However, I continued as a member of 13 Cdn FSS under a burden of suspicion. It appeared to me that I was viewed as a troublemaker who had laid charges against a superior officer and disturbed very important personnel at CMHQ.

Ten
The Aftermath

As far as my military career is concerned, everything that followed after l'affaire Flemming was an anti-climax. However military superiors may have regarded my conduct in this episode, it received general approbation amongst my associates in the Section and the result was accepted with evident satisfaction. With the relaxation of the tension that formerly gripped me, I resumed my normal activities in London. I enjoyed a variety of experiences, ranging from commonplace, amusing, entertaining, or interesting to noteworthy or profound. In the first category were my contacts with women who operated the counters, or waited on tables, in restaurants such as the Lyons chain. They tended to address the customers in extremely affectionate terms, such as "love," "dearie," or "duck." It was not intended as a special word of endearment, even when accompanied by a warm smile, but a regular salutation in business. On one occasion, when I approached the counter the attendant asked: "Wot'l you 'ave, Duckie?"

"Are there any more scones?" I inquired.

After a brief hesitation, the attendant bent under a bar to go to the rear of the shop and on returning bent under again and handed me a scone.

Ever polite, I said "Thank you very much."

"You orter," came the rejoinder. "I near broke me corsitts gittin it."

On another occasion I was waiting at a service club for the appointed hour for the pay parade to be held at the nearby CMHQ. It was the end of my fiscal period and I was short of cash. The club operated a "griddle bar." I approached and asked the girl at the coffee stand: "How much is the coffee?"

"Tuppence," she replied.

"And how much for the griddle cakes?"

There followed a short conference with another girl at the griddle counter. "Sixpence."

"I'll have some coffee," I said.

The girl regarded me in silence for a moment. "Are you that broke?" she asked, sympathetically.

Embarrassed, I protested I was just waiting to go on pay parade, but somehow displayed my total wealth, which was fourpence and a farthing. The girls insisted on giving me a "slightly hard" griddlecake "on the house."

One day I learned that an international conference was being held in one of the royal buildings near the palace and I went to investigate. Of course, I could not gain admission despite my possession of a card certifying to my singular importance as a member of a select Canadian army unit. I loitered in front of the entrance and, by chance, entered into conversation with a British soldier in riding gear standing beside a motorcycle. He told me, to my delight, that he was a dispatch rider attached to the personal staff of Winston Churchill, an attendee at the conference. He regaled me with anecdotes about the strange working habits and eccentricities of Churchill in wartime: invitations to members of his cabinet for weekends at Chertwell, causing them to remain until the early hours of the morning to watch his favourite film, *Gone with the Wind*, late morning risings and baths, sudden spurts of activity late at night. These eccentricities were not widely known at the time, but have been well chronicled afterwards. I was amused at the attitude of my acquaintance. His impressive boss did not impress him. He was full of grievance and complaint about his lot in the army: interminably required to stand by, and then sent on a moment's notice to deliver dispatches, at any time of the day or night, at the call of his unpredictable master.

I had a strong desire to observe the British wartime leaders in action and, one day, I struck oil. I was invited by Sir Jocelyn Lucas, MP, to attend a session of the House of Commons. Actually, Sir Jocelyn did not issue the invitation to me directly. I obtained it through one of the women in charge of a service club who, after numerous requests, decided she could "squeeze me in" for the concluding session before the House was to rise for the Christmas vacation. I was expecting only a routine agenda, merely to clear up a miscellaneous collection of minor items. It happened, however, that the opposition in Parliament was pressing for a debate on an important controversial issue of the day, the intervention of Britain allegedly in support of reactionary elements in Greece. Suddenly, it was announced that the government yielded to the demand and the last day before rising would include a debate on the situation in Greece.

I was seething with excitement when I attended the "Mother of all Parliaments" at the designated time and place. The Commons were not then meeting as usual in the "House of Commons." It had been damaged in the German raids of 1940-1941. Instead, the session was held in the chamber of the House of Lords where the Commons had been meeting ever since. The seating capacity for visitors was severely limited. In the morning, I was unable to obtain a seat. I was standing in the corridor leading to the legislative chamber as the Speaker of the House, clad in his official robes, passed by me. He was in a procession led by a solemn gentleman, attired in eighteenth century breeches, and followed by another carrying the mace that symbolized the powers of the Commons.

In the afternoon, I obtained a seat in the visitors' gallery well before the debate commenced on British policy in Greece. After preliminary matters, which I still followed with interest, Arthur Greenwood, Leader of the Opposition and a socialist, opened the debate on Greece. An excellent debater, he criticized the Government in a strong, well-reasoned address. He was followed by a number of the leading statesmen of the day. For sheer debating skill, I considered Aneurin Bevan to be outstanding. He lived up to his reputation. I enjoyed the entire debate, including even the fiery speech of Gallagher, the lone communist in the House. He was a colourful personality and was severely heckled. However, I was told that he was personally well liked by his colleagues. Anthony Eden, then British Foreign Secretary and leader of the Government in the House, closed the debate. He explained British policy in Greece to a hushed House

141

in a speech that appeared to me to be clear, logical and reasonable, and without any attempt at showmanship. I finally withdrew from the gallery, while he was still speaking, at about 5:30 p.m. I had witnessed a superb performance by skilful protagonists in the art of debate. The debate was on a subject of major importance and took place in the most historic of all parliaments. It also demonstrated the merits of the democratic system at a decisive time in history. It was an exhilarating and memorable experience.

In about March 1945, I was entitled to a furlough. Through one of the service clubs, I was lucky to be able to arrange for a one-week leave course in Balliol College at Oxford University. The College was founded in the year 1260; it was a very old and respected centre of learning. For one week, I dropped my character as a private soldier and adopted the mantle of an academician. I was able to enjoy lectures by renowned teachers, the luxury of one of the rooms in residence, and the amenities normally available to regular students in full-time enrolment. The program included an introduction to the College and the University, and lectures on political science, foreign affairs, and Shakespeare. The Dean and Master of Balliol College were amongst the lecturers. The program also included an informal party at Rhodes House; and, on my own, I attended a parliamentary debate at the Oxford Union. I found the course to be most stimulating; it was an idyllic interval in my military career. On leaving, I carried with me the motto of the College as translated from Latin by Dean Bryson that I now claimed as my own: "I too was once a Balliol man!"

Shortly after my return from furlough and sparked by a simple phone call from CMHQ, on Thursday, April 19,1945, a wave of wild excitement struck No. 13 Cdn FSS like a shock of electricity. All FSP were to be on hand on Friday afternoon for an inspection by high ranking officers from Military Intelligence. Two of our men, who had been sent out of London on detachment, were instructed immediately to return to headquarters. In our Section an inspection by officers from CMHQ was an extraordinary event — almost unprecedented. So on Friday, all FSP presented themselves, meticulously clad in uniform and gaiters, ready for inspection. It turned out to be not an inspection at all, but an examination. This requires an explanation.

Several months previously, the governing authorities had introduced into our Section a training course in the German language. Since then, we had spent an hour or two once or twice each week in lessons intended to help us achieve proficiency in this language. Our teacher was a prim English spinster, whom we addressed as "Madame" George, in some cases in an overtone of mild amusement. She had the thankless job of trying to teach a foreign language to a group of mature adults, most of whom attended with resignation and disinterest. Two members of our group ultimately pleaded inability and were excused further attendance. While I enjoyed some of the joking about Madame George, I took the Course seriously — although without special application. The text we used bore the title "Jock und Bill in Deutchland." I regarded the book with some amusement; it appeared to me to embody the view of its British authors in the military establishment about what would interest two ordinary British soldiers who found themselves in Germany as part of the post-war army of occupation. The assumed interests were beer, girls and directions. Consequently the story dealt with *dos wirtshaus*, how to get there, *rechts oder links, helles oder dunkeless bier*, and, of course, *die maedchen*.

It was generally acknowledged that I was the best student of this language in the Section. At all events, when on Friday a Sergeant fluent in the German language arrived at our headquarters, not for the purpose of an inspection but to test the FSP on their knowledge of the German language, I realized immediately that I was to be on the move again. The Sergeant gave each Section member in turn an oral examination. Then a general staff officer from Military Intelligence arrived and conducted a written test. On Saturday, I was duty NCO and could not avoid overhearing part of a phone call. I heard the OC saying: "Yes...Clarke ...Vanek...that soon ...Oh well, I had better run them out in the wagon." On Sunday, Brooker, our batman-driver, drove me in our station wagon. I was accompanied by the OC and delivered by them once again to CGRU, the Canadian army holding unit adjacent to the town of Aldershot.

I was assigned to the Intelligence Company. One of the first persons to greet me was the man who was responsible for bringing me back to the holding unit, Sergeant John White. He was an instructor in German in the Intelligence Company and had administered the oral tests at No.13 Cdn FSS. He apologized for having taken me away from the comforts of London to the dreariness of life in a military camp. At this time, however, I had no complaint. I anticipated that I would be transported with all dispatch to the continent, probably to act as an interpreter. In fact, I was placed with a select, small group of soldiers fluent in the German language, intended to constitute the next draft for Germany, and expected to leave shortly. Clarke, on the other hand, was considered not quite ready for draft as he needed further training.

I spent the next few days with this group of German speakers. We were under instructions to converse solely in German. We would go on a modified type of route march at an ambling gate speaking to one another in German. It would have been most perplexing for a stranger to have observed this unlikely assortment of Canadian soldiers who were conversing in a foreign tongue. In these several days, however, my proficiency in the language increased considerably. Then disaster struck; I became ill. It was a recurrence of a malady I had suffered in London. I had the untimely misfortune of going on sick parade with the consequence that I was immediately confined to bed in the Sick Bay. I remained in the Sick Bay for two weeks while the M.D. loaded me with a variety of drugs intended to drive the malady from my system. The upshot was that I was removed from the draft for Germany, replaced by Clarke, and the draft departed without me.

From my bed in the Sick Bay, I followed with increasing excitement the concluding events of the war on the continent: Himmler's offer of unconditional surrender to the Allies, exclusive of Russia; Mussolini's capture and execution; the surrender of all German forces in Italy; and finally, by order of Grand Admiral Doenitz, the unconditional surrender of Germany. On May 8, 1945, VE Day, I was still in bed in Sick Bay. Not only did I fail to get to Germany, I also missed the celebrations marking the end of the war in Europe.

On May 17, 1945, when at last I was discharged from Sick Bay, I expected to be included in the next draft for Germany. In the meantime, with other aspirants, I continued my studies in German under the tutelage of Sergeant John White. Gradually, it dawned on me that there would never be another draft. Just as I had missed the last draft for officers' training school at Three Rivers, so it transpired that I now also missed the last draft for the continent. The zeal both for learning and teaching the German language lessened proportionate to its need; finally, the course ground to an end. By this time, the military authorities virtually abandoned training programs at CGRU altogether. Nevertheless, I remained in the Intelligence Company at CGRU under military discipline. I passed my time in idleness and boredom, only partially relieved by organized sightseeing expeditions and occasional forays into London.

At this juncture, an atmosphere of uncertainty enveloped the Canadian forces regarding any further military service that might still be required of them, either as part of the army of occupation in Germany or in the continuing war against Japan. I believed it highly unlikely that I would be called upon to serve in the east and I had no intention to volunteer for service in the army of occupation. Instead, I wanted to get home to my wife in Canada as quickly as possible. I began to look about for an educational course that might be made available to me. It would occupy my time more profitably than languishing in a military holding unit until arrangements could be made for early discharge or repatriation. Naturally, my preference was to take a refresher course in law or a specialty of it, such as labour law. It occurred to me to make inquiries at Oxford University as to the possibilities in either respect.

Thus it came about that on Thursday, July 24, 1945, I returned to my Alma Mater, Balliol College, and presented myself to the Secretary for Leave Courses, Mr. Allington. He invited me to remain overnight in order to meet an individual he thought could be helpful to me. The next day, I was introduced to this person, Professor Hanbury, a professor of law at Lincoln College. He was well acquainted with Dean Kennedy and Professor Auld of the Law Department at Toronto and, to my delight, I found his specialty happened to be labour law. He had to leave, but invited me to visit him that evening in his rooms at Lincoln College. Later that day, I had another stroke of good fortune. The Secretary, who was having tea on the lawn, called me over and introduced me to two other gentlemen. They were "brass hats," a Colonel and Lt. Colonel, and were none other than the two top officers in charge of the Canadian Educational Corps. When they learned of my quest, they appeared to be supportive of my taking a course at Oxford. In the evening, I called upon Professor Hanbury at Lincoln College expecting a private meeting with him. To my complete astonishment, I walked into a room where I found assembled what appeared to be the entire governing body of Lincoln College — the Rector and Fellows — prepared to deliberate whether to allow me to study at their College.

I must have made a good impression. They decided at this meeting that I should make application for a one-term course at Oxford to study labour law at Lincoln College. I was to begin immediately to work informally doing research under Professor

Hanbury until the official commencement of the course. I returned to Aldershot greatly satisfied with this success. There were, however, certain obstacles to overcome. I required the consent both of my OC and the officer in charge of the unit. Neither of them was prepared to deal with the matter of a course at Oxford because another disposition was pending at this time. I was about to be transferred to another unit. Nevertheless, I submitted to the Educational Branch at CGRU an application for a course at Oxford University, precisely in the terms suggested in my interview at Lincoln College. Some weeks later, I attended before the Educational and Rehabilitation Board at Camberly in support of my application. My application foundered for failure of any means of financing the project. The Board would have required me to pay not only for the tuition, but also my maintenance while taking the course. This, in my financial circumstances, or lack thereof, was impossible. On return to Canada, veterans were allowed not merely a single term, but their entire university education, at governmental expense. However, that was in the future and did not help me before the Board.

Meanwhile, my anticipated transfer to another unit occurred. I was transferred to No. 12 Cdn FSS with headquarters at Farnborough, about two miles from Aldershot. It was smaller than Aldershot and had even fewer facilities for the comfort and recreation of the troops. I was transferred as "supernumerary to the establishment." The negative consequences of this classification were an aggravation of what I considered to be a previous injustice. When I was brought back to CGRU from London on April 26, the following item appeared in Orders: "Effective 25 April 1945 B62876 L/Cpl D.C.Vanek reverts to rank of Trooper at rate of pay of $1.50 per diem." Not only was I deprived of subsistence allowance and expense account, but suffered the loss of my rank and reduction of pay to the lowest level in the Canadian army. Now, on being posted to another Security Section, as supernumerary to the establishment, neither rank nor pay was restored and, in addition, I lost the use of a motorcycle. While I was allowed a subsistence allowance, it was barely sufficient to cover the exorbitant amount of the rent I had to pay for an unheated, dimly lit, room in Farnborough.

To be transferred from Aldershot to Farnborough was like being pushed from the frying pan into the fire. Instead of languishing in CGRU, I was destined to languish in Farnborough in idleness, impecuniosity, and without means of transport. This would last until the army could get around to repatriating me to Canada, unless somehow I could change the course of events.

I made few friends at my new Section. The FSP were billeted at different locations throughout the vicinity and I encountered them only rarely. I found the continuing exercise of military discipline, arbitrary and irksome in the current circumstances. The town itself was dull and boring; it boasted only a single cinema exhibiting films that were generally outdated and not at all to my taste. I tended to walk aimlessly in solitude about Farnborough, trudge the two miles to Aldershot, and spend the rest of the day at one or other of the two service clubs that would open about four o'clock in the afternoon.

It was at about this time that World War II finally came to an end, precipitated by the most catastrophic single event in the history of the world. The sensational news about the dropping of an atom bomb on Hiroshima, and the devastating loss of life and destruction caused by it, broke on August 7, 1945. This occurred the very day that I was posted to No. 12 Cdn FSS. A day or two later a second atom bomb was dropped on Nagasaki, with similar results. The unconditional surrender of Japan followed a few days later. In Britain the conclusion of the war was announced officially on August 15, that became popularly known as VJ Day. I heard the news early in the morning and was determined not to miss the joyous celebrations anticipated to occur in London to commemorate this longed-for event. Without seeking authorization, I quietly slipped out of Farnborough and took the train to London. I was one of the huge throng that lined Whitehall to witness the procession of royalty for the opening of Parliament that day. I was also amongst the huge gathering of people, joyous and tearful, celebrating VJ Day at Trafalgar Square and Piccadilly Circle. Finally, I was crammed within the immense gathering in front of the palace wildly cheering the royal family as the King, Queen and Princesses appeared on the balcony and waived to their subjects and well-wishers. Then I returned to my monotonous existence at Farnborough.

I intensified my efforts to improve my condition, either by obtaining early discharge from the army, repatriation, educational courses, or training that could utilize my time to better advantage. A possibility of early discharge failed to materialize. I made an application for a short course on Shakespeare at Stratford and, after every encouragement, was ultimately told it was unavailable. I endeavoured to secure employment with a firm of solicitors in London. This episode simply got me into trouble with my OC, who reprimanded me for going "over his head" in applying to civilians in order to secure a personal advantage. At one time, I was led to believe that No. 13 Cdn FSS was officially seeking my recall to London, but this possibility failed as well. Finally, having exhausted every avenue, I gave up all further efforts and simply waited for my turn to be repatriated to Canada in accordance with the point system. Joyce constantly beseeched me by a stream of letters as to specific dates and times. I had no answer.

Meanwhile, I continued my routine of wandering through the streets of Farnborough and Aldershot but was able to add an activity that somewhat relieved the tedium. In the writing room of the YMCA Service Club in Farnborough I came upon a tattered volume of the complete works of William Shakespeare. For lack of other outlet, I adopted a project of reading through the entire volume, copying large extracts into a pocket notebook, and memorizing these passages during my perambulations. This activity gave me some degree of satisfaction and pleasure. However, as autumn approached, there was a dramatic change in the weather; it began to rain, turned very cold, and I was almost constantly in a state of discomfort. My most abiding recollection of the last few months of my sojourn in England is of heavy interminable rainfall, early morning mist and enveloping fog, and shivering overnight under blankets in an unheated room. The discomfort increased my frustration and despondency, which may be gathered from a few lines I wrote. This was prompted by a conversation that I overheard between two disgruntled soldiers who, like myself, were awaiting repatriation. I reproduce this opus with apologies to Shakespeare and the courageous British people. I hasten to add that I acquired the greatest admiration for this happy breed of men and women and sincere appreciation of their traditions, institutions and beautiful country.

REFLECTIONS OF A CANADIAN SOLDIER AWAITING REPATRIATION

This royal throne of kings, this scepter'd isle;
This earth of fish and chips, this seat of spam —

This other delight, demi-ham —
This NAAFI which men created for themselves,
To aid infestation with a pack of Woodbines;
This happy breed of drinkers, this world of tea;
This precious Mild and Bitters, on draft, unbottled,
Which serves them in the office of a beverage,
Or, as a tonic like Guinness, for Strength imbibed,
Yet not the envy of less foggier lands;
This blessed fish, this bitters, this spam — this England!

At long last, on November 29, 1945 the order came from CMHQ authorizing the movement on December 5 of a draft of Canadian troops to a repatriation depot. Thankfully, I was included. I remained at the repatriation depot for one month. It was my last taste of barracks-room living. On December 27, my draft proceeded to Liverpool, the port of embarkation. We sailed for Canada on the "Scythia" on December 29 and arrived in Halifax on January 5, 1946. Two days later, I was back at Exhibition Park in Toronto, where my military career had begun, marching in a parade of the homecoming troops. I kept my chin up and arms swinging high, probably out of step with my companions, as we came to a halt and fell into the arms and embrace of our loved ones. For me, it was a happy, tearful, and sobering moment. I returned from service to shoulder my responsibilities as a married man, without rank, financial resources, and even fewer prospects than when I had enlisted in the army. Under the constraints of honesty, I would have to concede, by way of understatement, that as a soldier I was not very successful.

Eleven
Picking Up the Threads

"No man is an island, entire of itself.... Any man's death diminishes me, because I am involved in mankind; and therefore, never send to know for whom the bell tolls; it tolls for thee."

These words, written in the seventeeth century by John Donne, graphically emphasize the interdependence of nations and peoples. They are even more applicable in modern times than when originally written. The world has shrunk considerably; what happens in one corner of the earth often produces profound effects in other parts of the globe. On an individual basis, we are not only influenced by one another but stand in need of each other. A man of my acquaintance, in retirement and comfortably endowed with the world's goods, has a standard response upon any reference to his material well being. "I am entitled," he would say. "I've paid my dues!" Apart from the arrogance and smugness of this observation, he is quite wrong. He assumes life is a club and he has earned a paid-up membership through his years of service. But life is not a club, and if his labours are dues, they are never fully paid. Inferentially, he suggests he is wholly a self-made man. If there is any such individual, he must be a rarity. From time to time, as we travel through life, we all need and receive the occasional benefit of a helping hand.

When I came home from the war and fell into the arms of my dear wife, I had no money and no plans and was in a state of acute apprehension. I did not know where I could find employment, either in my profession or in other gainful work. How was I going to be able to support myself and a wife and where would we even rest our heads at night? Joyce did not share the latter concern.

As soon as it could be arranged, Joyce led me to a newly constructed group of houses on Chiltern Hill Road in the vicinity of Eglinton Avenue and Bathurst Street. She had rented from the builder the rooms on the second floor of one of these houses. The builder resided with his family on the ground floor and basement. Obviously, he required the rent to help finance further building operations. With great pride, Joyce conducted me through the apartment that was to constitute our first marital abode. The rooms included a bedroom, living quarters and kitchen, all freshly painted and spanking clean. I was overwhelmed. To my further astonishment, all the rooms were tastefully furnished with newly acquired furniture. Joyce's father had paid for all the furnishings. Joyce had paid the rent for the first month of the tenancy. Needless to say, I tried adequately to express my amazement, pleasure and appreciation. However, this grand presentation served also to heighten my anxiety about our future. What I most particularly required was assistance to get quickly established in work that would enable me to earn a livelihood for myself and, according to the custom of the times, my wife.

It seemed hopeless to expect any help from my own family. While I had been away, the inevitable had befallen my father: Merchants Trading Company Limited had gone into receivership. Not only did my father lose his business and any investment he had made, he caused my brother Tom also to suffer a loss in an amount that was never disclosed to me. The ultimate disaster had been foreshadowed by a bitter quarrel between my father and Norman, which had occurred before I went overseas. Whatever harsh words were exchanged between them, Norman never forgave my father. In anger and abiding resentment, Norman left Merchants Trading. He took his customers with him and continued in the same business on his own account. Of course, he had to look after his family, my sister Faye and their children, June and Raymond. By this time, Norman, Faye, and their children had moved from Shaw Street and were residing nearby on Heyden Park Crescent. Incidentally, when I was overseas, my loyal retainer, June, did her part to maintain the morale of her warrior-uncle by a warm and affectionate series of letters.

Shortly after this fateful quarrel with Norman, my brother Morris also left Merchants Trading. Morris found employment as a salesman with a firm that manufactured corrugated cartons and other paper products. Almost contemporaneously, he enlisted in the Canadian air force and was waiting to be called to service. When he finally returned to Canada after the end of the war, he was moderately better off than I was. At least he had a job to which to go back — and that is exactly what he did. Several months later, in December, he married Feigie Halpern. It did not take long afterwards for them to produce the first of their three sons, Leonard. It was at Leonard's briss that the statement was made to me that I commemorated at the beginning of this narrative. Within a not unusual period of time, and in succession, Robert and Arthur made their appearance to complete their family.

When Merchants Trading finally succumbed to adversity, my father, who was left without other resources or alternatives, simply took over from my mother the control and management of the Lake Wilcox property. By this time, my mother had abandoned any attempt to operate a hotel; even the refreshment booth was being operated by other people under a lease. The other buildings on the land had been allowed to deteriorate. My father caused one or more of them to be improved to a condition barely sufficient to accommodate occupation in winter and endeavoured to maintain himself and his wife from the revenue he could produce from this property. At the time of my repatriation, my parents were living in a state of profound marital discord interspersed by periods of separation and brief reconciliation.

Whatever money Tom lost in the bankruptcy of Merchants Trading did not seriously impair his own business. It was making steady progress, especially the wholesale tobacco business that he had begun as a sideline. Tom and Anna, his wife, were pre-occupied at this time with all the problems of raising a family of growing boys: Paul, Roy and Sheldon. Anna was an intelligent, capable helpmate and caring mother. She could hardly be blamed for her attitude towards her husband's family: Tom had shouldered quite enough of responsibility toward them; enough was enough; and he had his own family to look after.

All the other members of my family were heavily absorbed in their own affairs and in coping with their own problems.

Mary and Sam were living in Sudbury where Sam had by now become well established in practice as a chartered accountant. He was also assisting his father, Jerry, who was engaged in the booming post-war construction business. A second son, Jonathan, had now arrived to join their first-born, Mitchell, with whom Mary had been pregnant at the time I married.

My next older brother, Abe, was married to Nina Pearl. My mother constantly referred to Abe with great sympathy as "poor Abe," mainly because, in addition to his daughter, Toba, his wife Nina had presented him with the further burden of raising and supporting a set of twins: Judith and Elizabeth.

My sister Faye, married to Norman, had the delicate task of dealing with a situation where her husband no longer would speak to her father.

Finally, not to be overlooked in this catalogue of family members, is my well-intentioned and steadfast eldest sister, Laura. For some reason beyond my comprehension, Laura had been unable to attract a suitor and for a while was in danger of remaining unmarried. Fortunately, she was rescued from spinsterhood when she met and married Nathan Polevoy, a man of ripe marriageable age, equally good-natured and good-hearted. Nat was an electrician who suffered from a serious impairment of his ability to engage in trade. He was chronically unable to charge an adequate price for his services. With my father's assistance, Laura had acquired a hardware store on College Street and, upon my homecoming, was supplementing Nat's earnings with the profits from the store.

Not long after I returned to Canada, Joyce shyly confided to me that she was pregnant. These joyful tidings were tempered by several obvious sober considerations. For starters, we would be required to give up our shared accommodation on Chiltern Hill Road. Joyce and I began to look for a habitation suitable for us and our anticipated contribution to the baby-boomer generation. Ultimately, we set our hearts and hopes on a pretty little dwelling on Bowie Avenue in a working man's district. The district, west of Dufferin Street and north of Eglinton Avenue, was then regarded as the northwest segment of

Toronto. With a degree of *chutzpa*, Joyce and I contemplated the possibility of buying this property.

The asking price was $8,500.00 with a cash payment of $3,500.00. Our only asset was the allowance to which I was entitled from the government by reason of my service in the army. Like all pay and allowances to military personnel, the amount of the individual payments to veterans was sharply graduated on the basis of rank. Of course, I came back to Canada without rank as an ordinary private. I therefore fell into the lowest category and drew the lowest allowance. Place and nature of service were also taken into account, but my personal service was not particularly notable in either respect. I still retain my pencilled computation of the amount of compensation to which I was entitled: a basic gratuity for service in Canada — $165.00; for service overseas — $315.00; a supplementary gratuity — $95.90; and a re-establishment credit — $480.00. Including a clothing allowance of $100.00 and one month's pay and allowances of $109.60, already spent, I reached a grand total of $1,265.50. It was far from enough to make the cash payment on the house.

I cast about for a loan of $2,500.00 to complete the purchase and, ultimately, was led to believe that this amount would be made available from the Vanek family. With this expectation, I submitted an offer to purchase and put up the full amount of my re-establishment credit as a deposit. Alas, when the time for closing the deal approached, the Vanek money was simply not forthcoming. I fell into deep despair. It appeared that we would not only lose the house, but would also forfeit our deposit, our only financial stake in the world. In this extremity, without a word to me, Joyce went to see her father and came back with a cheque for $2,500.00. With this money, we paid the balance of cash required to complete the purchase of 161 Bowie Avenue and took possession of the dwelling.

Joyce's parents did not attach any condition of repayment when they advanced the money that rescued us from financial ruin. The money, which I accepted as a gift, not a loan, was never repaid. Instead, I tried to repay in kind, by good conduct and deeds in the manner of an affectionate son toward loving parents. My in-laws were always supportive of Joyce and me. I became very fond of them and, reciprocally, they liked me very well. Joyce used to say that her mother, in particular, doted upon me. If, on occasion, I had a disagreement with my wife, in a humorous vein I would threaten: "If you don't give in, I'll go home to *your* mother!" That usually provoked a laugh that enabled me to win the dispute.

Joyce was one of three sisters. The eldest, Doris, married Morris Lefko, who had arrived as an immigrant from Poland a few years before the outbreak of the war. Despite his old-fashioned ways and religious orthodoxy, I got along well with him. Morris was a relative of Aaron Ladovsky, a contemporary of my father, who operated a popular restaurant on Spadina Avenue. The restaurant operated under the name "United Bakers" and honoured the Jewish *kashruth* by avoiding meat and serving only dairy dishes, including some favourites of the patrons: boiled white fish and "gefilte fish." The restaurant also became famous for its use of the honour system in the payment of customers' bills. Patrons would approach the cash register, orally list the food consumed and pay according to the tally of the person in charge. The elder Ladovsky took Morris Lefko into the business and, upon the death of the elder Ladovsky, Morris operated the business in partnership with Ladovsky's son Herman. I occasionally frequented the restaurant, but was always embarrassed. Morris treated me as an honoured guest and invariably refused to allow me to pay my bill.

Joyce's second sister, Phyllis, committed the unpardonable sin of Jewish orthodoxy of marrying Ronald Bryce, a gentile. My in-laws reacted to their daughter's marriage to a gentile in the typical, traditional manner of Jewish parents. They rejected both their daughter and her husband and refused to see either of them. Joyce and I got an early opportunity to perform an important act of reciprocal kindness for her parents. Notwithstanding that Joyce's relations with Phyllis were plagued by sibling rivalry, we arranged a special occasion to meet with "Mother" and "Dad" (as distinguished from my parents who were always "Ma" and "Pa") to deal with this issue. We strongly urged them to reconcile. I like to believe that our advocacy helped to end the estrangement. Joyce's parents did what their hearts told them to do anyway: they forgave their errant daughter and accepted Ron as a son-in-law. Possibly as an expression of gratitude, Phyllis and Ron presented Mother and Dad with two grandchildren, first Karen and then Allan. This family unit became well integrated into the Lester family and the Lester/Alexander clan of families.

At the time that Joyce's father gave us the $2,500.00 to buy our first house, I did not realize the extent that this advance, together with his outlay to purchase our furniture, constituted a drain on his own financial resources. Joyce's parents were by no means wealthy. They made a modest living operating the Doric Theatre. However, it was not enough to justify continuing Joyce's education at the University. During the war, the business fared reasonably well because, given the wartime regulations and particularly the rationing of gasoline, people favoured attendance at the neighbourhood theatres rather than travelling downtown to patronise the more expensive, large theatres. This changed with the end of the war, the lifting of the wartime restrictions, and the advent of television. Business at the local theatres, including the Doric, fell off dramatically. One by one, the neighbourhood theatres began to close. A few years later, I discovered, to my astonishment, that Dad did not even own the theatre he had operated for decades. He simply held a lease that was renewed periodically and that, ultimately, was not renewed. Joyce's parents lost their theatre business. It was an ungracious and inauspicious ending for the man who had been the first to operate a motion picture theatre in Toronto.

By the time I returned to Canada, I had been away from the law, and contact with lawyers, for almost four years. I was not in a financial position that enabled me even to undertake a refresher course in the law, let alone commence post-graduate studies. I required immediate gainful employment. To this end, one of my first acts was to see Sam Cohen. It may be recalled that Sam was a lawyer who carried on a busy practice. He had also been the president of the now defunct Fairmount Golf and Country Club, the Club of which I had been the secretary. The Club had been foreclosed during the war for failure to pay an indebtedness of about $40,000.00. It was an insignificant sum in relation to the actual value of the property, property from which successive owners realized millions of dollars. Today, a cluster of high rise apartment buildings occupies the land.

Sam Cohen took me into his office and put me to work at a salary so moderate that I am unable to recollect the amount, or even the range, of the remuneration. I hoped to refresh my knowledge of the law and gain the practical experience that I was unable to acquire either as a student under articles with HSR or in my abortive pre-war attempt to engage in private practice. Unfortunately, I became increasingly disappointed. Sam also took his nephew, a recent graduate, into the office. The nephew handled a great deal of the overflow and there was rather little of the work left for me. Although Sam's practice was substantial, it was largely of a personal nature and the volume of business did not seem to justify employing additional staff. I sometimes felt that he regarded my employment as an act of charity.

I recollect only one significant item of practical training with Sam. Sam dispatched me to argue a motion in Weekly Court. He cautioned me strongly that when I first opened before the judge, I should speak distinctly at dictation speed: "Your Honour, this...is...an application...under the...Vendors' and Purchasers' Act...for an Order...etc. etc." Why? Because if I observed the judge, I would find that he was bent over his desk making a verbatim note of my remarks for later use in his judgement.

Regardless, I was becoming ever more frustrated and uneasy with Sam Cohen. On one occasion, in most amiable and friendly tones, Sam confided: "Do you know what I like about you, Dave? It is that you are not aggressive." It was intended as a compliment, but I was deeply insulted. I knew then there was no future for me with Sam Cohen.

It was at about this juncture that fate stepped in and extended the helping hand I so desperately needed. I received a telephone call from Professor Jacob Finkelman. He told me that Dean Kennedy was contemplating offering me a position as a lecturer in the School of Law at the University and wanted to know if I was interested. It was like throwing a lifeline to a drowning man. I lost no time in stating that I would be delighted to accept the appointment if offered to me. A day or two later I received a letter from C.E. Higginbottom, Treasurer and Secretary of the Board of Governors, dated July 4th, 1946, which read as follows:

Dear Mr. Vanek:-

The Board of Governors at their meeting held on Thursday last, June 27th, appointed you to the position of Lecturer in the School of Law, for the academic year 1946-47, at a salary of $2,550.00. The official notice of appointment is enclosed herewith.

I promptly left my employment with Sam Cohen, went to see Dean Kennedy, and began to try to organize some courses.

Twelve
Lecturer in Law

In September 1946, I embarked upon my new career at the University of Toronto. I do not know whether my first attendance as a full-time lecturer in Law at the university may properly be characterised as an encounter or a confrontation. I do know that, for me, it was a harrowing experience. Lecturer and students subjected one another to a cautious scrutiny and appraisal. Now thirty-one, approaching thirty-two, years of age, I still appeared quite youthful. My first class was composed of about twenty to twenty-five students, several of whom were World War II veterans and almost as old as I. Chastened by this experience, I immediately acquired a formal hat and dark, sober, conservative clothing to emphasize my age and status as a member of the teaching staff. Thus attired, in fair weather I travelled daily by bicycle to and from the Law Building on St. George Street where, prior to the war, I had been a mere lowly undergraduate. By this time, Joyce and I were already residing at 161 Bowie Avenue.

In our new home, we were awaiting the imminent arrival of our first child, who was beginning to show definite signs of eagerness to make an appearance into the world. Joyce's mother, despite her natural reserve, was in a flutter of anxiety about this upcoming event. Joyce entered into an elaborate conspiracy with Phyllis to keep from her mother the state of the pregnancy as it approached the usual climax. Joyce did not want her mother to worry or fuss about her condition. Finally, it appeared that the significant day had dawned. A small bag was packed containing the clothing and articles Joyce intended to take to the hospital. Towards evening, we were in the living room as I helped Joyce count the frequency and estimate the intensity of her pains. At last, Joyce signalled that it was time to leave for the hospital. I picked up the bag of clothing and we took about two steps out the front door. Lo and behold, there were Mother and Dad seated in the front seat of their automobile. They had been patiently waiting for us to make an appearance. They then followed us to the hospital. There was, however, a slight deviation from our course, because Joyce expressed a sudden desire for nourishment. We stopped at Diana Sweets, a well known soda bar and restaurant, for an ice-cream soda. The rest of this occurrence proceeded in normal fashion and we became the proud parents of our first child whom we named Peter Daniel. It was November 7, 1946.

In the midst of preparing courses for the instruction of my students, I now found it necessary to give myself an immersion course in the care and attention of a baby. After the baby was brought home, Joyce had to return to the hospital because she began haemorrhaging. I was left with the responsibility, with whatever assistance could be mustered, to look after Peter. I learned to feed, clean and bathe him, change his diapers, and even operate our old-fashioned washing machine. Thankfully, after a few days at the hospital, Joyce was well and came home to assume the major responsibility for his care. Then, as a family, we started on the path to live happily ever after in empathy with a popular song of my youth:

Just Molly and me
And baby makes three
We're happy in our
Blue heaven!

Our happiness was tempered somewhat by the exigencies of rearing a child and the constraints of a limited budget. One of our problems with Peter was that he learned to climb before he learned to walk. We had great difficulty keeping him in his crib. For instance, after we put him to bed, we would suddenly discover he was sitting on the landing at the top of the stairs to the second floor. No matter how often he would be put back in his crib, we would again come upon him at the top of the stairs. One day, alerted by calls of distress, we found him hanging out of an open second floor window.

Our pretty little house was physically somewhat restrictive. While it boasted a sizeable living room and kitchen, the bedrooms were very small. The baby's room could have passed for a large closet or pantry. Our master bedroom, as well, was altogether too small; it could barely accommodate a double bed and dresser. If Joyce was already in bed, I had to climb over her to get to my side of the bed.

We shared a narrow driveway with the occupants of an adjoining house. The driveway led to garages at rear of our respective premises. One day, in dead of winter and late at night, I tried to drive my father's car into our garage. The driveway was covered with snow and ice and the car skidded into the side of the garage causing damage to both garage and vehicle. In a white heat of anger, I bounded from the car, ran up the stairs to our bedroom and sat down heavily on the bed. Mattress, box spring, Joyce and I fell through to the floor. I was too tired and it was too late to restore the bed to a proper condition. Disconsolately, I dragged the mattress down the stairs to the living room and Joyce and I slept overnight on the floor.

We found it difficult to live well on a salary that, in our opinion, was also not commensurate with the importance of the service and the prestige of a full-time lecturer at the University. My salary was payable monthly. Similarly, the payments on our mortgage were due monthly. Fortunately, those payments were very reasonable. Blended payments of principal, interest and taxes amounted to $32.50 per month. Despite these moderate mortgage payments, Joyce used to observe, wryly: "In the first week we ate steak, the next week, fish, the third week, hamburger, and the fourth week, at Mother's."

Nevertheless, despite a tight budget, we managed to purchase an automobile. It was an old, second-hand car that I bought for only a moderate outlay of cash. Straightway, Joyce and I picked up Mother and Dad at their home and took them for a drive so that they would be the first to share our pleasure in this acquisition. Within a distance of about 500 metres, we suffered a blowout; our spirits were also considerably deflated.

I still owned either this or some other second-hand vehicle, when Joyce decided that she wanted to learn to drive a car. I hesitate to admit the hazardous circumstances under which I undertook to teach her to drive. Joyce was about eight months into her second pregnancy and Peter, about three years of age, was allowed the freedom of riding in the back seat while the lessons proceeded. It is a tribute to the strength of our marriage bond that we persevered with the lessons to the end. One day, Joyce announced that she had made an appointment for the required driving test and that Phyllis was going to drive her for the examination. Later she called on the telephone to declare, in triumph, that she had passed the test. In a reflex reaction I responded: "You may have passed the official test but you have not yet passed mine." In fact, she conquered this last hurdle as well. Today, as she is seated beside me while I drive, she constantly instructs me in proper driving standards. She claims to be a far better driver than her former teacher.

Shortly after we moved into 161 Bowie Avenue, a young woman, who lived a few doors away, knocked at our door to introduce herself as a neighbour. In consequence, we became lifelong friends with Sarah and David Kachuk. Dave Kachuk was a member of a family of which the elders were contemporaries of my parents and, like them, had emigrated from the town of Uman in the Ukraine. In other words, they were "Landsleit." That helped to cement our friendship. The Kachuks were also in process of raising a family. As young housewives, Joyce and Sarah passed many hours in companionship and teaching one another the delicate arts of cooking and baking. With the Kachuks, we joined the baby carriage brigade.

Upon the termination of wartime service and our return to Canada, Saul Wolfe and I automatically resumed our relationship as best friends. Saul married Jeraldine (Gerry) Singer who, within the usual time frame, presented him with progeny. Saul and Gerry acquired an oversized baby carriage to accommodate their twins and immediately joined the baby carriage brigade. As we were obliged to live frugally, we tended to spend our leisure hours in an exchange of visits with friends. We made an arrangement with the Wolfes to divide between us the cost of hiring baby-sitters.

While I was happy in my blue heaven, it did not follow that I was isolated from all unhappiness or even grief. On the very day Joyce gave birth to our first child, bursting with desire to bring the happy tidings to my parents, I received an urgent call to come to 637 Shaw

Street for an entirely different reason. I was summoned to resolve a bitter quarrel that had erupted between my parents. I arrived to find them in an angry confrontation. My father was in a blind rage. I had never seen him so furious. The quarrel had something to do with getting rid of tenants who occupied the second floor, my father's physical condition, and my mother's rights in the maintenance of "her" home. I do not know why I was called instead of Tom; I assume he was not readily available. I had looked forward with keen anticipation to announcing my wonderful news, accepting "mazel tov" (congratulations), and basking in their delight. Instead, my euphoria was wholly overshadowed by their distress. I was left with heartache and depression. I tried to calm them, but was quite unable to settle their differences. It was at about this time that my parents separated for good. Not long afterwards, Tom sold the house on Shaw Street that, at my father's behest, Tom had purchased as a residence for my parents, and my mother went to live with Faye and Norman.

About three years later, the Vanek family suffered a grievous blow. On a summer weekend, almost all of us were at Lake Wilcox when word came that Tom had died. He was alone in his home when he succumbed to a massive heart attack. He was only forty-nine years of age. My mother and father were devastated by their loss. Their eldest son was the light of their life. Master peacemaker, chairman of the board of arbitration, he was the cement that had kept them together for most of their days. His death was a tragedy. His wife, Anna, and their three boys survived him. The tragedy was compounded three years later when Anna also died. She had been diagnosed shortly after Tom's death as suffering from incurable cancer. Anna, who was intelligent and capable, bore her misfortune with courage and fortitude. During a long illness, she made appropriate arrangements for her children. As long as she was able, she attended Tom's store and supervised his businesses. Ultimately she sold the wholesale tobacco business and, as well, disposed of all other business interests. She made a will appointing her brother Alex Wolgeruch, a confirmed bachelor, as executor. He was an excellent choice, trustworthy, prudent and reliable. When all these arrangements had been made, it seemed to me on occasional visits to her that Anna waited in calmness of spirit to die.

The one decision Anna failed to make was who, physically, would take care of her three growing boys after she was gone. Paul, the eldest, was only thirteen years of age. There was an immediate need to provide the meals, send the boys to school, and attend to the numerous duties of managing a busy household. In this extremity, my mother elected to fill the breach. She moved into the family home with the boys and took upon herself the functions of their deceased mother. At the same time, Alex dealt with financial matters, including payment of the household expenses. However, by then nearing her seventieth birthday, my mother found it increasingly difficult to attend to these demanding duties. Then my good-hearted sister Laura came to the aid of her beleaguered mother and three orphaned nephews. Laura came into the household on a regular basis and, still operating the hardware store, helped look after the children and her mother, always subject, however, to her mother's directions. With all this help, the boys were brought to maturity and to a condition in which they were capable of managing their own affairs.

I had infrequent contacts with my father after his separation from my mother. In 1955, about three years after Anna's death, my father suffered a heart attack. I attended at the hospital and was there when my mother arrived as well. We both stood at his bedside in tears. My father was in a desperate condition. Gangrene had set in on one leg. He was scheduled for surgery in the morning for the amputation of his leg. I made many promises I knew I could not keep. I told him I would look after him after the operation. Alas! If I could not look after him when he was whole, how could I do better when his leg had been amputated? My father regarded us in silence. I could tell he had lost his will to live. He did not survive the amputation. In the morning, he died.

I grieved for my father. He had endured a hard, unrewarding life. I was well aware of all his faults, which were myriad. However, he possessed a variety of good qualities and virtues as well. He kept well abreast of the news by subscribing to newspapers in the Yiddish language, such as the *Journal*, published in Toronto, and *Der Tag* in New York. He was capable of exerting considerable charm. Despite his difficulties in the English language, he was an excellent salesman. He worked very hard all his life to support his family, but was constantly frustrated by his failure to apply his ability in business to conditions as he found them in Canada. Nevertheless, he put his first son into a thriving business in a store for which he arranged the purchase. He acquired and built up the property at Lake Wilcox. He helped Laura to purchase a store for her hardware business. He took his wife's nephew into his family when, as a young man, Norman fled to Canada from

Russia. He took a leading role in organizing a religious congregation, of which he became the first president, and in the construction of a modest synagogue. It was he who got Norman's father, my mother's brother, installed as the "Shamas" (a caretaker with special religious duties) of that synagogue. This appointment rescued my uncle from a life of idleness because of his chronic inability to obtain any remunerative employment after coming to Canada a few years prior to the outbreak of the war.

I remember my father at his best when he presided over the "seder" feast on Passover, the festival commemorating the exodus of the Jews from Egypt in biblical times. As the youngest male member of the family, it was usually my responsibility to ask the four questions: "Why the unleavened bread? Why the bitter herbs? Etc." In response, he would lead the family in reading from the "Haggadah," in Hebrew, the story of the exodus. When all the food had been eaten and this recitation come to an end, my father would become particularly joyful. With gusto, we would join him in the traditional songs of Passover, sung in my father's special version. At such times, my father was no longer a frustrated businessman; to me, he was then a veritable Prince of Zion.

My mother, who was herself not without fault in her past relations with my father, survived him by about eight years. For most of this period, she continued to reside with Faye and Norman. She had been so accustomed to managing her own home, however, that she tended to manage Faye's home as well. In time, this tendency, more evident as she aged, came to be a considerable irritant. Finally, after a family conference, it was considered strategic to arrange other accommodation for her. We rented a suite in a high rise apartment building on Bathurst Street south of Eglinton and installed her in her own apartment. It turned out to be a very happy choice. We provided for her upkeep by using the dwindling revenue from the Lake Wilcox property, supplemented by equal contributions from members of the family. As master of her own destiny in her own apartment, Ma brightened perceptibly. She made a number of friends with elderly ladies who also lived in the building; she played bridge and otherwise socialized with them. Of course, she could not resist scolding me, for general neglect and other defaults, when I visited from time to time. I loved her, regardless of her faults. She also had many virtues. She worked hard in raising a family and helping to earn a livelihood. She was a superb cook and baker and, with great respect to Joyce, who also excelled in these arts, I miss Ma's strudel!

When I joined the University of Toronto Law School as a lecturer, the staff still included the Dean, Dr. W.P.M. Kennedy, F.C. Auld and Jacob Finkelman, all of whom had been my teachers when I was an undergraduate. Norman Mackenzie, who had taught public international law, had left Toronto to become president of the University of New Brunswick, and later, president of the University of British Columbia. Finkelman had recently returned to the University after a leave of absence spent as Registrar of the Ontario Labour Relations Board; previously he had been responsible for drafting the Labour Relations Act, under which the Board had been established. Three younger men were appointed to the staff about contemporaneously with my appointment: F.E.(Gene) LaBrie; Sylvan (Van) Sommerfeld; and William (Bill) Reed. The earliest of these appointees was LaBrie, who was already on staff at the time I arrived. He had been appointed after about three years in post-graduate studies. Two years later, LaBrie achieved tenure upon promotion to Assistant Professor. I shared an office with Sommerfeld and we became particularly good friends. From the outset of my career as a teacher, there existed a strong spirit of collegiality amongst the staff. The younger members looked particularly to Finkelman for guidance and support and Finkelman assumed the mantel of mentor and advisor.

The subjects assigned to me included two courses that I took over from Gilbert Kennedy, the Dean's son, who had been lecturing at the University on a part-time basis. Gilbert was leaving Toronto for a full-time position as a professor at the University of British Columbia. Later he became Deputy Attorney General for that province. On one of these subjects, legal bibliography, Gilbert handed me a detailed set of notes that he had compiled and that I found most useful. This was an introductory course for first year students that dealt with the sources of the law — statutes, law reports, text books, periodicals, digests — and, in general, the use of a law library in order to ascertain the state of the law on any given question. With the assistance of Gilbert's notes, I had no difficulty teaching this subject. It was essentially a practical subject intended to provide persons aspiring to become lawyers with the tools of their trade. Curiously, it was not a subject offered at Osgoode Hall Law School, where one might have expected a subject of such obvious utility to be taught. I was rather gratified to find it was not overlooked at the University law school.

My principal assignments were real property and public international law. I undertook to teach these subjects without casebooks or other written material or even a proper outline as a foundation for the courses. Inevitably, I found myself scurrying to make up the courses as I went along and trying to stay a few steps ahead of my class. Real property concerns the selling, buying, mortgaging, leasing or otherwise dealing with land, including structures erected on the land. It constitutes a substantial part of the practice of lawyers and law firms. In organizing this course, I tended to minimize matters of conveyancing that students could learn by employment in a law office and to stress the evolutionary and historical aspects of the subject. The subject was not my particular interest and I was never quite satisfied with my handling of the course.

Public international law, sometimes known as the law of nations, is a body of rules that regulates the relations between states. It is a subject especially useful to students aspiring to a legal career in the Department of External Affairs but with little apparent utility in an ordinary legal practice. At this time, it was not taught at Osgoode Hall or any other university in Canada, with the possible exception of Dalhousie University. Students tended to be sceptical about the existence of this alleged body of rules and whether they truly qualified as law in the absence of any agency to enforce the rules. I taught that public international law was in an early stage of development, roughly equivalent to the evolution and early development of the English common law. With a touch of idealism, I ventured the view that its further development should be encouraged to ensure that law and peace prevailed amongst the community of nations, as well as amongst peoples throughout the globe. In contrasting my two major assignments, I used to remark that in one subject I had to keep my feet firmly on the ground and, in the other, my head up in the clouds.

I dealt with two other assignments, one of which I found particularly helpful in later life; from teaching the other, I simply felt a feeling of satisfaction. The first was criminal law. In this subject, I confined myself to general principles and only the most serious specific offences, such as murder and manslaughter. I was greatly assisted in this assignment by a casebook Professor Finkelman had created. The second subject was one I taught to a class in Pass Arts to students not majoring in law, but seeking a general introduction to the law. The course I developed began with a description of the nature and sources of the law in our Canadian federal system. This was followed by a consideration of our Constitution, at that time known as the British North America Act, with reference to the distribution of legislative powers between the federal and provincial legislatures. We discussed a few leading decisions of the courts, such as the Judicial Committee of the Privy Council. The course included an examination of municipal structure and government. To conclude the course, I dealt with public international law and world order, with emphasis upon the recently created United Nations. I was rather proud of this course. I believed it provided a good overview of the law that would affect the students as citizens of Canada and as individuals within the international community of nations.

By the time I was appointed, the Department of Law I had known as an undergraduate had been transformed in status to become the Faculty of Law of the University. As such, it acquired the authority to confer academic degrees senior to the ordinary Bachelor degrees. Accordingly, it undertook to grant the degree of LL.B. (Bachelor of Laws) to students who had completed an undergraduate course and also satisfied the requirements of the graduate course, either on a full or part-time basis. I was gratified by the fact that, even in my junior role on the staff, I had been assigned tutelage of a candidate for the D. Jur. degree (Doctor of Jurisprudence), the highest degree the University bestowed. Jim Northey came to us from the University of Auckland in New Zealand. I worked with him on a thesis he was preparing on the topic of treaties in international law. Upon achieving his goal, Northey returned to New Zealand and became a professor at the University of Auckland.

As a member of the staff, I attended meetings of the Faculty of Law. Board meetings were concerned with academic matters, such as qualifications of candidates for admission to the law school, course content, and the like. Dean Kennedy presided as chairman of the Faculty Board and LaBrie was the secretary. Kennedy displayed a side of his character and abilities that I had never noted before. As chairman, Kennedy was business-like, precise and efficient. He also displayed good ability as an administrator.

As time passed, I became increasingly absorbed in public international law. I found it to be a subject that called for a degree of expertise in Canadian constitutional law, comparative constitutional law and an appreciation of jurisprudence, which is the philosophy of law. It was surprising that a subject of such complexity had been entrusted to a junior member of staff. It attracted numerous scholars of eminence in the United States, Britain and Europe. Moreover, a variety of circumstances of the day tended to focus attention on the subject. World War II had ended and leading statesmen were seeking a new world order that would maintain the peace. International meetings had resulted in the creation of the United Nations and the International Court of Justice. At Nuremberg, the trial of major war criminals for crimes against humanity had resulted not only in the conviction and sentencing of offenders but also the formulation of certain rules or principles of international criminal law. I was caught up in an atmosphere of excitement that pervaded the teaching of this branch of law.

Dean Kennedy was quietly very supportive of me in my work, particularly in respect of my interest in international law. He arranged for me to attend conferences of the American Society of International Law. At a conference of the Society held at the Hotel Algonquin in New York, famous as a meeting place for the literati, I met a host of teachers and educators, several with worldwide reputations for eminence in this subject. Professor Brierly, a leading scholar, came from Britain to address the conference. I was introduced to Justice Robert Jackson, formerly the American prosecutor at the Nuremberg trials. I met Judge G.H. Hackworth, a judge of the International Court of Justice. It was an exhilarating experience. A year or two later, I attended another conference of the Society, this time held in Washington D.C., where I renewed acquaintances with teachers I had met in New York.

I had taken a book with me for reading en route to the Washington conference. I was to review it for our University of Toronto Law Journal. I travelled by bus and, not having room in my baggage for an additional item, the book was lying on the seat beside me as we approached the US border. An American customs officer came on board and, attracted by the title, picked up the book and began thumbing through it. A peculiar expression passed across his face. It was only then that I realized the impression that the book was creating, especially in light of the climate of the times in the U.S.A. The book bore the title, *The Seizure of Territory*. I made haste to explain I was merely an ordinary academic and had no intention of engaging in the conquest of the United States of America. After the officer examined the book carefully, at last he put it down. I asked him how he had enjoyed the book. He confessed he was unable to get past the Latin quotations.

In Washington, I was the houseguest of Professor Murdoch who taught public international law at George Washington University. John Foster Dulles, who had just been appointed Secretary of State of the United States, delivered the main address at this conference. At this time, the US. was in confrontation with the USSR and both the Senate and House of Representatives were heavily involved in ferreting out communists and so-called fellow travellers. I was frankly disappointed in Dulles' address. I felt he had little to offer of a constructive nature in dealing with foreign affairs, specifically in relation to Russia. I had hoped to attend a meeting of the Senate sub-committee on what was called un-American activities, but was unable to arrange an attendance.

Toward the end of his career, Dean Kennedy sadly remarked to me that he was "the last of the characters" at the University. I find difficulty in applying appropriate adjectives to accurately depict the character of this man. Each person on staff in Law, with the exception of Professor Auld, had been his student, at one time or another, and had benefited from exposure to his influence. He was on easy terms with the president and chancellor of the University. Amongst his peers — the professors of faculties within the University — he was an acknowledged leader. Amongst his accomplishments, he took pride in being the billiards champion of the Faculty Club. The one word that best sums up his personality is "overpowering." That is why, one day when Dean Kennedy extended an invitation to me and my wife to spend a weekend with him and his family at their summer cottage, I was suddenly terror-stricken. The prospect of spending several days, subjected to his personality, one on one, on a full-time basis was utterly daunting.

When I told Joyce this "good news," to my distress she flatly refused to go; and I could not change her mind. How, I asked, could I explain to the Dean her rejection of an invitation that he had extended as indication of our acceptance and his friendship? Moreover, as she must know, such an invitation from the Dean of the law school was akin to a command. Not at all moved by my arguments, Joyce told me to convey, as her excuse, that she was pregnant. It was true, for she was later to give birth to our second child, Nancy; but, at the time, her condition was not a critical disability. Nevertheless, upon her instruction, we pleaded pregnancy, on the strength of which Joyce was found not guilty and excused. Inevitably, however, the Dean turned to me and said, "then you will come up yourself."

Thus the die was cast; I was committed. I went to see Professor Finkelman for advice. When Finkelman learned that I had been invited by the Dean for a weekend at "Narrow Waters," he became most solicitous. Out of the background of his experience, he tried to prepare me for the situation I was about to encounter. He cautioned me that the Dean directed his family like a commander of a military establishment. An atmosphere of strict discipline prevailed. Activities were regulated for each segment of the day. Meals were frugal. "You will be hungry," he warned, "so take along some chocolate bars." "There will be no snacks between meals and no food after dinner, which will be held early. After dinner, the Dean will turn on the radio for the news. When the news is over, he will examine his pocket watch and announce it is time for bed." My anxiety was not much relieved by this information.

On a lovely summer day, I found myself on a train headed for a resort area in the District of Haliburton, north of Toronto. Eventually, the train stopped at a milk stand in open country. There I was met by the Dean's wife, Pauline Kennedy, in charge of a car of ancient vintage and accompanied by her daughter Shelagh. Pauline drove to a gate across a lane where she alighted, put her hand to her mouth and, to my astonishment, called in a loud, clear, soprano voice, "cooie." From the distance came back the answering call of the mate in a high-pitched male voice, "cooie." We opened the gate, got back in the car, and Pauline drove down the lane. There, standing in the lane, we came upon William Paul McClure Kennedy, appearing as I had never before beheld him. He was clad in knee high boots, breeches, cowboy hat, and no shirt. With his thin frame, the sun outlined every rib of his body. Sudden brashness overcame my temerity. "Dean, don't move," I said; "I have my camera and I want to take a picture." I descended from the car with my camera; and the Dean suffered me to take a snapshot of him. The rest of my weekend passed almost exactly as Finkelman had foretold.

Narrow Waters was a comfortable summer cottage that stood on a substantial tract of land partially covered by forest. It fronted on a lovely little lake, typical of this resort area of Ontario. I had brought my bathing suit and was aching to go swimming in those inviting waters. Not once did the possibility of water sports even arise. Instead, it was the Dean's pleasure to take me for walks through his forest. It appeared that he caused some of the trees to be cut for firewood. He told me that he put his guests to work from time to time cutting trees. Without the slightest embarrassment, indeed with considerable pride, he pointed to trees that had been felled by good friends. In one instance he pointed to a stump and, with relish, commented: "This one was cut down by Innis." Harold Innis was a highly respected professor in the Political Science Department of the University. "If you will look there, you can see where he carved his initials into the stump," the Dean continued. Thankfully, I was not invited to join the Dean's illustrious collection of woodsmen. I have no recollection of any discourse with Shelagh or Frere, Kennedy's second son. I spent the weekend almost wholly in the company of the Dean, listening to what amounted to a steady monologue on a variety of legal and other erudite subjects. I was a good listener. Occasionally, when he posed a question on a topic with which I was unfamiliar, he would save me the embarrassment of venturing an answer by stating his own opinion anyway. Finkelman was right about the food. I ate a number of chocolate bars.

There is a sequel to this story. Many years later I was attending a function in late spring held on the quadrangle behind Hart House. Drinks were being served. I was conversing with a younger man whom I had not met before. He mentioned to me what apparently was uppermost in his mind at the time: "I have just come back from Haliburton; I bought a summer cottage; I dealt with a cleric..." It was this last remark that caused my mind to click.

"Don't tell me you bought Narrow Waters!" I exclaimed.

"Yes, I did." There followed mutual introductions; and I found I was chatting with Martin Friedland, the former Dean of the Faculty of Law and author of several books on law including an exceptionally good treatise on double jeopardy.

"Then you just bought W.P.M. Kennedy's place in the country," I continued. "In that case, I must tell you a story." I launched into an account of my visit and mentioned that I had taken a picture of Kennedy. "So," I concluded, "since you are now the owner of Kennedy's

Narrow Waters, and also a former Dean of the Law School, you should be put in possession of my prized snapshot of Kennedy." Later, I found the picture, had a print of it made up, and sent him the print.

About two years after I began teaching at the University, I approached Professor Finkelman with an offer to write an article for the University of Toronto Law Journal. Amongst his other responsibilities, Finkelman was the editor of the Law Journal that, in a few years, achieved a reputation for excellence as a learned publication. Finkelman encouraged me to proceed with this project. The subject I had chosen is well indicated by the title I had selected — "Is International Law Part of the Law of Canada?" To this question, I gave an affirmative answer. I set out to demonstrate that the rules governing the relations between states have a practical application internally within Canada; and that these rules must be applied where relevant to the disposition of issues arising in our courts. I worked painstakingly on this article and finally brought the finished product to Finkelman. Professor Finkelman then put me through the following process. We read through the entire article together, interrupted at about every sentence by Finkelman questioning words, clauses, and sentence structures, querying clarity of meaning, and stressing simplicity of expression and grammatical construction. Never did he suggest any specific changes. Indeed, he exhibited scrupulous regard for my work. It was to remain wholly my article; but the concern he expressed always was whether it could not be further improved. After this session, I took away the article, practically re-wrote it and brought it back to him. Finkelman put me through precisely the same process a second time. Nothing seemed to satisfy him. He was by this time my very good friend. On a personal basis, he showed me great kindness; but on an academic footing he was a hard taskmaster. Only once during the joint process of review did he allow me a glimpse of his softer nature.

Toward the end of the article I had prefaced my conclusions with a sub-heading in Latin: *De Lege Ferenda.* When we came to this part of the article, after all the preceding criticism, somewhat crestfallen, I conceded, "This will have to come out, I suppose."

To the contrary, Finkelman rather liked it. "Oh no," he responded with a smile, "a little class does no harm at all!"

Again, I made extensive corrections. When he was finally satisfied with my article, Finkelman turned to me and in his most amiable tones offered the following explanation of the inquisition to which I had been subjected: "I want you to know, Dave, I have been doing you a favour. What I did for you is what Kennedy did for me when we were writing a tract together. Kennedy put me through exactly the same exercise. He insisted on precision. He said he intended to make me think and write clearly. That is what I have been trying to do for you too." After about forty-five years, I recently reread the article. I consider it to be the best work I have done.

For a number of years, a dispute had been waging amongst the Benchers of the Law Society of Upper Canada about the future of legal education. It stemmed from dissatisfaction with the current system under which the Law Society exercised control over legal education by virtue of its statutory authority over admission to the Bar of Ontario. Qualification for the practice of law required satisfactory completion of a course operated by the Law Society involving three years of lectures and contemporaneous service under articles in a law office. One faction argued for the retention of the current system. The other claimed that it was too narrow and tended to treat the profession as a trade; and that to produce lawyers of intellectual breadth and professional capacity required the Law Society to yield a major role in legal education to the universities. The dispute spread amongst the teachers at Osgoode Hall Law School. Like everyone in the profession, I was aware of the dispute. However, I played no part in it. To his credit, I believe Kennedy did not interfere or seek to influence the result. By its very existence, his law school spoke volumes on this issue.

Suddenly, at about the end of the school year in 1949, three of the top teachers at Osgoode resigned and were immediately appointed to the Faculty of Law of the University of Toronto. The leader was Dr. Cecil Wright. He brought with him Bora Laskin and John Willis. At the University of Toronto, Dr. Kennedy was overdue for retirement. He retired and Caesar Wright was appointed Dean in his place. Thus came about a new regime at the University's Faculty of Law. Not long afterwards, the opposition to change in the Law Society collapsed and the present system came into effect. A candidate now needed to successfully complete a course in a recognized university leading to the LL.B. degree; one year of training in a law office under articles; and a further six months in a course at Osgoode in the practical aspects of the profession.

The accession of Dr. Wright and his associates to the University signalled the victory in the struggle for reform of legal education and the transfer of considerable power to the universities. It might have been supposed that my colleagues and I would have greeted this change with enthusiasm. Instead, we met it with mingled apprehension and gloom. Dr. W.P.M. Kennedy, who had founded the first law school at a university in Ontario, possibly the first in Canada, went into retirement and was allowed to slip quietly into relative obscurity. He left without fanfare or special recognition of his immense contribution to the cause of legal education. Bill Reed left Toronto to accept a teaching position at another university. Sommerfeld took a post with the Combines Investigation Branch of the federal Department of Justice.

To my surprise, I was allowed to remain on staff, although I soon realized that, like Sommerfeld and Reed, I was also slated for departure at the end of my one-year with Wright and his associates. I surmised that I was regarded as dispensable because I lacked academic tenure. Even more relevant was the fact that I held no academic degrees, except for my B.A., acquired as an undergraduate, and my LL.B., acquired from the University while engaged as a lecturer. Unlike Wright and Laskin, I never attained the distinction of post-graduate studies and the acquisition of degrees from Harvard or other prestigious universities. Whatever reason there may have been for letting me go did not justify parting with Finkelman or LaBrie. Finkelman was an experienced and respected professor of long-standing and LaBrie had displayed proven competence and had acquired tenure. Within a year or two after I left, Finkelman resigned to resume his former position as Chairman of the Ontario Labour Relations Board; later he went to Ottawa as chair of the newly created Public Services Staff Relations Board where he enjoyed a long and distinguished career. Shortly afterwards, LaBrie also tendered his resignation and left for private practice to specialize in taxation, a subject in which he had acquired a particular expertise. Once he departed, no more members of the Kennedy regime remained on the staff of the Faculty of Law.

With the advent of Dr. Cecil Wright to the Faculty of Law, so far as I was concerned, there was a decided change in the atmosphere and environment under which I went about my duties. The former aura of friendliness, collegiality and support were gone. Wright assumed an attitude of camaraderie and affability at odds with the name "Caesar" by which he was widely known. Although he was invariably polite, I could detect no warmth in his casual contacts with me. Never did he even mention my article on public international law even though it was published in the University of Toronto Law Journal during the very year of my service with him. Never did he extend the slightest encouragement or indicate any appreciation of my efforts.

At an early meeting in his office to allocate assignments for the academic year, Wright turned to me and said: "Dave, you will take agency."

"But,"' I stuttered in protest, "I have never taught agency. I hardly remember any agency law."

"Don't worry," he responded, "You can use my casebook."

My concern was increased rather than allayed. My mind flashed back about thirteen years when I was a student at Osgoode Hall where Wright taught agency using the casebook method of instruction that had been popularized at Harvard University. Wright's casebook was a compilation of judgements of the courts in leading cases in the broad area covered by the law of agency. Following each case or group of cases, Wright had inserted a number of hypothetical situations designed to question the validity of the principle to be deduced from the decided cases and showing that a variety of alternative solutions were plausible. The supporters of this methodology maintain that the object is not merely to convey information, but to train the mind to think clearly and logically. It was my experience, however, that by the time Wright's course ended, I was aware only of numerous inconsistencies in the law. I had the uneasy feeling that I had acquired little knowledge of the actual state of the law on any specific matter — even when well settled by decisions of the courts. I am prepared, nevertheless, to concede that the fault may lie with the apprentice and not the master. Regrettably, I was a poor imitation of Caesar Wright in the teaching of his course on agency. Burdened as I was by other assignments, I enjoyed little success and derived no satisfaction in teaching a subject assigned to me on short notice and about which I retained little familiarity.

By the time the year ended I was not unhappy to part company with Dr. Wright. Of course, I was anxious about my prospects of obtaining other employment. In light of my interest in public international law, I contemplated making overtures for a position with the Department of External Affairs, but never took any step to that end. I could not afford to await their process of selection of candidates by written or oral examination. I was troubled by the practical necessity of supporting a family. By this time, our Nancy had been born and in the next year, Howard likewise came along to round out our family of three children. Accordingly, when I received an offer of employment that was extended to me on the recommendation of Professor Finkelman, I felt that I should not wait for some other or better opportunity and I accepted the offer. My career then took an abrupt turn. I took employment with a company engaged in the business of construction and land development and gave myself the title of general counsel.

I enjoyed my few years as a teacher at the University. My contact with the students was a source of considerable satisfaction. It is difficult to describe the gratification one derives from dealing with keen minds at the university level of students on a quest for higher education and admission into a learned profession. I never was so foolish as to suppose that in my four years I became an exceptional teacher. I did my very best to teach the subjects entrusted to me and tried to inspire my students much as I had been inspired by the likes of Professors Kennedy and Finkelman. It has been one of the delights of my life, occasionally, to meet a former student; invariably I have been greeted with respect, warmth and, I believe, even affection.

For years after I left the University, I received periodic letters from the Faculty of Law addressed to me in my capacity as a graduate. These letters usually described recent activities at the law school and often included an effort to raise funds for one purpose or another. Inevitably, the letters ended with words extolling the contribution to the teaching of law at the University by Dr. Wright and his associates and rarely, if at all, paid homage to Wright's predecessors. This ongoing process of deification of Wright and his followers and, by negative inference, virtually denigrating the achievement of the founding fathers of the University Law School, finally provoked me, many years later, to write a letter of protest that, for the record, is reproduced below:

Dean Robert J. Sharpe
Faculty of Law
University of Toronto
78 Queen's Park

Toronto, Ontario
M5S 2C5

Dear Dean Sharpe:

Thank you for your letter of October 10, 1992, addressed to me as a graduate of the Faculty of Law and in which you report on the progress of the Law School.

I wish to draw your attention to the penultimate paragraph in which you remark on 'the vision of Wright, Laskin, Willis and Abel.'

Lost seems to be the vision of Kennedy, Finkelman, Mackenzie and Auld who were the School of Law that constituted the foundation for the teaching of law at the University level as a condition of qualification and practice at the Bar. Their contribution to the cause of legal education in Canada was enormous.

Missing as well in your remarks is any reference to any of the lesser lights such as LaBrie, Sommerfeld, Reid, or even this correspondent who devoted four years to the teaching of law at the U. of T.

I forgo any personal recognition. It seems to me, however, that the late Dr. W.P.M. Kennedy, founding Dean of the School of Law, Finkelman, and the others who produced such illustrious graduates as Laskin, C.J.C., Howland, C.J.O., Martin, J.A., and the present Chief Justice of Ontario, might be given permanent recognition and the same approbation for their contribution as is constantly afforded to Caesar Wright and company.

Yours truly,

I had hoped that this letter might help to achieve a more balanced perspective in the history of the teaching of law at the University of Toronto.

Thirteen
Principal Investments to
Private Practice

Principal Investments Limited, to which I now devoted my energy and talent as legal counsel, was a private corporation wholly owned by the Bennett family. Four Bennetts operated the company: brothers Dave, Archie, and Jack, and Archie's son, Avie. I almost invariably referred to them by the initials of their given names. Shortly before my arrival, the founder of the firm, the father of the Bennett brothers, and a fourth brother had died.

Principal Investments was a construction company that confined its operations mainly to the development of commercial properties and holding the completed projects for investment. Its offices were located at 67 Richmond Street West but, shortly after I started work, it took over a floor in one of its buildings, an eight-story structure at 133 Richmond Street. Principal Investments' projects were usually substantial. They involved the purchase of land and construction of large buildings, financed by mortgage loans. Generally, the financing was dependent on the leases arranged and the financial strength of the tenants. The legal work to accommodate these projects required a good knowledge of the law of real property. My academic experience in this area of the law stood me in good stead.

Fulfilment

The four Bennetts jointly ran the company. I never knew any of them to have a particular designation, such as president, chairman of the board, or chief executive officer. They made important decisions at meetings behind closed doors, somewhat akin to a football team huddling behind the line of scrimmage.

I never took part in company business decisions. Whether by circumstance or design, my activities were confined to the legal aspects of its operations. The Bennetts restricted my business information on a need-to-know basis.

I believe it was Avie who brought the concept of the modern shopping centre to Principal Investments. He probably got the notion of building shopping centres on a visit to the United States where he would have observed this novel type of merchandising in operation. The company experimented with this concept in a development at the corner of Bayview and Eglinton Avenue in Toronto. It built the first shopping centre in Canada, however, at the corner of Lawrence and Bathurst Street. They called it the Lawrence Plaza. Thereafter, the company specialized in the construction of shopping centres. At its zenith, it had built, owned, controlled and managed the largest number of shopping centres of any company in Canada.

The advent of the shopping centre created a huge expansion of my legal responsibilities and work. Shopping centres were usually located outside of congested urban areas on land acquired as "raw" or unserviced. It would be necessary, therefore, for the developer to install all municipal services, such as water lines and sanitary and storm sewers, or to ensure they had already been installed. Often it would be strategic to acquire a tract of land of which only part was intended for use as a shopping centre. This would involve the developer in all the problems of land subdivision. Finally, it would be essential to determine that the land could lawfully be used for the purpose for which it was being acquired; namely, that it was zoned or could be rezoned pursuant to any governing zoning by-law for use as a shopping centre. All these matters required applications, attendances before a variety of governmental authorities and, often, appearances before the Ontario Municipal Board, the administrative tribunal that was vested with the authority of final decision in most cases.

In one instance, the owners of a shopping centre near a project of Principal Investments opposed its application to rezone its land for use as a shopping centre. The matter came on appeal before the Ontario

Municipal Board. The owners of the adjoining shopping centre argued that there was an insufficient amount of business, actual or projected, to justify the operation of two shopping centres in the area. They argued that, if Principal Investments were allowed to proceed with its project, it was likely that neither shopping centre would survive. I contended that it was not the proper function of the Ontario Municipal Board, in the regulation of land use, to restrict or eliminate competition, and in effect to confer a monopoly. In this case, my argument prevailed and Principal Investments completed its project in due course. To the best of my knowledge, both shopping centres have enjoyed good success.

Many municipalities had by-laws that had accumulated over the years prohibiting the opening of stores on specified days during the week. To similar effect were the provincial "blue" laws that prohibited the carrying on of business on Sundays and holidays. All these laws offended the basic principle underlying the existence of shopping centres, which is that all stores should be required to remain open for business at all times and days when customers could reasonably be expected to have the desire and the opportunity to do their shopping. In opposition to these laws, which generally were supported by merchants of strip developments, I attended public meetings and appeared before municipal councils and Magistrates Courts on various occasions.

The special nature of the shopping centre was also reflected in the form of lease that merchants, who occupied space as tenants, were required to execute. The form of lease we developed at Principal Investments contained a clause granting exclusive possession of specific store premises to each tenant, together with rights in common with all other tenants similarly entitled over the parking areas and all other common areas of the shopping centre. I probably drafted the first clause of a shopping centre lease in Canada dealing with what I described as rights in common. I adopted a wording by analogy to rights of way and easements, both well-known concepts of the law of real property. Our form of lease contained a rental clause that required payment of three types of rent: a basic rent in a fixed amount; a percentage rent computed as a percentage of the gross annual sales of merchandise in the tenant's store; and an additional rent to cover a proportionate part of the expenses of operating the shopping centre.

Principal Investments' duty to provide parking for all tenants led to serious difficulties in its first development — Lawrence Plaza. A successful shopping centre needed to boast a full complement of shopping facilities, particularly a food supermarket and at least one major department store. Principal Investments was initially unable to attract a department store to the Plaza until the shopping centre had been built and leased. Only then did The Bay, probably the most substantial chain of department stores in Canada, decide to open, at this location, their first department store in Toronto. The Bennetts scrambled to accept this opportunity and began construction of the department store on part of the parking area previously allocated to other tenants. Of course, this was a gross violation of the company's obligations under the clause granting rights in common to the other tenants. Principal Investments had the delicate task of obtaining the consent of each tenant to this invasion of the tenants' rights.

The Bennetts attracted capable and dedicated employees. One of these was A.E. (Eph) Diamond. Eph was a graduate engineer who had served in the navy in wartime. The Bennetts put him in charge of the construction of Lawrence Plaza. He was a person of exceptional ability with whom I had increasing contact. We became very good friends. In the course of planning the shopping centre, Eph showed me two conceptual drawings of it. One depicted stores in the open in form of an "L" and the other an enclosed mall. Eph had wanted to build the mall, but the Bennetts decided that the mall was too advanced for the times because customers expected to view individual stores from the street and obtain access to each store from an exterior entrance.

At Principal Investments I received some sound advice and valuable experience in practicality and realism. It was common practice in the legal profession when acting for a purchaser of real estate to write a long letter of requisitions questioning every possible defect that might appear upon a search of the title. It was also common on behalf of the vendor to respond at length on each point but often with the simple message "satisfy yourself." An insistent requisitioner on some minor discrepancy could sometimes accomplish more harm than good. Jack, who was himself a lawyer, made a special point of cautioning me on this subject. He told me that when the Principal Investments entered into an agreement to purchase a property, they really wanted the deal consummated, they did not want it aborted. They did not want me to place roadblocks in the path of accomplishing this object.

Nevertheless, I may sometimes have been overzealous in the protection of my client. On one occasion, instead of drafting a lease for execution by a prospective tenant, I received a form of lease drafted by the tenant's lawyer, Louis Singer, who was a senior member of the Bar for whom I had great respect. I wrote one of those long letters, about which Jack had cautioned me, in which I questioned a variety of items in the draft lease. Louis Singer's response was to invite me to lunch at the Royal York Hotel. After an enjoyable lunch, we got down to business.

"Now tell me," Louis Singer asked, producing his form of lease and my letter, "What is wrong with my lease?"

We examined each item of my letter. On each point, he posed the same question. In each instance, I was unable to justify my objection and ended by waiving it. By the time we finished, I had waived everything and accepted his draft of the lease altogether.

After this defeat, which I accepted as gracefully as I could, I took the opportunity of telling this much older lawyer how he had won my admiration when I was still a law student. I was an observer in a courtroom at Osgoode Hall when Louis Singer acted as counsel for the plaintiff, the owner of a cut-rate tobacco store on Yonge Street, in an action against all the tobacco companies in Canada as defendants. The tobacco companies had refused to supply the plaintiff with merchandise for sale in his store. He sued for damages alleging a conspiracy in restraint of trade.

"You were all alone acting for the plaintiff. Against you were no less than three of the leading counsel of the day: Helmuth, Tilley and Robertson. Robertson was an expert in evidence. His only function at the trial, it appeared, was to raise objections on points of evidence." Later, he became Chief Justice of Ontario. Warming to my account, I continued: "I can not tell you how much I admired your cross-examination of the sales manager of the Imperial Tobacco Company who was on the stand that day. You spoke quietly, never raising your voice. The witness, a portly man, became increasingly flustered; his face reddened; he faltered. I thought your cross-examination was classic, superb."

Louis Singer listened impassively to my enthusiastic adulation. "Yes," he said, "I worked hard on that case. But I want you to know I worked just as hard *on this lease*. It did not come easy. It took me a long time to draft. I worked as hard on the lease and got the same satisfaction as I did that day in court."

Jack would sometimes refer former clients to me. Generally, it was a welcome diversion from my ordinary responsibilities and, on occasion, it was exhilarating. I remember Julius Seltzer particularly. He was the father of my fraternity brother, Gilbert Seltzer. Julius Seltzer was first and foremost a Jew, yet not a particularly religious Jew; he was devoted more to Jewish culture than to religious observance. Despite his background as a businessman and employer, he was mildly socialist in political orientation and a member of the movement known as the "Arbeiter Ring" or Workmen's Circle. For many years of his life, Julius Seltzer was a resident of the West Toronto Junction. He had been engaged in partnership in the operation of a woollen knitting mill. Now retired, he informed me that he had a problem. I asked him what it was.

"Well," he began, in a Talmudic cadence and inflection; "I am selling and buying a house."

"So what," I remarked, "there is nothing unusual about that; so what is the problem?"

"Well," he continued, "after I signed the deal to buy the house, friends came to me and said: Seltzer, this house you are buying is a house with a reputation. The house takes water in the basement. Seltzer, you bought a lemon!"

Mr. Seltzer went on to explain: "When I heard that the house was a house with a reputation I thought to myself, either it's true or it's not true. It is like if you agree to marry a woman and someone comes to you and tells you the woman you agreed to marry is a bad woman, a tramp. What should you do? You marry her. If after you marry it turns out it's true she is a tramp, what do you do? You divorce her! The same with the house. People tell me it's a house with a reputation. What should I do? Buy the house and move in? If after I move in I find its true, the house takes water, what should I do?"

In triumph he answered his own rhetorical question: "I DIVORCE IT!"

"So, Mr. Seltzer," I finally asked my philosophical elder, "What do you want me to do about the house?"

Oh," he responded without hesitation, "close the deal." That is what I did. I completed both transactions and, so far as I am aware, the elder Seltzer lived the rest of his days in his new home and I heard nothing more about water in the basement.

No doubt, not only Jack but all the Bennetts were well acquainted with Julius Seltzer. They shared with him a connection to the West

Toronto Junction. Many years previously when their father was in charge of the business, the Bennetts built a large proportion of the houses on the Maria Street I knew as a boy.

In their personal relations, the Bennetts were easy-going and affable. In an expansive mood, Dave could relate a variety of anecdotes and offer incisive observations about people he knew. With regard to Louis Singer, for instance, Dave once remarked wryly: "Louis Singer's problem is that it was not enough for him that he was clever; people had to be shown how clever he was and, in the process of displaying his cleverness, he lost most of his cases."

I never knew any of the Bennetts to have any particular ability in sports but they were enthusiastic baseball fans. On May 1 in each year, they effectively closed their business to attend the opening baseball game of the year. On occasion Dave would call for me, at too early an hour in the morning for me, so that we could play nine holes of golf before work. It had to be very early in the morning so Dave could afterwards go on a tour of inspection of current projects and still get to the office at the same time as everyone else.

Unfortunately, Principal Investments ultimately fell into hard times. Almost invariably, Principal Investments was a purchaser of property; it was rarely a vendor. It was my impression that Dave could not bear to part with any of the company's assets. Over the course of the years, Principal Investments had accumulated a huge inventory of real estate. The problem was that all the properties were heavily mortgaged. It suffered from a chronic lack of adequate financing. To add to their problems, serious differences arose amongst the Bennetts themselves. It became clear to me that Principal Investments was headed for bankruptcy.

I had been very comfortable at Principal Investments for upwards of eight years and had enjoyed working for the Bennetts. The work was interesting and the Bennetts had treated me very well. However, by this time I was economically responsible for a wife and three children. I was forced to make a hard decision. I could not afford to wait for the inevitable disaster. I agonized over my decision about which there was no realistic alternative. Finally, I made up my mind to leave the company and, despite my disastrous experience after my call to the Bar, I opened a small office and launched again into private practice. As before, it was a step into the dark.

Fourteen
Raising a Family

Meanwhile, on the home front, life was just as full of interest, challenge and exhilaration as it was in my regular work at Principal Investments. Upon joining Principal Investments, I acquired a considerable increase of remuneration. The extra money was particularly important because, instead of Molly and me and baby who made three, we had Joyce and me and babies who made five. Nancy was born just prior to my joining Principal Investments and Howard came along the following year.

I chose the name Howard for my younger son because of Howard Bowman, an old friend of whom I was very fond. By Jewish tradition, however, babies were named after ancestors, not living persons. So, to justify my choice, I selected an uncle, Herschel, the husband of my mother's sister, who had lived in Brooklyn and recently died, and named Howard for the Hebrew equivalent of Herschel. I had rarely come into contact with this uncle for he never moved out of Brooklyn. When it became known that I had named my newborn son after my deceased uncle, I received a long letter from cousins in Brooklyn thanking me profusely for the honour I had conferred upon their family. Unfortunately, I had made a sad mistake. My uncle was not

Herschel. To my discomfiture, I discovered that his name was actually Israel! I was most embarrassed about this little error. Happily, it seems to have passed relatively unnoticed. I assume that his lapse on my part has not adversely affected the course of Howard's life.

Shortly after I took employment with Principal Investments, we sold our house and moved to another dwelling. Joyce and I differ about the reason for this important change. She says we moved because our house was too small and we urgently needed larger premises. I claim we moved because of a mouse. I had a heavy distaste for rodents. One night, after my family was asleep, I was seated alone in the kitchen when, to my horror, I noticed a "wee sleekit beastie" poke its nose out of a hole in the wall. The mouse took a few steps forward, regarded me in contemptuous silence, and returned whence it had come. Alarmed by this sudden intrusion into my domain, I grabbed a broom and waited for the mouse to come out again. After a few minutes, as anticipated, the mouse emerged again and took a few steps into the room. We scrutinized one another with interest. Then I lunged forward, brought the broom down with a resounding blow — and missed. The mouse scampered back to its hiding place. There followed one or two repetitions of the same incident. I learned to entertain respect for the little creature. Still, firmly resolved, broom in hand, I waited. But my antagonist seemed to have given up the sport. I waited all night in the hope that I might get a last chance at the mouse. Finally, in the early hours of the morning, it emerged and took tentative steps in my direction. I waited as long as I could endure the tension, then aimed a wild blow with my broom. Again I missed. The mouse returned to its home behind the wall. I never encountered it again. Shortly afterwards, we moved.

We sold our modest little house of two tiny bedrooms and bought a slightly larger house of three tiny bedrooms in a new housing project. It was a major development that was under way on a large tract of land adjacent to the north of Lawrence Plaza in the Township of North York. It was possibly the first large-scale National Housing Act subdivision in Canada and was named Lawrence Manor. The NHA was the principal vehicle under which the federal government endeavoured to satisfy the post-war demand for moderately priced housing. Individuals who qualified under the NHA were enabled to purchase houses, built under regulated conditions, and financed by mortgages at relatively low rates of interest. The government guaranteed payment of the money secured by these mortgages.

The NHA was responsible for a prolonged period of residential construction and the extension of urban development into suburban and rural areas. The creation of Lawrence Manor coincided roughly with a number of advances in town planning and municipal organization. In Ontario the legislature enacted statutes to control the use and subdivision of land. It also brought into existence the Corporation of Metropolitan Toronto as an additional municipal organization with specified authority over an area that included Toronto and its adjacent suburbs. The main object of the legislature was to promote the planned development of land and facilitate the installation of municipal services throughout the entire area. At about this time, the Township of North York passed its first zoning by-law to govern and regulate the uses to which land would be permitted in designated areas, a by-law that became a prototype for the rest of Canada.

Joyce and I were in the first wave of purchasers of houses in Lawrence Manor when we moved into our new home at 77 Brucewood Crescent. The developer considered it finished to a degree sufficient to justify occupation, although not to the extent required by our contract. The lack of sod at front and rear of the premises was particularly irksome. Houses were under construction throughout the subdivision. Even the installation of municipal services was far from complete. Months passed before the roads within the subdivision were paved. When it rained, the area became a virtual quagmire. Rubber boots were a necessity. According to the plan of subdivision, a substantial parcel of land in the centre of the development was designated for use as a public park. An immense mound of earth had been dumped on this prime parkland, topsoil collected during the excavation for the houses throughout the area. This unsightly mess remained to impair the landscape and was only removed when the roads were paved as a last step in the development of Lawrence Manor.

Accustomed to all the amenities of the City, Joyce and I felt like pioneers being exposed to the hardships of life in a suburban subdivision still under construction. Our problems were aggravated by the initial unavailability of private telephone and individual postal delivery service. Private telephones could only be acquired in due time after lines had been brought into the area and there was a long waiting list of applicants. Joyce again used her plea of pregnancy as grounds for priority. This time she was about to come to term with Howard. This excuse accelerated our application by a few months. After we acquired our telephone, we provided a popular telephone service for all of our neighbours still on the waiting list.

Our neighbours and we complained to one another about the treatment we were being accorded by builders, tradesmen, developers, and municipal and governmental officials. There was a general tendency amongst all these people, it seemed, to disregard the complaints and concerns of the purchasers of houses in the development. What was needed was some means of protecting the legitimate interests of the purchasers; for instance, to ensure the due and timely performance of the subdividers' obligations under the subdivision agreement with the Township. In general, however, there was a great deal of excitement and enthusiasm amongst the purchasers about their adventure in suburban living. As residents in this new subdivision, the purchasers wanted the opportunity to participate in the development by arranging for the facilities and amenities that would make it a model community in which to live and raise a family.

Somebody mentioned the notion of a ratepayers association as a vehicle for providing some self-help. Although I had no previous experience with this type of organization, the suggestion struck me as a very good idea, and I immediately sprang into action. It took the form of a simple letter circulated amongst the residents calling a public meeting. The letter received an enthusiastic response. The meeting, held at the local Saranac Public School, attracted a full attendance. I acted as chairman. By unanimous vote of the residents, the Lawrence Manor Ratepayers Association was constituted. Inevitably, as organizer and chairman of the meeting, I was elected the first president. Officers elected at the meeting included Irv Paisley and Sol Cowan. Together we acted as a triumvirate in the leadership of the Association.

The Association became a powerful force in the Township. We held meetings with builders and officials and, as occasion required, attended meetings of the Planning Board and Council of the Township. Additionally, the Association undertook projects designed to improve the community. An early undertaking was a tree-planting project the object of which was to promote the planting of a tree on the lawn in front of each house, preferably of the same type, to ensure a uniformity of trees along each street. Later, the Township itself adopted this project and made it a standard requirement by inclusion in its form of subdivision agreement. Individual members took a particular interest in our local school through the Home and School

Association. The Cowans were particularly involved in the matter of a public library. With other members, they arranged for our community to be served on a regular basis by bookmobile until a branch library could be built to provide regular library service. Irv Paisley was involved in a variety of projects.

The women became equally involved with the men. Joyce, for instance, suggested an excellent program for the children on Halloween. Her thought was that, instead of a night of childish pranks, our children should be encouraged to use the occasion for helping less fortunate children. It was her suggestion that we provide the children with slotted receptacles for soliciting contributions of money for the Save-the-Children's Fund of the United Nations. Typically, the Save-the-Children's Fund gave the idea a lukewarm reception. Later, they seized upon the project as a money-raising enterprise and gave it widespread extension. On the first experiment in Lawrence Manor, the executive members of the Association and their wives spent the early hours of the morning after Halloween prying open the tin cans to gain access to the coins the children had collected.

Normally, the Association adopted and carried out the programs proposed by the leadership. In one instance, however, serious differences arose among the members regarding the development of the central parcel of land covered by the huge mound of earth. The dispute arose over a plan prepared by a landscape architect to improve the site as a public park. The architect proposed the installation of an expanse of lawn, the planting of flowers and shrubs, and the allocation of a corner of the property for use as a children's playground. The plan was brought to the Association by Curly Posen who was so favourably impressed with it himself as to expect it would immediately be accepted and implemented by the Association. Curly Posen was a good-natured jovial individual with a rotund frame. He was familiarly known as "Curly," illogically, because he was wholly bald except for a sparse fringe of hair at the back of a large head. The dispute raged between the owners of houses on the street along the perimeter of the intended park who sought the visual enjoyment of an attractive open area and residents at a distance who wanted some recreational use of the park for their younger children. The dispute became so acrimonious that it threatened the disintegration of the Association. Ultimately, we deemed it expedient to abandon the project and leave the matter of the improvement of the land to the developers and the Township.

Unfortunately, ratepayers' organizations may sometimes operate not to protect a legitimate interest but as a means of exerting pressure to gain an advantage not socially justified. Our Association was no exception. The first Chairman of Metropolitan Toronto was Fred Gardiner, a forceful, domineering personality who was popularly known as "Big Daddy." Gardiner wanted to demonstrate the efficacy of the new municipal entity as a means not only of bringing municipal services into the outlying reaches of Metropolitan Toronto, but also for the provision of housing for lower income people. Accordingly, he promoted a proposal for a high density subsidized housing project to be located immediately to the west of Lawrence Manor. When this became known, the residents of Lawrence Manor became greatly alarmed at the prospect of their ideal, model, middle-class community being threatened by its proximity to this proposed high density, low income development. Curiously, for this project to be allowed to proceed, Metropolitan Toronto required an amendment of the zoning by-law of North York. This project was so important to Metropolitan Toronto that "Big Daddy" attended personally before the Township Council in support of the application by Metropolitan Toronto for amendment of the by-law. On behalf of the Lawrence Manor Ratepayers Association, I also attended the meeting, flanked by Paisley and Cowan, and spoke in opposition to the application. The application was deferred.

Fred Gardiner was furious with our Association and, I fear, with me personally, for our interference in the plans of Metropolitan Toronto. Actually, I felt somewhat embarrassed about our opposition. Although a local ratepayers' organization might cause some delay, it was highly unlikely to defeat an application by such an important applicant. Fortunately, we were able to achieve an honourable resolution of the issue in another way. We negotiated a settlement with Metropolitan Toronto. As the first large-scale NHA subdivision in North York, and the whole of Canada, the subdivision agreement applicable to Lawrence Manor omitted the installation of many items in a full range of municipal services. We settled on terms that additional services should now be installed throughout Lawrence Manor, including storm sewers and curbs. In exchange, the Association withdrew its opposition to Metro's application. Accordingly, "Big Daddy's" favourite project was allowed to proceed to completion.

Despite my regular work for Principal Investments and my

voluntary activities on behalf of the Association, I still found time to spend with my family. It soon became evident that our new dwelling was still too small to accommodate us adequately. The main problem this time was the kitchen. When our family ate meals in the kitchen, which was usual, it was not possible to open the door of the refrigerator or the oven; and if anyone tried to gain access through the rear entrance, little Howie and his high chair had to be moved out of the way. To relieve the congestion, we decided to add a small room. With my connection to the building trades, I was able to arrange for the work to be done without delay. The room was about completed when I arrived home from work one day to find my wife in tears.

A man had come to the back door. He said he was from the Township offices and asked: "Is this your house?" Upon her response in the affirmative, he continued: "This room will have to come down. It is in breach of the building by-law." "Our lovely room," she wailed. "Just as the last nail was being hammered home, we must pull the room down?"

Greatly shaken by this sad report, I set to work to find a solution to the problem. I gave the building by-law a critical examination, spoke to municipal officials, and embarked upon an inconclusive correspondence with the Township solicitor. It was my position that the room was not in breach at all, but even if there were an infringement, it was minor and could readily be corrected. I kept up a regular barrage of letters and arguments. Finally, I received a strange letter from the Township solicitor that I accepted as a conclusion to our correspondence and this episode. Unfortunately, it is no longer available. In effect it stated: "Please, Mr. Vanek, about your room, if you will stop bothering us, we will stop bothering you. Yours truly." In this oblique way, the defect, if there was one, was cured. As a reward for good service rendered, although perhaps not in this affair, the Township solicitor was promoted to be the solicitor for Metropolitan Toronto.

I then arranged with my next door neighbour, Mac Wellwood, that we would help one another install a slab of concrete at the rear of our houses to serve as patios. I mistakenly believed that Mac was experienced in household chores of this kind and discovered later that he was just as inept as I was. One morning, a truck of Principal Investments arrived at my dwelling and deposited a pick, a shovel, and a wheelbarrow. In the late afternoon, I set to work to create a shallow excavation that I intended to fill with concrete. I took the pick firmly in my hands and brought it down on the hard earth with full force. It simply bounced back. After several minutes in this futile endeavour, I gave up. Joyce came to my rescue. She claimed this was not work to suit my abilities. She hired a labourer for the job. When I met him I was appalled. He was a little, thin old man. "Good heavens," I thought, "if we let this fellow do this work, we could be responsible for his death!" But when I saw him in operation, stripped to the waist, I felt re-assured. This little old man possessed bulging muscles and superior strength. With one blow of the pick, earth was shattered. When I returned from work a shallow trench had been created and we were ready for the concrete.

Early the following morning, there was wild excitement in the neighbourhood as a huge ready-mix truck was brought to my house and parked in the driveway. Mac Wellwood and I were ready. I brought the wheelbarrow to the chute at rear of the truck. Seated in the cab, the driver pulled a lever, and concrete poured into the wheelbarrow like molten lava. I lifted upward on the wheelbarrow with all my strength; nothing happened. I could not get it to budge. Mac tried as well, and failed. The driver, still seated in the cab, gave us a look of utter contempt, alighted, lifted the wheelbarrow with ease, rolled it to the excavation, and dumped the contents. Lacking any other alternative, the driver continued the process, working both the lever and the wheelbarrow, until the excavation had been filled with concrete. Meanwhile, Mac and I, on hands and knees, worked furiously to level the concrete before it hardened. When the job was finished, the truck-driver was still with us. I do not know how many deliveries of concrete were delayed that day because of his enforced co-operation in my cause. I do not recall whether I gave him a gratuity. I know I could not have managed without him.

We derived a great deal of pleasure from our children in these days. We used to read to them on a regular basis. They loved the stories I invented for them best of all. My stories dealt with a group of little creatures that inhabited the mound of earth that marred the Lawrence Manor Park. These creatures I called "Shmowies." The leading characters amongst the Shmowies had names strangely reminiscent of my children. They were Howie Shmowie, Nancy Pantsy, and Peter Shmeeter. As well, the stories bore a curious parallel to my experiences in the Lawrence Manor Ratepayers Association. Usually, each episode began with my being hailed by Howie Shmowie as I entered Lawrence Manor on my way home from work. We enjoyed the singular ability to converse with one another. Invariably Howie Shmowie was seeking my help because of a serious problem of the Shmowies, usually concerning relations with builders and subdividers; in a word, problems similar to those affecting the human population.

One of my best stories, which I was called upon to repeat many times, dealt with an occasion when all the Shmowies had been laid low by an epidemic of "haddack" — our Howie's word for headache. Howie Shmowie begged me to send to Sudbury for Legal Speigel to come to the rescue of the Shmowies with his magic pillbox. Joyce and I used to get as much amusement from this story as the children because, of course, I was joking mildly at the expense of my brother-in-law whom we loved dearly, but regarded as somewhat of a hypochondriac. In fact, poor Sam (as his mother used to call him) did suffer from severe headaches and in his travels to and from Toronto often displayed a pillbox that contained an astonishing assortment of pills. In my story, Legal Speigel always came to the rescue of the Shmowies in as many ways as I could devise.

I may have overdone these fanciful stories. I took the same approach to the music that I enjoyed and that I wanted the children to learn to enjoy as well. For instance, I used to play a recording of the Beethoven pastoral symphony and provide a descriptive commentary. As the record approached the fourth movement, I would urge the children to get under the table to avoid the fierce thunderstorm to be depicted in the music.

The children did not need any enhancement of their imaginative faculties. Little Howie, for example, was quite fanciful enough. One day Joyce took him with her when she went shopping at Lawrence Plaza. Upon leaving a shop, she was walking along the sidewalk with a friend and Howie, then a toddler, also walking at her side. Suddenly Howie burst into tears. He was inconsolable. It took Joyce several moments to discover the cause of this outburst. Howie had left behind an imaginary horse in the store. They had to go back to the store to retrieve it. On another occasion, Howie was in the back seat of our car when again he came to tears. This time we learned that a car following us had come too close and was interfering with his horse who was tethered to the back of our car. We enjoyed all these antics and even the escapades of our children.

It was because of my children that I became involved in a religious organization that at the time was far removed from my thoughts and inclination. It may be recalled that I came to Judaism with impeccable credentials; after all, my maternal grandfather was a "sofer," my paternal grandfather a "melamed," and my parents were staunchly orthodox Jews. However, in ecclesiastical matters I have never been the very model of an observant Jew. Thus Irv Paisley assumed a difficult task in trying to convince me to join a new religious congregation founded about one year previously by a nucleus of individuals resident in Bathurst Manor, a development located about a mile north of Lawrence Manor. Paisley's final argument, however, was enough to crush all opposition: "What about the children," he asked? "Aren't you going to give your kids a Jewish education?" The argument was irresistible. So I joined the new congregation, Temple Sinai Congregation of Toronto.

Holy Blossom was the first reform congregation in Toronto. From rented quarters above a drug store, it moved to its own building on Richmond Street, then to another building on Bond Street, and finally to its present stately edifice on Bathurst Street south of Eglinton. Originally, Holy Blossom was organized as a traditional orthodox institution. Gradually, its services and practices were relaxed to conform to social and economic conditions in Canada. Finally, in 1921, Holy Blossom joined the reform movement by affiliating with the Union of American Hebrew Congregations (UAHC), centred in the United States. Reform is a branch of Judaism that originated in Germany. Immigrants brought it to the United States where it enjoyed phenomenal growth. It brought to Judaism a process of rationalization of religious belief and liberalization of practice and observance. Temple Sinai was the second reform congregation in Toronto, intended to accept the overflow of people wanting membership in a reform synagogue or temple.

In one year Temple Sinai had already become a thriving concern. It had acquired a substantial and enthusiastic membership. The first president of Temple Sinai was Harry Pollock, a partner in an advertising firm. He was primarily responsible for the founding of the Temple. A board of directors and an executive committee operated Temple Sinai, with the assistance of a number of other committees, including a building committee and a building fund committee. The building committee had begun a search for an appropriate site and was considering plans for the construction of a synagogue. The Brotherhood and a Sisterhood comprised two other arms of Temple Sinai. Each had its own board of directors and each conducted social and cultural events and fund-raising programs. Through the help of the UAHC, the Temple acquired the services of a student rabbi, Jordan Pearlson, who was still studying at the reform seminary in Cincinnati and came to Toronto to conduct religious services on weekends. Upon his ordination, Jordan Pearlson became the full-time rabbi of Temple Sinai where he served with distinction until his retirement just a few years ago.

Pending the erection of its own synagogue, Temple Sinai held services and meetings in various temporary premises. The High Holy Day services were held in a local theatre. Temple Sinai was conducting a religious school for its children in several classrooms of the Saranac Public School and a Hebrew school above a hardware store on Bathurst Street. In an exemplary exhibition of ecumenical co-operation that received much praise in the press, the Astbury and West United Church was made available to Temple Sinai for its Sabbath evening services on Fridays. Members of the Pulpit and Services Committee transported the holy arc and religious paraphernalia to and from temporary premises.

I had a previous acquaintance with Irving Siegel who was the president of the Brotherhood. Initially, I had no intention of participating actively in the affairs of the Temple but, at his invitation, I joined the Brotherhood board. There, I made the acquaintance of Roy Berk, who was the vice-president of Brotherhood. Soon I learned that serious differences had arisen between the Brotherhood and the board of directors of the Temple. Roy Berk, supported by Irving Siegel, was the leader of the opposition to the current administration. They claimed that the affairs of the Temple were being mismanaged and, short of alleging any wrongdoing, filled my head with stories about Harry Pollock, the president. I was unable to keep myself immune from Temple politics. The annual meeting for the election of officers was approaching. Roy Berk was sponsoring his own candidate for president of the Temple, in opposition to Harry Pollock who was standing for re-election. The candidate, he assured me, was far and away the most competent person for the job — a man, he said who possessed vast ability and leadership experience in Jewish organizations. At the instance of Roy Berk, I wrote a letter, which was

197

circulated amongst the membership, in opposition to Harry Pollock and in support of Roy's candidate. The letter contained strongly worded criticism of Harry Pollock and his leadership of the Temple.

Alas, the letter brought down upon my head the wrath and condemnation of the membership. It occurred to me, belatedly, that I had been manoeuvred into leading the charge of the Light Brigade. I have no recollection of the detail contained in the letter. Happily, I believe no copies are still to be found. It caused such ill feeling that I was in fear of being impeached, excommunicated, or at least expelled from the religious institution I had so recently joined. Fortunately, none of these consequences came to pass. On the day of the annual meeting of Temple Sinai, in some trepidation, I was in attendance with Eph Diamond. He came with me, I believed, for moral support and a show of solidarity. The meeting got under way in an atmosphere of great excitement and tension. I consoled myself about the effect of my letter by the thought that at least it created interest in the election and attracted a full attendance.

My first encounter with Roy Berk's candidate occurred when he addressed the congregation in support of his nomination as president. To my discomfiture, his speech was astonishingly inept. It attracted almost total disapproval from the membership; I was embarrassed. Harry Pollock was re-elected president for a further term of one year. Nominations for directors were accompanied by varied and numerous extreme and vituperative remarks. Much to my surprise, Eph Diamond, who had just joined the Temple, rose to his feet and was allowed to address the congregation. He spoke in calm, measured tones, in an endeavour to calm the raging controversy that had characterized the proceedings and restore peaceful relations amongst the members. So reasonable were his remarks, and acceptable to the meeting, that he was immediately nominated for election to the board of directors. Eph turned to me and offered to stand for election, if I also would stand for election to the board. I agreed and we were both elected to the board of directors. Thus it came about that after Harry Pollock completed his further term in office, Eph Diamond became the second president, and in the year following I became the third president of Temple Sinai. Eph presided over the planning of the synagogue; I had the good fortune to be president in the year the synagogue was built; and my friend, Saul Wolfe, as fourth president, presided over the consolidation of Temple Sinai as an ongoing institution.

In my year as president, I took particular pleasure in the sod-turning ceremony to mark the commencement of operations for the erection of our synagogue on Wilson Avenue. I keep with me an image of my little daughter, Nancy, then about six years old, applying a heavy spade to the good earth in symbolic support of a good work — the creation of a much needed religious institution to serve the Jewish population of Toronto.

Fifteen
Politics, Credit Counselling, and the Bench

W e were still living in Lawrence Manor when a neighbour, with whom, at best, I had only a nodding acquaintance, came calling upon me. He brought with him a gentleman he wanted me to meet. The neighbour was Joe Eisenberg, a widower about fifteen years my senior. He was living with a married daughter and her family. I used to see him in the summer seated on the front veranda of his home. He wanted me to meet our riding candidate for the Progressive Conservative Party in a forthcoming election to the Parliament of Canada. The candidate was Roy Thomson, a newspaper tycoon who had acquired an impressive collection of newspapers, mostly from locations in northern Ontario. They came to solicit my support for Mr. Thomson in the election, presumably on the assumption that as president of the Lawrence Manor Ratepayers Association, I was a person of influence in the area. I was not particularly conscious of any political influence that I wielded and had no commitment or connection to any political party. I told Roy Thomson bluntly — and rather tactlessly — that I could not support his candidacy because I had decided to cast my vote for his opponent, a worthy young lawyer who was the candidate for the

Liberal Party. That ended our meeting except for pleasantries exchanged amongst us in an amicable parting.

In this election there was a general sweep in favour of the Liberal Party on the strength of which the young lawyer was elected. He served one term in office and was never re-elected. Defeated by a younger, relatively unknown opponent, less qualified in the world of affairs, Roy Thomson forsook Canada for the United Kingdom. There, perhaps as a consolation prize, he bought the most prestigious newspaper in London and, ultimately, was transformed to become Lord Thomson of Fleet.

One might have expected that my brash rejection of the powerful magnate he was sponsoring for election would have brought me into permanent disfavour with my neighbour. Quite to the contrary, we became very good friends. Joe Eisenberg was rather short and round. He had a large head and creased face. Inevitably, a thick cigar was stuck in the corner of his mouth, as though it was part of his costume. His fondness for cigars was a holdover from his youth when he was employed in a tobacco factory rolling tobacco leaf into cigars. Now in retirement, Joe spent an inordinate amount of his time and energy in politics. He was particularly well connected with the hierarchy of the Conservative Party. He lived modestly and frugally and served the party on a voluntary basis. He came to this association with the Conservative Party through his father who, in earlier times, was a staunch party man. The party depended on his father to get out the Jewish vote in the central section of Toronto where the bulk of the Jewish population resided. This area was known simply as "The Ward." It was an area west of Yonge Street and east of University Avenue between Queen and College Streets. The official name of the party was the Progressive Conservative Party but Joe eschewed that part of the title denoted by the word "Progressive". "He was," he would proclaim uncompromisingly, "a Tory" — the old-fashioned designation of Conservatives who had strong beliefs in the British connection, British justice and right-wing political ideology. On my part, I enjoyed his good humour and loyalty and tolerated his occasional extreme political comments as a form of eccentricity.

Joe may have been intrigued either by my forthright rejection of the chance to cultivate the good will of his powerful friend or by my artlessness and naivety. In either case, he must have decided to take in hand my training in politics. He took me to party headquarters where I renewed acquaintances with Hugh Latimer who was employed full-time in an executive position. My association with Latimer went back to my days in Farnborough where Latimer had been a sergeant in the 12 Canadian Field Security Section. In those days, Latimer had an overriding interest in photography and had given me a superb portrait of a grieving Winston Churchill descending the steps of St. Paul's Cathedral following Franklin D. Roosevelt's memorial service in England.

Under the wing of Joe Eisenberg, I attended numerous political gatherings and functions. On one occasion, I accompanied Joe to a meeting at the Ontario Club, a Conservative stronghold, for an address to be given by John Diefenbaker, then an embattled Prime Minister of Canada who was faced with a revolt of party faithful. I was standing on the sidewalk at the front entrance when a limousine pulled to the curb. Several people emerged, including Diefenbaker whom I instantly recognized. The wonder was that he recognized me; we had never met. He went directly to me and shook my hand warmly. No doubt he mistook me for the leader of the welcoming committee. I enjoyed the incident anyway. I also enjoyed the speech of the "Chief," as he was known, who soundly berated detractors for disloyalty, much to the embarrassment of some of them who were seated nearby.

On another occasion, Joe, as if by magic, produced for Joyce and me an official invitation by the Lieutenant Governor of Ontario to attend a state dinner to be held at the Royal York Hotel. The invitation stated that the dinner was "In Honour of His Imperial Majesty The Shah of Iran and The Empress Farah Pahlavi." Needless to say it was a lavish dinner and a gala event. Even Joe looked good in his rented formal suit and Joyce and I delighted in our names being announced as we entered the dining hall. It was a memorable event that became more memorable in light of subsequent developments in Iran.

One day Joe asked me if I would consider standing for election to the Provincial legislature as a candidate for the Progressive Conservative Party in the September 25, 1963 election. He told me the nomination was available for the Downsview riding, a substantial area that included Lawrence Manor. I knew that the time for campaigning was short and it would be not only a formidable, but perhaps hopeless, assignment. Downsview was considered a safe, strong Liberal riding. The frontrunner for the Liberal Party was Vernon Singer, a popular local politician, a former Reeve of North York, and the current Liberal member of the legislature seeking re-election. The standard bearer for the New Democratic Party, A. Alan Borovoy, was likewise a well-known candidate particularly on account of his work as executive director of the Civil Liberties Association. Nevertheless, intrigued by the slim possibility of success, I agreed to stand, subject to the party underwriting the expense of the campaign and my partner agreeing to my taking a leave of absence from our firm. I received the assurances I was seeking. On August 27, I presented myself at a nomination meeting and, unopposed, was duly nominated the official Progressive Conservative candidate for the Downsview riding.

Joe attended to most of the arrangements for the campaign. A suitable location was acquired to serve as campaign headquarters. Bess Godfrey was assigned to me as campaign director. Her son Paul, then a young man, was an eager campaigner in my cause. Later he entered politics on his own behalf, became a councillor in North York, rose to become chairman of Metropolitan Toronto, and eventually the publisher of *The Sun*, a Toronto newspaper. Fred Stinson, a former member of the federal parliament, was my advisor and finance director. The party contributed a budget of about $8,000.00. Eph Diamond headed a finance committee that brought in a significant additional sum for expenses. Saul Wolfe, then in the silk screen and display business, produced all the signs for the campaign. I received very good general assistance from Joyce and the family. My favourite memento of the election is a photograph that appeared in the press showing Joyce and the children in line each carrying my campaign sign soliciting a vote for husband and father. I gave the campaign my best effort. As generally anticipated, Vernon Singer won re-election, Borovoy was second, and I was third. I was told that the leaders of the Party establishment were not disappointed; I had still brought in a substantial vote. It was a respectable, creditable showing.

In the aftermath of the election, I put aside all ambition about a political career and resumed the private practice of law. When I left Principal Investments, I had opened an office in partnership with Ben Sichy, who had been my articling student and later my associate at Principal Investments. Shortly afterwards, however, Ben left me because he wanted to work in court as litigation counsel. I might also have enjoyed the prospect of appearing in court as counsel but I did not attract that type of practice. I took another person as junior who remained about a year or two and also departed. Thereafter I became associated in partnership with David Baum with whom I have always maintained a good relationship and who remained with me to the end of my time in practice. I like to believe that we carried on a general practice, but it was heavily weighted by the same kind of work as I had done at Principal Investments — real estate and land development.

Although some matters we dealt with were interesting, the incidents that remain in memory are only incidentally related to my practice or any legal accomplishment. One example is my experience with Bill Studer. He had urged me to accompany him to Florida to help negotiate what appeared to be a very lucrative deal.

Bill Studer was my client and also a good friend. He had spent many years in the hotel business. When I knew him, however, he was trying to make a living in real estate. In this instance, he was negotiating to build a hotel for lease or purchase by the operators of a major international chain of hotels. With reluctance, because I did not want to absent myself from other clients in Toronto, I accompanied Bill to Miami where we took rooms in the hotel built directly over the Miami airport. For a full week, confined to the hotel, I drafted, revised, and re-drafted forms of agreement and otherwise assisted in the negotiations. By late Friday afternoon, we brought the negotiations to a successful conclusion and achieved a signed agreement. At this time, in an expansive mood, Studer said: "Dave, we have done a good job; we're entitled to some relaxation. Let's go down to the Beach for the weekend."

Tempted, I reflected briefly on this proposal, and responded: "Ah, Bill. How can I do that? Joyce is at home looking after our three children; she hasn't had a holiday in ages. I'd rather meet her in New York and give her a holiday too!"

Bill immediately picked up this thought: "What a great idea! What a fine, thoughtful husband you are! Look, not just the manager, but the boss over the manager at the New Americana Hotel in New York is a very close friend of mine. I'll phone him right away and you can have a suite at the Hotel."

Under Bill's guidance, for he was an experienced traveller, we arranged all the details, and then I phoned home and spoke to Joyce:

"Dear, how would you like to spend the weekend with me in New York?"

"Are you crazy," was her reply. "Just how am I supposed to manage that? Who is to look after the children?"

"That is up to you, sweetheart, but listen: Bill and I have checked plane times. Your plane will leave Toronto at 8:00 p.m. and arrive at Idlewild International Airport by 9:05. My plane will arrive about ten minutes later. We can meet at the airport and stay at the New Americana Hotel. The manager is Bill's very good friend and will be expecting us."

"Impossible," Joyce muttered. Her voice trailed off, and then she added briskly: "I'll call you back."

Moments later she was on the phone to me: "Don't hold me up. I have no time to lose. I have arranged for Howie to stay with the Frewens, next door; Aunt Esther will look after Nancy; and Dad will take Peter."

"Great, wonderful, sweetheart; I'll see you at the airport."

"Don't hold me up," she repeated. "I'm in a hurry; I have only a half hour to make the plane."

Studer was as pleased as I was. "What a wonderful thing you are doing!" he repeated. "You're such a good husband!"

My bag was packed ready for departure about an hour or two later when Bill said: "Let's go up to the bar at the top of the hotel for a drink, to celebrate."

So we proceeded to the bar. Bill bought me a drink and I listened to part of the story of his life, much of which I had heard before. According to custom, of course, I had to buy a drink back for Bill. Finally, we got to our feet. We went back to our rooms for my bag and shook hands in farewell. I took the elevator down to the ramp leading to the airplane where the attendant stopped me at the entrance.

"Sorry, I can't let you go through," he remarked.

"But," I spluttered, taken aback. "I have my ticket and ..."

"Sorry," he repeated adamantly; the plane is being revved up; nobody is allowed to board after the plane is being warmed up."

Entirely crestfallen, bag in hand, I dragged myself back to the room I had just left and knocked at the door. Bill regarded me in disbelief. "What are you doing here?"

Bill listened sympathetically to my explanation and then took control of the situation: "Don't worry," he said: "Joyce will be at Idlewild in about 10 minutes. We'll call the airport and have her paged and you can explain the whole situation to her."

We phoned the airport. I heard the name "Joyce Vanek" called on the loud speaker and after a short interval heard a quavering voice on the telephone:

"Where are you?" she asked.

"Listen, dear, I was unable to make the plane; I'm still in Miami, but ..."

"What!" is what I heard, in a tone of utter incredulity.

"But not to worry; I'm booked on the next plane. There is a suite for us at the New Americana Hotel. Bill's best friend is expecting you. Just take a cab and tell the driver to take you to the New Americana Hotel."

"I can't," came back a tearful voice. "I don't have any American money."

"Well, dear, you can change..."

It was at this precise moment that Joyce hung up on me.

Chastened, tired, and disconsolate, it was about 2:30 a.m. when I finally knocked on the door to a suite at the Americana Hotel. Joyce would not let me in. Finally, she relented. Thereafter, I showed her a very good time in New York. I took her for a drive by horse and carriage through Central Park and otherwise we passed a most enjoyable weekend in New York. Joyce finally forgave me for my sins of omission but on terms that I must never, ever, tell anybody this story, a condition that she only recently waived.

Unrelated to the above affair, but within much the same time frame, is an episode that began when I was seated at dinner with my family. By this time, we had moved from Lawrence Manor and were living at 9 Mead Court, a short keyhole street located just east of Bayview and North of York Mills Road. Somebody happened to refer to the strong box that I brought back to Toronto after the War. The remark set me to ruminating, nostalgically, about the box and its contents. It was a large, heavy, metal ammunition case I had packed with letters, books, and a variety of acquisitions, including a prized Beretta automatic revolver. I had never actually discharged the revolver. I never had any ammunition for it. I was never able to strip the gun or put it together again. I can not even remember how I came into possession of it. It was simply a finely engineered piece of equipment for which, unaccountably, I had conceived an abiding affection. The box had lain dormant for years in a remote corner of the family dwelling. Reminded of the revolver, I interrupted my ruminations to state: "I really should take the gun from the strong box and oil it."

Howard, now in his early teens, quietly observed: "You can go to the box but you won't find it, Dad."

"What do you mean, won't find it? It's always there, in the metal ammunition box."

"Oh Dad," remonstrated my number two son, in a tone as if marvelling at the naivety of the older generation. "When you and mother used to go out on weekends, what do you think Nancy and I would do? We would go to the strong box, take out the Beretta revolver and play with it. After we finished playing with it, we would usually put it back or we would hide it under the grate of the fireplace in the living room so it would be there when we wanted to play with it again."

Joyce and I listened to this narrative in shocked disbelief.

Howard continued: "One day we hid the revolver under the grate. The next time we went to get the gun to play with it, the fireplace was sealed up. Don't you remember, Dad, when you and mother had the house remodelled, the fireplace in the living room was blocked and plastered over because you thought the one fireplace in the basement was enough for us."

It seemed incredible. "Do you mean to tell me my prized Beretta is gone forever?" I lamented.

Two or three years passed. We sold our spacious remodelled dwelling because none of the children were then living with us and moved to an apartment in a high rise building. One day the purchaser of our house on Mead Court came to pay off the mortgage and, in the process, asked: "By the way, wasn't there a fireplace at one time in the living room?"

Taken aback, of course I acknowledged the former existence of the fireplace. "The reason I ask," continued the purchaser, "is that we are considering remodelling the house and if you can tell us the precise location we would like to re-open the fireplace."

"Good heavens," I exclaimed, or some similar expletive. Then I related the entire story regarding the disappearance of the revolver, concluding: "And if upon uncovering the fireplace you find a Beretta revolver, don't expect to find a body; for there is none; but I would certainly appreciate your returning the gun to me."

Months later the purchaser again called upon us and this time delivered to me my Beretta revolver. It was much the worse for the misadventure it had undergone — heavily tarnished and corroded. I was immensely gratified to repossess it anyway.

At this time, I was a Provincial Court Judge. One day there was a judges' conference at the Royal York Hotel. One of the police officers guarding the entrance door to the meeting hall was Sergeant McKie, who was in charge of security at the Old City Hall and with whom I was well acquainted. When I came upon him, suddenly, I bethought myself of my revolver, and upon impulse, said: "Sergeant McKie, I have a revolver that is all tarnished and corroded. You fellows must know how to get this kind of equipment cleaned up. Can you suggest how I can go about getting my gun cleaned."

"What kind of gun is it, your Honour?"

"Oh," I replied with pride: "It's a Beretta automatic repeater pistol. Why, with one pressure of the trigger it can let loose six bullets in succession. It's a magnificent piece of mechanical equipment!"

"Have you ever had the weapon registered?" asked the Sergeant, an excellent officer.

The question caused me suddenly to lose my enthusiasm. Startled, I spluttered: "Why no. I didn't think of it. I brought it back from the War. I never considered it necessary." It was a weak response. I was embarrassed. I found it impossible to reconcile my own possession of a gun with the dim view I entertained as a judge of the possession of firearms by others.

Sergeant McKie then addressed me in kindly tones with only a slight hint of condescension: "Your Honour, why don't you do yourself a favour? Bring the gun to me and I will have it destroyed."

That is what I did. The next day, meekly, I surrendered my cherished Beretta to Sergeant McKie. I presume it was immediately destroyed and its ashes scattered over the earth. Nowadays, occasionally, I contemplate with regret my unused automatic repeater Beretta revolver, the spirit of which is floating about somewhere in the Nirvana of confiscated firearms.

About one year after my unsuccessful attempt to represent the Downsview riding in the Ontario legislature, I received a telephone call from a woman who said she was calling on behalf of the North York and Weston Area Social Planning Council. She told me that this agency had become very concerned about the deleterious effects on family life by the increasing use of consumer credit. The Council wanted to establish an agency to deal with this problem as a social service in the public interest. She asked me to accept the leadership in an effort to organize a credit counselling service for Metropolitan Toronto. She must have been particularly persuasive or I was rather pliable. I agreed to expend a great deal of my time and energy in this undertaking during a single telephone conversation with a person I did not know in a matter about which I had no special expertise.

It was this woman, I believe, who referred me to a member of the North York municipal council, interested in the creation of a credit counselling service. He in turn brought me into contact with Arthur Bray, with whom I established a productive working relationship. Arthur Bray was an executive of the Household Finance Corporation. I learned from him that businesses involved in the granting of credit were similarly interested in the creation of a credit counselling service. It seemed that some members of the public needed help with problems in the use, or stemming from the abuse, of consumer credit. Arthur Bray and I put together a joint initiating committee of about twenty-five members composed about equally of people active in social work and related areas and representatives of the major credit granting organizations.

I felt the future credit counselling service would be a partnership between the social services, the credit granting businesses, and the government. Therefore, it was my view that the capital and operating costs should be spread equally amongst the three partners. Our first priority, however, was to enlist a prestigious and broadly acceptable sponsor for the project. None could more suitably fill this role than the Social Planning Council of Metropolitan Toronto with which the local Planning Council was affiliated. Accordingly, I led a delegation of the joint initiating committee and made a presentation to a meeting of the Social Planning Council with gratifying results. The Social Planning Council endorsed our project as a valuable social service for Metropolitan Toronto.

My next effort was to try to obtain the general public's approval of the project. I made a simple telephone call to J.D. MacFarlane who was then the editor of the *Toronto Evening Telegram*, a highly influential newspaper of the day. I then met with Mr. MacFarlane. He listened to my explanation of the object and need of the proposed new agency with interest and approval. The very next day there appeared an editorial in his newspaper in support of the project. The editorial sparked a more general interest and a number of reports in the press.

My next step was to prepare a brief for submission to the Government of Ontario in support of an application for governmental assistance. I obtained an appointment and led a deputation of the initiating committee to a meeting with Arthur Wishart who was then the Attorney General for Ontario. I explained our purpose and tendered my brief at this meeting. It was well received. At about this time, Bill 100 was before the legislature. It was later enacted as the Consumer Protection Act. Based upon the brief and my presentation, the government added to the Act a clause that read: "The Consumer Protection Bureau shall promote and assist existing Counselling Services in respect of consumer credit." The government also agreed to make a financial contribution to the establishment of our proposed counselling service and later to provide an annual allowance as a contribution toward its operating costs.

Next we had to incorporate and organize the bylaws of the new entity. The agency was incorporated on September 28, 1965 as The Credit Counselling Service of Metropolitan Toronto. It was a non-profit corporation without share capital. There were three objects of the corporation: first, counselling in respect of the use and abuse of consumer credit, including budgeting and money management; second, assistance in debt management programs including the orderly payment of debts; and third, a general educational function in respect of the proper use of consumer credit. I also applied for and secured federal recognition of the new corporation as a charitable organization.

The first annual meeting of the Service was held in December 1965, at which time a board of directors and officers were elected. The board included substantially all the members of the initiating committee. I was elected president and retained that office for three years. George Penfold, who had retired from another long-time occupation, took on the challenge of becoming the executive-director of the Service on June 1, 1966. He tackled his new employment with vigour and enthusiasm. George Penfold made numerous and varied administrative arrangements, hired a staff, opened an office, and carried on the actual operation of credit counselling as a social service. He guided the Service throughout its formative years and for many years after it became firmly established in public acceptance.

After the Service became operative in Toronto, I began to receive enquiries on how to organize similar counselling services in other localities throughout Ontario. I made it a practice to send copies of the organizational documents to persons wanting to create a counselling service. A set of the documents was included in a publication entitled "Consumer and the Law," edited by William A. Neilson, then associated with the Osgoode Hall Law School. Currently there are six offices in Metropolitan Toronto and about thirty credit counselling services throughout Ontario organized on the same model.

After the Service became operational, I received an invitation from the Canadian Broadcasting Corporation to appear on a television program to be broadcast coast to coast in Canada. I had never appeared on television and felt greatly honoured by the invitation. I vividly recall the day fixed for the telecast. It was a winter day but there had been a sudden thaw. The streets and sidewalks were full of melting snow and ice. I had been through a busy day at the office and finally set off on foot to reach the Jarvis Street studios of the CBC. I had forgotten to take my rubbers and my feet were wet. I dashed into Simpson's Department Store to buy new rubbers, and left in frustration because I could find no one to wait on me.

I arrived at the studios feeling quite uncomfortable and apprehensive. I was wholly lacking any experience in the production of these broadcasts. My apprehension increased while I was being made-up for the performance and waited for my call. Then I discovered that other persons, who had made some contribution to society, were to appear on the same program. Indeed, I was only one of four individuals scheduled for interview.

We went through a dry run for all four interviews. Finally the time for the real thing approached. Each of the three other honourees was ushered in turn before the cameras for a live interview about his particular accomplishment. I listened and watched the interviews on a monitor in increasing nervousness. At last, when my nervousness was at its highest pitch my turn came. I heard the interviewer give his introduction ending with the words: "and here to represent The Credit Counselling Service of Metropolitan Toronto is its president, DAVID VANEK." Precisely upon the announcement of my name — the lights went out and the show went off the air. Transfixed, I could just imagine my children, glued to the television set at home, asking their mother, in wonderment, what happened to daddy. Nobody bothered to tell me what happened. I received no explanation or apology, nor was I even asked to return for an interview another day. The aborted interview was never rescheduled and, to this day, I have never had the experience of an appearance on television.

Since then, however, I have been honoured on several occasions for my contribution toward the establishment of the Service. On the occasion of my resignation as president, I was elected a life director of the Service. At a dinner held on January 22, 1969, I was presented with a fine oil painting in further recognition of my efforts. A number of years later, at a conference of the Ontario Association of Credit Counselling Services, I was presented with a plaque in commemoration of my assistance in the establishment of similar services throughout Ontario. Still later, on the occasion of the thirtieth anniversary of the Service, I was honoured by the designation of "Father of Credit Counselling," which I have accepted with deep satisfaction and as more than ample reward for my efforts.

It was not surprising that I should derive satisfaction from my involvement with credit counselling. There is an instinct in most of us to do something worthwhile with our lives. To make an important contribution to the public welfare is immensely gratifying. Conversely, the failure to use one's talents and energy for a socially desirable purpose leaves an individual unfulfilled.

My efforts toward the creation of the Service brought into focus deficiencies in my practice of law. I was becoming increasingly disenchanted with private practice. While it provided a reasonable level of income, I was unable to find any significant social value in what I was doing. Acting on behalf of a land developer seemed to be an insufficient justification for convincing a municipal council to change the use of the developer's land from low to high density. The end result would be to increase the value of the developer's land, but would not necessarily be a boon for society. One day, at a social gathering, I encountered an acquaintance of many years, whom I knew was politically well connected. In the course of general conversation, he abruptly asked me if I would consider taking public office in Ontario as a magistrate. Given the source, I had every reason to believe that this simple enquiry amounted to a proposal that he had the political influence to effect. Taken aback by this sudden proposal, I asked about the remuneration this office attracted. The amount was shockingly low. It appeared to me that the magistrates were being abysmally underpaid. I told my acquaintance frankly that at this level of remuneration, I could not possibly afford to accept an appointment. On this note, we ended our conversation on this subject.

I was greatly flattered by this proposal, however. I considered it most unusual for the government to be making an unsolicited offer of a judicial appointment to an individual. I was under the impression that the normal practice was for the government to entertain and pass upon applications made by persons seeking an appointment. Under our peculiar constitutional arrangements in Canada, the provincial government appointed magistrates and the federal government appointed the County Court and Supreme Court judges. The administration of all of the courts came within the provincial legislative authority.

The possibility of attaining judicial office tempted me. However, I entertained mixed feelings regarding the Magistrates Courts. Lawyers often referred to magistrates, disparagingly, as police magistrates, and their courts as police courts, because of their proximity and association with the police in each area where they presided. As well, magistrates were often appointed to Boards of Police Commissioners that controlled the organization and management of the police forces. A Board of Police Commissioners commonly was composed of the local magistrate, the mayor, and the County Court judge. Magistrates were not necessarily even lawyers. The nature of justice delivered by Magistrates Courts tended to be of poor quality. In too many instances, the decisions of magistrates were made without particular regard for the law and, in matters of sentencing, in the exercise of a broad, largely uncontrolled, discretion.

The statements of Colonel George T. Dennison give an example of the attitudes and principles that governed magistrates and reflect on the quality of justice dispensed by them. Colonel Dennison was a magistrate who presided in Toronto for about forty years to at least 1915. In *Recollections of a Police Magistrate* he stated:

> I will give an idea of the general principles upon which I have carried on my business. My main desire has been above all things to administer substantial justice in all cases coming before me. This I felt should be done in preference to following legal technicalities and rules, if close adherence to them would result in injustice... I never follow precedents unless they agree with my views... The best plan is to go into

the whole facts and decide what is fair and right between the parties... I may also say that I depend upon an intuitive feeling as to a man's guilt or innocence and not to weighing and balancing the evidence. I depend upon this feeling in spite of evidence, and will subsequently give illustrations of the advantage of doing so.

I recall making a strategic error on a rare appearance in Magistrates Court when, in addressing the Bench, I argued that the case should be dismissed because the prosecution had failed to disclose any evidence of *mens rea*, probably the most basic concept of the criminal law. It refers to a guilty mind or some quality of intention that is an essential ingredient of every criminal offence. It was obvious that the magistrate did not know what I was talking about.

However low may have been the regard for the magistrates by members of the legal profession, they undoubtedly possessed huge judicial powers. Magistrates presided over the trial of offences without a jury. They acted as judges of the facts as well as judges of the law. Their jurisdiction extended over a broad range of offences, from minor penal matters to the most serious indictable offences. With regard to sentencing, their powers extended to sentences of maximum severity under the criminal code, including life imprisonment. Authoritative reports on the administration of justice in the period under consideration state that Magistrates Courts had a broader jurisdiction and wider sentencing powers than any other lower court in the world that exercised criminal jurisdiction.

Several months after the conversation with my influential acquaintance, I went to see Rendall Dick who was the Deputy Attorney General for Ontario with whom I had some dealings about credit counselling. There was before the legislature at this time a bill intended to dramatically reform the administration of criminal justice in Magistrates Courts. The proposed legislation was the governmental response to a report by a commission headed by J.C. McRuer, formerly the Chief Justice of the Ontario High Court of Justice. The reform was to be accomplished by the establishment of a new court to take over the jurisdiction exercised by the magistrates. All of the magistrates were to be appointed as judges of the new court. The bill also provided for a provincial court to deal with family and civil matters. Most importantly, the bill established minimum professional qualifications of legal training as a condition of the new judges exercising jurisdiction in the more serious offences.

Rendall Dick encouraged me to submit an application in the usual manner for appointment as a magistrate. He anticipated that the bill would be enacted into law within about six months, with the strong likelihood of a substantial increase in remuneration for the newly appointed judges shortly thereafter. After further consideration, I tendered an application to the government together with two recommendations in support. In due course, I was appointed a magistrate by order in council effective September 1, 1968. A few months later, the bill was enacted into law by the legislature of Ontario as the Provincial Courts Act and, in common with all other magistrates, I became a judge of the Provincial Court, Criminal Division. By an amendment of the Act in about 1973, the qualification for appointment to office as a judge of the Provincial Court was raised to the same standard as the appointment of a judge of any other court — full qualification as a lawyer with at least ten years experience in the practice of law. With normal attrition, the Provincial Court of Ontario then became a fully professional court.

Sixteen
Criminal Court Judge

I n Gilbert and Sullivan's *Trial by Jury*, the Judge, upon entering the courtroom, regales the courtroom audience with an account of how he came to be a Judge. His song begins with the lines:

Judge
When I, good friends, was called to the bar,
I'd an appetite fresh and hearty,
But I was, as many young barristers are,
An impecunious party.

The cause of his sudden rise to eminence as an English barrister is explained in the following revelation:

Judge
So I fell in love with a rich attorney's
Elderly, ugly daughter.
The rich attorney, he jumped with joy,
And replied to my fond professions:
"You shall reap the reward of your pluck, my boy

At the Bailey and Middlesex Sessions."

At length the song reaches a climax when the judge proclaims to general approbation:

Judge
For now I am a Judge!

Chorus
And a good Judge too!

Judge
Yes, now I am a Judge!

Chorus
And a good Judge too!

The Judge's song concludes with the admission, recited *sotte voce*, in confidence: "It was managed by a job," to which the assembly responds: "And a good job too!"

The Judge's song is, of course, both amusing and satirical. I refer to it — not just because I too was once an "impecunious party" — to emphasize the differences, not the similarities between the fictional judge's circumstances and mine. He was elevated to the English judiciary and became a "nob" and I was appointed a magistrate and, later, a lower court judge in Canada. I never married my boss' daughter and was never made a "nob." I particularly dispute any suggestion my appointment was managed by a "job." I lay no claim even to having been "a good judge too." In fact, perversely, I keep in my possession a statement to the opposite effect. It is a letter in which the writer states bluntly in a single line: "Judge Vanek: You are a bad judge." I only claim to have done my best to be a good judge.

What is the function of a judge? I am unable to improve upon the statement made over two millennia ago and attributed to Aristotle or Socrates. I do not recall which.

Four things belong to a judge:
To hear courteously
To answer wisely

To consider soberly and
To decide impartially.

I have tried to follow these precepts, not invariably with success.

Upon appointment as a magistrate, I was assigned to the Toronto area. The Old City Hall, centrally located in downtown Toronto, became my base of operations. Automatically, I joined a select brotherhood of the judiciary. It was indeed a fraternal organization because not a woman graced the dais at this time or for several years thereafter. Twenty-six magistrates, about half of whom had never been trained as lawyers, presided in the Magistrates Courts at Toronto. Centred at the Old City Hall, they also serviced the area courts in North York, Scarborough, Etobicoke, and even Richmond Hill. A lesser number of magistrates presided in other cities such as Ottawa, London and Welland. Elsewhere in Ontario, a magistrate served each locality of sufficient size, normally a county town. Throughout the entire Province, a total of about 130 magistrates handled the work of the Magistrates Courts. Occasionally, the Toronto magistrates were dispatched to other localities in the Province to relieve a local magistrate incapacitated by illness or to enable him to take vacation leave. In special circumstances, where there was a possibility of a local magistrate being affected by even an appearance of partiality or interest in a case, an outside magistrate would be sent in to dispose of the matter. This practice of using the personnel at Toronto to service or assist other courts was continued after the magistrates were appointed as judges to the newly created Provincial Court (Criminal Division).

For many years prior to my appointment, the civic administration in Toronto shared its City Hall with a variety of courts. The Supreme and County Courts used courtrooms on the second floor. The lowly Division Court, now the Small Claims Court, occupied space on the third floor. The City Hall also accommodated the Magistrates Courts: at least one large courtroom on the east side of the ground floor, as well as a small, dingy, claustrophobic room in the basement known as the "women's court." The basement also contained cells for the prisoners who were brought in daily through an enclosed courtyard that also contained a limited number of spaces for the parking of vehicles of judges, police and favoured members of the staff. Prisoners were escorted from the cells up a set of stairs directly into the large courtroom to be dealt with by the presiding magistrate.

During Nathan Phillips' term in office as mayor of Toronto, a new, modern city hall was constructed immediately to the west of the Old City Hall. It was built on a tract of land that had been cleared of a row of decaying ancient buildings, including the Manning Chambers in which I had begun my legal career. The civic administration was moved from the Old City Hall into the new functional building. The Supreme and County Courts and the Division Court likewise abandoned their premises in the Old City Hall at various times.

The Magistrates Courts were left in sole occupancy of the Old City Hall and their use of the building was extended from time to time in accordance with the need for expansion. By the time I became a judge, the Criminal Division of the Provincial Court had taken over the entire building. The use of the Old City Hall as the main courthouse in Toronto for the criminal division of the Provincial Court was supposed to be temporary, pending construction of a modern courthouse for the Provincial Court. The new building was never constructed. The old building was, and still is, an ancient edifice with deteriorated services and facilities and inappropriate to the use to which it was and is being put. From time to time, additional courtrooms and chambers for the judges were created out of the available space, including even the old council chamber, and some effort may have been made to modernize the building. This piecemeal extension and adaptation failed to address a fundamental defect — the absence of a means of physical separation of the judges from the general public. There was nothing to safeguard the judges from interference and provide them an adequate measure of security.

At the time I arrived at the Old City Hall to take up my duties, no special training was prescribed to prepare a newly appointed magistrate for the exercise of his judicial responsibilities. It was the practice, carried over to the Provincial Court, to assign the appointee to the care of experienced magistrates in order for him to observe how they handled the task of presiding in court. Normally, this orientation period was about two weeks. Afterwards, it was considered improper for a judge to enter a courtroom in which another judge was holding court. Thus, the only opportunity that a judge was afforded to obtain first-hand knowledge about the performance in court of another judge was limited to this two-week period of observation. I spent a few days with each of Tupper Bigelow, Joe Addison, Mike Cloney and Peter Wilch.

I found my two weeks of observations of these magistrates to be helpful, as much for attitudes and practices of which I disapproved as for those that attracted my approbation. Tupper Bigelow was the senior magistrate in Toronto and had already served twenty-four years as a magistrate. He tended to operate his court in the manner reminiscent of an old-fashioned police magistrate. He told me, for instance, that he never gave reasons for his decisions: "They only provide the ammunition on which you can get shot down on appeal." I considered this statement to be astonishing, particularly since Tupper was an experienced lawyer and a person of high intelligence and accomplishment. I decided immediately always to give reasons, both for judgement and sentence, and it became my invariable practice. It was my view that an offender was entitled to be told precisely what he had done that was a criminal offence and why a particular sentence was appropriate to the crime. In a simple case, this could be done orally in a few words. In more complex matters, I prepared reasons in writing, as I considered necessary. In sentencing, Tupper had a list of fixed penalties he imposed for specific offences that tended to be somewhat draconian. I believed that the sentencing of an offender should be determined in accordance with the directions, or inferences from them, in the Criminal Code; the principles laid down by the Court of Appeal; the circumstances of the offence and the offender; and the overall interest of the public.

Tupper was a complex individual of considerable learning and broad interests. In court, he had the reputation of being strict and stern; but out of court, he was pleasant and affable. He wrote a manual of instruction for magistrates. He prepared a reference manuscript on courtroom etiquette and "orders of precedence" that I read and found useful. He also published an informal publication on legal subjects that he called the *Ontario Magistrates Quarterly*. Occasionally, I submitted a note or article but Tupper prepared most of the material himself. Tupper was a devotee of Sherlock Holmes and an enthusiastic bridge player. He possessed a fund of jokes and anecdotes.

Years after his retirement and shortly before his death, Tupper sent me copies of two stories that originally appeared in the Ontario Magistrates Quarterly, which I regarded as illustrative of his sense of humour. The first is a famous story about a true incident in a court presided over by Magistrate O.M. Martin who was a full-blooded Cree Indian. I had a dim memory of the incident. The magistrate called back an offender who, after sentencing and being led from the courtroom, supposedly under his breath muttered something about a "bloody Indian." The magistrate, who heard the remark, is reported to have said: "Listen here, paleface, me Big Chief here. You go pokey thirty more days for badmouthing Big Chief."

The other story is an apocryphal account about two magistrates, each of whom received a summons for speeding. They decided to try one another on these charges. At the first trial, on a plea of guilty, the magistrate declared a suspended sentence. At the second trial, upon a similar plea, the other magistrate imposed a substantial fine. "But just a minute," said the accused, "another offender just got a suspended sentence." The presiding magistrate lectured the offender on the necessity of imposing a draconian penalty to stop the carnage on the roads caused by this serious offence and advised the accused against any further complaint at the risk of being cited for contempt of court.

Joe Addison was also a lawyer of experience. He had been a magistrate for about ten years. Like Tupper, Joe was likewise infected by the magistrates' syndrome, although perhaps to a lesser extent. I considered Joe to be too close and friendly with the police. While there was nothing wrongful in this relationship, I felt it was desirable to avoid even an appearance of influence over a judge by persons associated with the justice system. I recall sitting in court with Joe Addison as part of my initial orientation when, in the course of the day, an accused came before him and pleaded guilty to the possession of a concealed weapon. He was a black man, had come from Buffalo by car, and had been stopped by police who found a loaded pistol in the car. I believe it had been affixed to the engine. The accused made an elaborate plea for leniency on grounds that because of the incidence of crime in the United States, it was necessary and acceptable to be in possession of a firearm for personal protection. He was under the impression that the law and the need for protection were the same in Canada. Joe Addison listened impassively, then simply spoke two words: "six months!"

Mike Cloney was a classmate of mine at Osgoode Hall Law School. He was known as a five-year man in that he qualified for the Bar in five years, by-passing a university course altogether. This was possible at that time but a rarely exercised option. He took a year of absence to work but returned and graduated with me. Mike was an average student but a huge success in the army. He joined the Judge Advocate General Branch and, at one point in his career, was Assistant Advocate General for Central Army Command. He left the army with the rank of Lieutenant-Colonel.

I spent two or three days in court with Peter Wilch. He came to the Bench as a magistrate without legal qualification. I strongly disapproved of the appointment to judicial office of individuals not trained as lawyers. Yet I found that Peter handled his court quite well.

Of the magistrates at Toronto not trained as lawyers, four or five rose to this position through the ranks, as it were — from years of employment as court clerk to justice of the peace and, finally, to magistrate. I considered this background of experience quite inappropriate and insufficient for a magistrate, let alone a judge. Most of the other non-legally trained magistrates were retired army or naval officers who had attained high rank after a career of meritorious service in the armed forces. Peter Wilch, for instance, was educated in Britain and had a distinguished career in the navy, rising ultimately to the rank of Commander. Norman Gianelli spent a good part of a lifetime in the army. He was a Brigadier-General and the Commandant at Camp Borden at the time I was there as an undistinguished Private. Bob Graham rose to the rank of Colonel and at one time was military adviser to the Canadian High Commissioner in New Delhi. Ben Greene was a Lieutenant-Colonel in the Intelligence Corps. These were superior types of individuals whose background included some exposure to military law. However, even these lay magistrates, who later became lay judges, lacked the depth and breadth of training in the law to reasonably ensure that their administration of criminal justice would be conducted according to law, and not their individual discretion, an indispensable requirement in a democratic country. A number of years passed until, by natural attrition and legislative decision, the Criminal Division of the Provincial Court became a fully professional court.

My best recollection is that I never quite completed my two-week tour of observations when Chief Magistrate Arthur Klein swore me in as a magistrate. The swearing in was far from the elaborate ceremony and social affair it became later. It happened without prior notice one morning when I was seated beside the Chief Magistrate, having a cup of coffee with the other magistrates, at a long rectangular table in the room that became known as the judges' common room. Arthur Klein casually turned toward me and remarked that it was about time I was sworn in as a magistrate. So I took the bible that was handed to me, raised my right hand, the Chief administered the prescribed oath of office, which I affirmed, and I signed a document in confirmation. I believe Arthur was short a magistrate that day because I was immediately put to work presiding in one of the courts at the Old City Hall.

Arthur Klein had an excellent reputation as a senior assistant crown attorney who had prosecuted some important criminal cases. Unfortunately, he was a disappointment as Chief Magistrate and later as Chief Judge of the Provincial Court (Criminal Division). He seemed to have no interest in the work and left the administration of the courts almost wholly in the hands of Fred Hayes who acted as his deputy. A few years after my arrival, Arthur Klein was moved back to the Ministry of the Attorney General as a senior adviser. Fred Hayes was appointed Chief Judge in his place and held this office during all my remaining years on the Bench. Fred possessed an extensive knowledge of criminal law, especially criminal procedure, and kept himself well abreast of current developments in the law. He arranged the assignments of the judges, mainly through a roster system. Although, he was almost invariably available for consultation, he was careful never to interfere in a case over which a judge was seized and showed scrupulous regard for the judicial independence of the judges under his administration. Fred Hayes was dedicated to the position of Chief Judge. He was supportive of his judges, arranged educational programs, and travelled extensively to visit the judges and courts throughout the Province. Despite all this activity, when he could find the time, he would take a tour of duty as a trial judge himself. We became very good friends and the friendship extended to our wives.

I got along very well with all my colleagues on the Toronto Bench on a personal level and benefited from my contacts with them. In general, they were a group of intelligent, knowledgeable and experienced individuals. I used to look forward to meeting the other judges in the morning prior to commencing my judicial duties for the day. Seated around the long table over a cup of coffee in the judges' common room, we would exchange amusing anecdotes or engage in a wide-ranging discussion on a variety of subjects, entertaining, stimulating and instructive. I also had the opportunity to meet a broader spectrum of judges. Several years before I took office, the magistrates of Ontario had organized an Association that held annual conferences and arranged educational seminars and meetings. After the magistrates became judges, the association continued to operate as the Provincial Judges Association of Ontario (Crim. Div.). Of course, I joined the Association.

Initially, I found the general meetings of the Association rather dull and uninspiring. Most of the discussion was devoted to securing an increase of remuneration and pensions, which were at unreasonably low levels, and improving working conditions. Unfortunately, an atmosphere of futility surrounded these discussions. These issues fell within the authority of a provincial government that disclosed no inclination to improve matters. Executive officers of the Association would address letters to the Premier, Attorney-General, or other governmental authorities, in exaggeratedly deferential terms, seeking an appointment. I found this embarrassing and inappropriate on the part of judicial officers. If an appointment were granted, it would often be cancelled at the last hour; or, in other cases, honoured by a lesser governmental official than the person who originally granted the appointment. This "cap in hand" approach to the government brought little improvement. The attitude of the Provincial government reflected the low regard in which it held the magistrates and Provincial Court judges in my early years on the Bench.

I developed an interest in the educational programs of the Association, although I found these also to be lacking in substance. They usually took the form of seminars that lapsed into a comparison of sentences for similar offences from locality to locality. I became a member of the educational committee and, in due course, chairman, a position I held for a few years. As chairman, I tried to make the sessions more meaningful. During my tenure, we held an annual educational conference of the entire membership and an educational program as part of the judges' annual conference, both of which occupied about two days on a weekend. As well, we held four regional sentencing seminars. We also carried on a program by which the judges, in rotation, observed the proceedings in the Court of Appeal. This attracted the support of Chief Justice Gale. Unfortunately, some of these programs were subsequently restricted or cancelled for lack of funding from the Province.

Fulfilment

In 1974 I made arrangements for an educational conference that was to have included a guest speaker. Shortly before the date of the conference, the invited guest notified us he was unable to honour his commitment. I discussed my dilemma with Cy Perkins, the local judge in Chatham who later became president of the Association. "Why don't you do it yourself?" he asked, with a smile. It was something that had never even crossed my mind. I was loathe to appear to be lecturing my brethren of the Provincial Court, many of whom had far more years of experience on the Bench than I. Still, I appeared to have no alternative and decided to make the main presentation myself.

My address was severely critical of my own court. I characterized the quality of justice in the Provincial Court as "bargain basement justice." For the first time, a few members of the press had been invited to this conference to participate with judges in a panel discussion. My characterization of the Provincial Court was reproduced in headlines of the Toronto newspapers. One newspaper proclaimed, "Bargain Basement Justice Condemned"; another read, "Judge Criticises Courtroom Deals, Bargain-Basement Justice." My criticism concerned practices of the police and Crown attorneys, apparently tolerated by the courts, that commonly were being used to exert pressure upon persons accused of offences to plead guilty and enable Crown counsel to dispose of heavy daily lists of cases without the necessity of conducting trials. The police laid multiple charges. This resulted in a plea of guilty to a lesser charge to avoid a possibility of conviction on much more serious charges. I took strong objection to the disposition of criminal charges by means of a "bargain" or "deal" between the Crown and defence counsel, thereby avoiding the scrutiny and authority of the presiding judge. A means toward this end was the jurisdiction assumed by Crown counsel of "withdrawing" a criminal charge, thereby again presuming to by-pass the authority and control of the court.

My address received considerable comment, including editorials in the press. Yet, if I had expected that my speech would immediately result in legislative or administrative reform of these practices, I would have been very disappointed. There were no such reforms and these practices continued unabated and unchallenged even by the courts. My brethren of the Provincial Court, however, received my address with satisfaction. It resulted in the considerable enhancement of my personal prestige and reputation, the more I suspect for my courage as a judge in speaking publicly about important matters — despite the tradition of the judiciary to refrain from pronouncements on public or political issues — than the substance of my remarks.

I was elected president of the Provincial Court Judges Association (Crim. Div.) for the years 1979-1980. In the intervening years, successive governments had been responsible for the enactment of a huge amount of legislation that added enormously to the importance and burden of the work in the Provincial Court. Amendments to the Criminal Code on a variety of topics, brought forth an entirely new spectrum of charges and defences. Provincial Court judges were being called upon to hear and determine issues of a very high order of complexity. Educational courses were necessary to keep the judges abreast of developments in the law and the educational conferences became more focused. Increasingly, the Provincial Court was gaining in recognition and status for its contribution to the criminal justice system.

In the other provinces of Canada, provincial judges of equivalent standing organized associations using the Provincial Judges Association of Ontario as a model. In addition, an association of all provincial judges associations was created. It was known as the Canadian Association of Provincial Court Judges. During my year in office as president of the Ontario Association, in addition to my regular judicial duties, I attended all four of the regional seminars, the educational and general conferences of the Ontario association, and the meetings of the Canadian association. I also received invitations to attend the annual conference of other provincial associations, which I often accepted. All of this activity gave me the opportunity to travel widely, meet judges from the various provinces, and gain an appreciation of Canada and some understanding of the problems we were facing in our country.

The highlight of my year as president was the annual conference of the Ontario Association. It was held at the Four Seasons Hotel on Avenue Road in Toronto. The closing event of the conference was the formal dinner with speeches, followed by dancing. In accordance with custom, I, as president, organized the conference with the assistance of a committee. I caused invitations to be sent to a list of eminent jurists with whom I had a substantial connection over the years. I was delighted by the response.

Bill Howland, The Chief Justice of Ontario, attended and delivered his usual graceful address. Bill Howland was a former classmate of mine. We spent seven years together, first in the Honour Law course at the University, and then at Osgoode Hall Law School.

I was particularly honoured by the attendance of the Chief Justice of Canada. To me, he was just Bora Laskin. I was also well acquainted with his wife, Peggy, who was raised in the West Toronto Junction. I believe Bora came to the conference as a special effort to please me. At this time, he was already in failing health. Bora was in the fourth year of the Honour Law Course when I was an undergraduate in the first year. Later, for a time, he taught under Dean Kennedy at the University School of Law. As a former protégé, Bora continued to enjoy a good personal relationship with Kennedy. After I joined the staff, Joyce and I occasionally came into contact with the Laskins, and for the one year I continued as a lecturer in Dr. Wright's administration, Bora and I were colleagues. As president of the Association, I had the pleasure of introducing the Chief Justice of Canada. Bora delivered a short address that was most warmly received. The judges were obviously delighted by the attendance of the chief judicial officer of the country and the interest and support for them that it conveyed.

The affair got under way with the guests of the head table being piped into the dinning hall to music of the bagpipes led by a piper in traditional Scottish attire. Someone took a photograph just as my wife came into full view. The photograph gives the impression that Joyce was leading the procession. Immediately behind her came the Chief Justice of Canada, then me, and then the Chief Justice of Ontario. Joyce had a broad, happy smile, her face flushed and radiant. Of course, I enjoyed immensely the formal dinner. Clearly my dear wife enjoyed it to the same degree.

In accordance with custom, I was elected to the office of president of the Association for only one year. Of course, during that year I had to fulfill my normal judicial responsibilities and two years as president would have been difficult. However, two of the judges of the Provincial Court provided outstanding service for many years while also performing their regular duties as a judge. Doug Latimer served as the Secretary of the Association and Bill Sharpe as Treasurer. In addition, Bill Sharpe was the Chairman of a committee of the Association called the Salary and Pensions Committee, which he with wry humour labelled the "avarice and greed committee." As president, I was *ex officio* a member of this Committee and took an active part in it. After my year as president, I remained a member of this Committee.

While the responsibilities of the provincial court judges had been steadily expanding and increasing in complexity, the provincial government continued to treat them as judges of a lower order of court. This was in contrast to federally appointed judges, whose salaries and other financial benefits were paid by the federal government under provisions of the Canadian Constitution. The Government of Ontario still approached the exercise of its administrative authority over the Provincial Court and provincial judges, including the salaries and pensions of the judges, as matters falling wholly within its discretion. Bill Sharpe's committee was encountering the usual difficulties, not only in obtaining increases to levels it regarded as reasonable but to get the government even to address the submissions of the Association. In this state of affairs, Bill convened a joint meeting of his committee with a similar committee of the Family Division of the Provincial Court.

The joint committee met in an atmosphere of dejection and frustration. No one seemed to know how to bring about a change of attitude of the provincial government or some improvement in the way the government was dealing with its judges. I was asked for an opinion and, without particular reflection, suggested a method commonly used in the settlement of disputes. My suggestion was to convince the government to agree to the establishment of a committee of three persons. One would be appointed by the government, one by the judges, and a third, who would act as chairman of the committee, jointly by the other two appointees. The committee would hold hearings and make recommendations to the government with respect to salaries, pensions and other financial benefits. My colleagues fastened upon this suggestion like shipwrecked sailors clinging to a lifeline.

I elaborated upon my proposal: "If we can get an appointment to meet with the Premier or the Attorney-General, we should argue as forcefully as we can, in support of this proposal. It is demeaning for the judges periodically to come to the government, cap in hand, begging for money. It is equally demeaning for the government to deal with the judges in a manner that could be considered arbitrary and inconsistent, as well, with the independence of the judiciary. Why, then, not appoint a committee to make recommendations to the government on financial matters as a mechanism to lighten the problem for the government and lead to fair and reasonable results for the judges?"

Previous to this meeting, Bill Sharpe had already written a long letter of complaint on the subject of the judges' remuneration to Bill Davis, the Premier of Ontario, in which he had asked for an appointment with the Premier. At long last, the Premier agreed to meet with some of the judges. I was a member of a small sub-committee that attended upon the Premier. We were pleased to find Roy McMurtry, then the Attorney-General for Ontario, also present. Our sub-committee made the submission for the establishment of a committee to deal with financial matters of concern to the judges almost exactly in the terms I had previously outlined. The Premier and Attorney-General conferred briefly and then — to our delight — agreed to our proposal! Joe James, representing the family division, either took notes of the meeting or drew up a short memorandum of the agreement in longhand. To the best of my recollection, the Premier and Attorney-General initialled this document, then and there. It was December 4, 1979, a historic moment in the relations between the judges of the Provincial Court and the Government of Ontario. I believe that the method agreed upon at this meeting was the first mechanism of its kind anywhere on this continent to deal with the remuneration and other financial benefits of judges.

A few days later, on December 13, 1979, the commitment made by the Premier and Attorney-General was honoured by the execution of an agreement. Bill Sharpe and Joe James signed the agreement on behalf of the judges. It provided for the establishment of a committee in accordance with the understanding reached in the meeting with the Premier and Attorney-General. As a sweetener, the judges were given an immediate increase of salary. The committee was established by an Order-in-Council, dated March 5, 1980 (OC-643/80), pursuant to the Provincial Courts Act, to be known as the Ontario Provincial Courts Committee.

In due course the government made the initial appointments to the Ontario Provincial Courts Committee. R.J. Butler was appointed upon the recommendation of the government; Arthur Maloney was appointed on the joint recommendation of the Associations of the Criminal Division and Family Division of the Provincial Court; and Clarence Sheppard was chosen as chairman. The judges retained Paul French as their counsel. The Committee conducted hearings and ultimately issued a unanimous report. The main recommendation of the report to the government was that the salaries of the judges should be increased to parity with the judges of the District Courts, whose salaries were paid by the federal government, by periodic increments over a period of about five years. Subsequently, with regard to pensions, the Committee, differently constituted, made recommendations that resulted in considerable improvement, although by no means entirely satisfactory to the judges. Meanwhile, without obtaining the concurrence of the judges of the criminal and family divisions, the government on its own initiative added the judges of the Civil Division to the process.

The culmination of the events stemming from my proposal to establish a mechanism to determine the remuneration, pensions, and other financial benefits of provincial court judges came about several years later. By this time, the Provincial Courts Committee had been transformed into a "Commission" and named the Provincial Judges' Remuneration Commission. The provincial judges associations had succeeded in pushing the government into making the ultimate refinement in the process, which I personally had never regarded as possible: the government agreed to make the recommendations of the Commission binding upon the government. A 1993 order-in-council made under the Courts of Justice Act (OR-407/93) states that the recommendations of the Commission have the same force and effect as if enacted by the Legislature and must be implemented by order-in-council within sixty days of the delivery of the Commission's report.

One paragraph in the document illustrates the immense achievement of the provincial judges associations over the years in raising the stature of the judges of the Provincial Court. They gained due recognition of their entitlement to be treated by the Government of Ontario upon the same principles as other judges in the judicial system. With reference to the framework agreement attached as a schedule to the order-in-council, it reads as follows:

> The purpose of this agreement is to establish a framework for the regulation of certain aspects of the relationship between the executive branch of the government and the Judges, including a binding process for the determination of Judges' compensation. It is intended that both the process of decision-making and the decisions made by the Commission shall contribute to securing and maintaining the independence of the Provincial Judges. Further, the agreement is intended to

promote co-operation between the executive branch of government and the judiciary and the efforts of both to develop a justice system which is both efficient and effective, while ensuring the dispensation of independent and impartial justice.

Before the judges attained the level of achievement reflected in the preceding paragraph, however, they passed through a particularly stormy period in their relations with the Government of Ontario. The government was failing to make the timely increases of remuneration to reach parity with the District Court in accordance with the unanimous recommendation of the Ontario Provincial Courts Committee. It appeared to the judges that the government was trying to back away from the process to which it had committed. As well, the unprecedented amount of Criminal Code amendments and the Charter of Rights and Freedoms resulted in the daily list of cases in the Criminal Division of the Provincial Court being heavily overloaded. The government, claiming it was a time of economic restraint, was reluctant to appoint new judges. Many cases, not reached at the end of the day for disposition, were adjourned, in many instances on several occasions. The Supreme Court of Canada later dealt with this situation in a landmark decision. It declared that a person charged with a criminal offence was entitled to a trial or other disposition within a reasonable time; and in the event of unreasonable delay because of a failure in the justice system, charges should be stayed. In consequence of this decision, numerous criminal cases, often involving very serious charges, were stayed for systemic delay and, in effect, dismissed without trial.

The turmoil in the Provincial Court (Crim. Div.) was aggravated by an antiquated system of courts that, despite the increased volume of work, had never been addressed. The ordinary citizen must have found the complex and unusual jurisdiction of the Criminal Division of the Provincial Court difficult, if not impossible, to comprehend. Briefly, the Provincial Court possessed absolute jurisdiction over minor offences, designated "summary conviction offences"; the Provincial Court shared jurisdiction with the then District and Supreme Courts over the major offences, designated "indictable offences." Upon a charge of an indictable offence, the accused was given an election whether to be tried in the Provincial Court or by a judge alone or judge and jury in "another" court. If the accused elected "another" court, the trial took place in the District Court of Ontario or the Supreme Court of Ontario. In a very few cases, of which a charge of murder is the most common, the accused had to be tried by a court composed of a judge and jury in the Supreme Court. In the trial of offences in the Provincial Court, the Provincial Court judge presided alone without a jury; the judge not only decided questions of law but was also the judge of the facts. Even where the accused elected trial in "another" court, the Provincial Court judge was required at the request of the accused to conduct a preliminary inquiry to determine if there was sufficient evidence to commit the accused for trial.

It appeared to one of the judges of the Provincial Court that the criminal justice system was headed for a complete breakdown. Norman Nadeau was a judge in the Criminal Division, with his base court in Barrie, who was highly respected by his brethren on the Bench. Norman had participated with two other individuals in the drafting of the "Provincial Offences Act," a statute that set up a full code of procedure for the trial of offences created by provincial legislation, as distinguished from criminal offences. Norman came to a general meeting of the Provincial Judges Association. He submitted that there was a great need for a critical examination of the criminal justice system to determine its defects and make recommendations for the reform of the system. He argued that the judges of the Criminal Division of the Provincial Court were best qualified to assess their own system under which they operated. They were the judges with the most experience in the criminal law, dealt with persons charged with criminal offences on a daily basis, and handled by far the highest volume of cases. He proposed to the meeting of the Association that it appoint a special committee to study the operation of the criminal justice system in Ontario and report its findings together with recommendations for improvement.

It was a novel proposal because it might have been considered a contravention of the tradition in the judiciary requiring judges to refrain from making pronouncements on public issues. Nevertheless the Association adopted it. A very strong committee was established composed of experienced and able judges chosen to represent various geographic areas in the Province. Upon the nomination of Norman Nadeau, I was appointed chairman of the committee; Norman was appointed vice-chairman. The committee was designated the

Provincial Criminal Court Judges Special Committee on Criminal Justice in Ontario. Ultimately, the Committee issued its report.

The main recommendation of the report was that the three courts in the existing three-tier structure of courts with jurisdiction over criminal law be unified and combined into a single trial court for the administration of justice in Ontario. The main thrust of the report was the need for simplification and rationalization of the criminal justice system. The report was published and broadly circulated amongst individuals, organizations and authorities with a particular interest in the subject. Occasionally it has been referred to as the "Vanek Report." I must acknowledge, however, that Norman Nadeau not only initiated the project, but was the guiding spirit throughout the study and was primarily responsible for the writing of the report.

I take some credit for organizing the project. Each of the members of the Committee was asked to prepare a paper on a specific aspect of the study. These papers were considered at meetings of the Committee. The results distilled by discussions in committee were taken into account in a draft report prepared by Norman. We submitted the draft report to a special general meeting of the Association where the members were broken into groups for detailed study of the report. Norman acted as rapporteur to whom the conclusions at the group sessions were transmitted. The Association gave the report draft approval. A final report was then prepared and reviewed by an editorial sub-committee composed of Bob Reilly, who was at that time president of the Association, Norman and me. The report was again brought to a general meeting of the Association in final form and approved and adopted by a unanimous vote. I believe that the report represented as nearly as possible the individual opinion of the approximately 160 judges that constituted the full membership of the Association at that time.

At about the stage when the report received draft approval by the Provincial Judges Association (Crim. Div.), the Government of Ontario suddenly appointed a royal commission of inquiry to report upon the administration of justice in Ontario, both in respect of the civil and the criminal system of justice. Mr. Justice Zuber of the Ontario Court of Appeal was appointed as the single commissioner to head the inquiry. No doubt Ian Scott, who was the Attorney-General for Ontario at this time and with whom the judges were in virtual confrontation, had learned of the judges' project. In any case, the

Royal Commission in effect pre-empted the judges' project. In due course, the Zuber Commission issued its report. Singularly, there is no reference in it whatsoever to the report of the provincial criminal court judges' special committee.

The principal recommendation of the Zuber report was that all the trial courts, both civil and criminal, should be amalgamated into a single trial court. The unification would be achieved in three stages. The provincial government acted quickly to implement the first and second stages: the District Court was amalgamated with the Supreme Court to create a single trial court, first called the Ontario Court (General Division) and now called the Superior Court of Justice. However, the third stage referred to in the report, the unification of the Provincial Court with the other courts, has never been implemented, except by a change of nomenclature. The former Provincial Court of Ontario was first changed to the Ontario Court (Provincial Division) and recently to the Ontario Court of Justice. This partial simplification of the justice system has left unchanged the basic structural defect about which the provincial court judges were complaining. The hierarchical structure of the criminal courts and the archaic procedure under the criminal code still remain.

WARTIME MARRIAGE

Joyce Vanek (née Lester)

Honeymooners

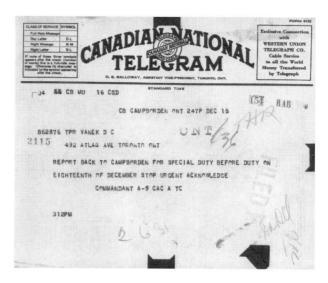

*Telegram from Military Headquarters summoning Vanek back to Camp
Borden from his honeymoon.*

*L/Cpl. Vanek as instructor in charge of a convoy in the Canadian
Armoured Corps at Camp Borden.*

Temple Sinai and Politics

*Temple Sinai President's Dinner. From left: Eph Diamond, David Vanek,
George Jessel, Harry Pollock, Rabbi Jordan Pearlson.*

Electioneering in 1963.

The Credit Counselling Service

Canada Pictures Ltd.

The first Board of Directors

In 1998, cutting the ribbon at the opening of new head offices in Toronto. Present with (left to right) Ed Heller (past president), Terri Williams (president), and C.M. (Duke) Stregger (executive director).

THE ANNUAL DINNER OF THE PROVINCIAL COURT JUDGES ASSOCIATION, (CRIM. DIV.)

Chief Justice Bora Laskin and President David Vanek at the 1980 annual conference

Joyce seems to be leading the procession of head table guests, followed by Bora Laskin, Chief Justice of Canada, David Vanek, and W.G.C. Howland, Chief Justice of Ontario.

SOME GOOD FRIENDS AND
ASSOCIATES OF THE BENCH

Association of Provincial Criminal Court Judges of Ontario

The Executive Committee of the Association for the year 1980–81. From left to right — Seated: William Sharpe (treasurer), Donald August, Gerald Michel (president), Robert Hutton, Douglas Latimer (secretary). Second row: James Crossland, Warren Eghoetz, Roderick Clarke, David Vanek (past president), Charles Scullion, C.E. (Cy) Perkins. Back row: Bernard Ryan, Clare Lewis, George Inrig, Richard Batten.

The editorial subcommittee of the judges' committee on criminal justice — Robert Reilly (standing left), Norman Nadeau (centre), and David Vanek (seated) — with Archie Campbell.

THE CHINA ADVENTURE

With judges of the American Academy of Trial Judges in Nanjing,
October 27, 1983

With Hugh Stewart, President of the American Academy, his wife, and
our interpreter, Guan Yun Le, in front of the 392 steps leading to the
mausoleum of Sun Yat Sen

THE NELLES CASE

Drawing shows Susan Nelles, left, at preliminary hearing before Judge David Vanek

An artist's sketch of a scene at the preliminary hearing.

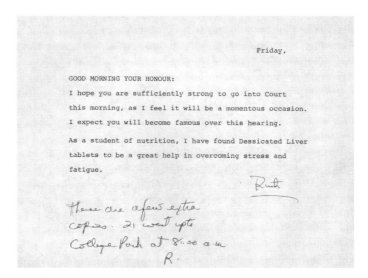

Friday,

GOOD MORNING YOUR HONOUR:

I hope you are sufficiently strong to go into Court
this morning, as I feel it will be a momentous occasion.
I expect you will become famous over this hearing.

As a student of nutrition, I have found Dessicated Liver
tablets to be a great help in overcoming stress and
fatigue.

Ruth

These are a few extra
copies. 2, went upto
College Park at 8.00 a.m.
R.

Advice from my secretary, Ruth, received just prior to delivering judgment

Seventeen
My Days in Court

My day in court used to begin when the court clerk came to my chambers to escort me to the courtroom. At the Old City Hall, sadly lacking in security, he also unwittingly served as my bodyguard. As I entered the courtroom, an official would exclaim in a loud voice: "All Rise!" I would bow to counsel appearing before me who would respond in like manner. Then I would seat myself on the podium. The clerk would take his place at his seat and desk at a slightly lower level. The court clerk kept a copy of the docket containing a list of the cases for disposition and a package of documents called "Informations." An Information contains a statement of the charge(s) against a person accused of an offence.

In a first-appearance court, I would deal first with requests for adjournment followed by taking the pleas of persons wishing to plead guilty. Then I would proceed to hear the rest of the cases on the docket. When a case is "called" and the accused stands before the court, the clerk "arraigns" the accused by reading the charge(s). If an offence is an indictable offence, the clerk will put the accused, if entitled, to an election whether to be tried by the provincial court judge or, in another court, by a judge alone or a judge and jury. If the accused elects to be tried in another court, the judge may proceed to hold a preliminary inquiry. If the accused elects to be tried by a provincial court judge or the offence is a summary conviction offence, regarded as a more minor offence, the clerk asks the accused, "How do you plead, guilty or not guilty?" If the accused pleads "guilty," the assistant crown attorney, often referred to simply as the "Crown," reads to the court a bare statement of the facts, which, if admitted by the accused, justifies the judge in registering a conviction for the offence charged. The judge may then pass sentence on the accused or remand the accused to another day for sentence. If the accused pleads "not guilty," the judge will proceed to hold a trial or, upon request, may adjourn the case to another day for trial.

The clerk administers the "oath" to persons called as witnesses to testify at the trial. The clerk also takes charge of the documentary evidence filed in court as exhibits. In general, the clerk is the administrative assistant of the judge and performs all the clerical work in court, including the preparation of a large number of documents for the signature of the judge. Every order made by a judge must be verified by an official document. As the day wears on, the clerk is endlessly passing paper up to the judge for signature. As well, after court the clerk may attend in the judge's chambers for signature of final documents to give effect to the informal papers signed in court.

The assistant crown attorney, who has been assigned to the court, prosecutes the cases on the docket. Defence counsel normally assists the accused. Defence counsel is either a lawyer retained by and at the expense of the accused, or a lawyer chosen by the accused who is paid under the Legal Aid Plan.

Two other participants play an important role in court. Every word spoken in the proceedings must be recorded. This is the duty of the official court reporter who takes notes in shorthand or speaks in a low voice into a tape-recorder and subsequently, if requested, prepares a typewritten transcript of the proceedings. The other participant is the official court interpreter who is present as needed to assist persons who are unable to make themselves understood in the English language. Occasionally, the court administration encounters difficulty in procuring an interpreter with sufficient facility in a particular language. I was sometimes concerned whether the court was being given an accurate translation of the substance, let alone every word, of the testimony purportedly being translated. On the other hand, at the Old

City Hall, for many years, we were privileged to have the services of Mary Apa, the regular court interpreter in the Italian language, who was an excellent interpreter. Mary Apa was possessed of a pleasant, modulated, rich voice. It was like listening to an aria from a Puccini opera to hear her rendition in Italian of the oath administered by the clerk: "Do you swear to tell the truth, the whole truth and nothing but the truth, so help you God?"

During my twenty-one years on the Bench in the Provincial Court, I dealt with an extremely broad spectrum of cases. They ranged from minor regulatory offences under provincial and federal statutes to the most serious offences in the Criminal Code and from the most simple to the most complex points of law. The first-appearance court on the ground floor of the Old City Hall was an exceptionally busy court. This is where persons charged with an offence attended in the first instance, under arrest, by other process, or on remand. The presiding judge had the task of processing the cases on a heavy docket, granting adjournments, taking pleas, sentencing offenders and, if there was still time available, conducting short trials or preliminary inquiries. On pleas of not guilty, however, generally trials would be held in other courtrooms with a much-reduced caseload and in a more relaxed atmosphere. In my early years, a judge also used to be assigned to perform what we sometimes referred to as a "gaol delivery." In a dingy courtroom located in the basement, the judge disposed of cases relating to drunks and prostitutes, the daily unfortunates of society swept in by the police the previous night.

The volume of work in the Provincial Court increased dramatically over the years while the government appeared disinclined to make timely appointments of additional judges to handle the increased caseload. Even in the earliest of my days as a judge, some courts were heavily overburdened. In the Scarborough court, for instance, a single judge handled the entire caseload of this large municipality with a population at that time of perhaps 125,000 people. I recollect days when I alone was the presiding judge in Scarborough. About midway through my term of office, four or five judges were permanently assigned to the Scarborough court. A typical daily list of cases at that time might include highway traffic offences but also include serious driving offences under the Criminal Code, such as impaired driving, dangerous driving and failing to remain at the scene of an accident. It could include minor offences, such as shoplifting, and even mere breaches of municipal by-laws. However, it could also include assaults of varying degrees of severity, break and enter, and other serious criminal offences.

In the more minor category, for instance, I recall dealing with two counts of keeping vicious dogs contrary to a local by-law. The offences were charged against the owner of the dogs. However, I used to consider the matter as if the dogs themselves were being charged because if, in effect, the dogs were convicted, the judge was required under the by-law to direct that the dogs be destroyed. I was cautioned by more experienced judges to beware of convicting a dog as a vicious dog. The uproar from the dog-loving community could be more than the judge or the justice system would wish to withstand. I resolved my case by sending one dog in exile to a farm and confining the other to an enclosure. Thus, I managed to spare the dogs and keep my reputation intact as a humane judge.

It was during a stint of duty in Scarborough that I first encountered a man whom I shall refer to as "Petrodopoulos." He came before me charged with a highway traffic offence. A police officer testified that he was patrolling traffic at the bottom of a deep valley. The officer stood at about the centre of the road and put up his arm to stop a car that came roaring down the hill. He had to jump out of the way in order to avoid being struck as the car passed him and climbed the opposite hill. Moments later, the same car returned in the reverse direction and again the officer had to jump out of its path to avoid being struck. Evidently, Petrodopoulos was playing games with the officer, who finally managed to apprehend and bring him to court. I do not remember how I disposed of this charge but, in any event, it did not conclude the matter. Soon afterwards, he again appeared before me charged with a more serious driving offence, which must have resulted in an order depriving him of his license to drive a motor vehicle for a period of time. A few days later, Petrodopoulos was back again, this time charged with driving while disqualified.

I was in my chambers preparing for my duties in court, when my clerk came running, breathless. "You won't believe this, Your Honour," he began, "Petrodopoulos is in the corridor and, as he passed by the arresting officer, he was deliberately tossing his car keys in the air to show he was driving his car on his way to court despite your order!" Again, I do not recall what disposition I made on this occasion. However, several months after these events ceased to occupy my mind, I was seated in my chambers at the Old City Hall and responded to the ringing of the telephone:

"Your Excellency," said a voice, without preliminary, "I've got to get out of here!"

"What? Who is that?"

"Petrodopoulos, Your Excellency, Don't you remember me?"

"Where are you?" I asked, weakly.

"I'm here where you sent me. Your Excellency, You have to get me out of here. I've got work to do."

"Petrodopoulos, You must not be phoning the judge." I tried my best to convey the message that I was not to be contacted in this informal manner and hung up. Then I fretted and fumed about staff who would, without notice, dump the judge into a confrontation over the telephone with an unhappy customer. Then Petrodopoulos made a big mistake. He called again, this time to my home, and got my wife on the telephone.

"If you ever, ever call again," she said, emphatically, as reported to me, "the police will be after you and you will be in deep, deep trouble!" He never called again. But this is when we changed our telephone listing.

I was again holding court in Scarborough when two young men, twenty-one and nineteen years of age, pleaded guilty before me to armed robbery. Actually, there were several charges of armed robbery. The older offender pleaded guilty to six charges and the younger man to five charges. Upon these pleas, Crown counsel read into the record a statement of the facts that the accused both admitted. They were shocking. The two accused specialized in robbing small convenience stores. The "take" in each instance was relatively light — a few hundred dollars in each case — but their conduct included just about every facet of vicious criminality. In each robbery, they wore masks and were armed with weapons including sawed-off shotguns and rifles. They terrorized the occupants of the premises — persons in charge as well as customers who happened to be there. They forced the victims to lie on the floor and, in some instances, pistol-whipped or otherwise brutalized the victims.

At this time, I was deeply concerned about the proliferation of serious, hard crime in Scarborough, which I thought was disproportionate to other sectors of the greater Toronto area. In passing sentence, my judgement was no doubt affected by this concern. I delivered reasons for sentence orally as the two accused stood before me. I told them bluntly that these offences, particularly in the vicious conduct of their commission, could not be tolerated by society. Moreover, there were multiple offences and each offence called for the imposition of a separate consecutive sentence. I took into account that a first offence attracted a lesser penalty, which, nevertheless, could not be less than a term of imprisonment for one year. However, they could not expect such leniency for second or further offences that were an aggravation of their conduct. The sentence for the second offence, therefore, was two years imprisonment. For the further offences, I increased the sentences in an arithmetic progression. By the time I finished, I found I had sentenced the older man to imprisonment for twenty-one years and the younger one to eighteen years in the penitentiary. Afterwards, I think I might have been somewhat surprised by the severity of these sentences. Regardless, I was satisfied and let them stand. Predictably, both offenders appealed against sentence and, on appeal, the Ontario Court of Appeal reduced the sentences.

Shortly after I learned of this decision, I was walking along Queen Street and came upon Charles Dubin who had recently been appointed to the Court of Appeal and later became Chief Justice of Ontario. Dubin invited me to join him for a cup of coffee. Over coffee, in kindly fashion, Dubin tried to explain or justify the action of the Court of Appeal in tampering with my sentencing:

"Dave," he said, "You made a big mistake. You forgot about the *totality* of the sentences."

I had to concede that he and the Court of Appeal were right. However, I was gratified to learn that the reduction in the sentences was relatively moderate and still left them with a sentence in double digits. Upon reflection, I drew solace from the consideration that the sentences as reduced still satisfied the principles and objects I had tried to uphold.

I should explain that I was relatively well-acquainted with Charlie Dubin. As a lawyer, he was for many years one of the most able and sought-after counsel in Toronto, with proficiency both in civil and criminal law. When I was in practice, I spent about a week with Dubin in Europe trying to settle a dispute with people on the continent involving a great deal of money. Dubin was retained as counsel. We went overseas to meet with a French lawyer who had been described to us as "the foremost advocate in Paris." We were told that "Maitre F" was in contact with the opposite parties and would be acting as mediator in this dispute.

Upon arrival in Paris, Dubin and I were greeted by persons acting in the same interest with us and next morning our entire party set off to attend upon Maitre F for a meeting scheduled for 11:00 a.m. We were taken to a luxurious apartment building in one of the most fashionable sections of Paris, adjacent to the Bois de Boulogne. It appeared that the conference was to take place in the advocate's residence. We were admitted by the concierge and led to an apartment where, at the entrance, visitors were expected to deposit a calling card onto a tray. We were suitably impressed upon passing through a dining room in which a table was laden with gold plate for dinner. Finally we were conducted to a sizeable, well-furnished living room and were seated. An adjoining door opened and the great man appeared. He was clad in bedroom slippers, pyjamas and housecoat. Maitre F padded into the room and immediately entered into a spirited conversation in French with one or other of our party who was to serve as our interpreter. With our poor high school French, Dubin and I were quite unable to follow this discussion. Maitre F became increasingly agitated, his arms gesticulating wildly. At last, the conversation came to an end. "What did he say, What did he say?" we both asked.

"Before we arrived," our interpreter explained, "the other party personally came to the apartment and met with Maitre F. They had words. The argument became very bitter. The other party insulted Maitre F. He had the other party thrown out of the apartment and now Maitre F is washing his hands of the whole affair. He is withdrawing from the case." In this, he was adamant.

Dubin and I were aghast. For this, we had travelled some thousands of miles across an ocean! Disconsolate, we left the apartment and pondered what could be done to restore the atmosphere in which it might still be possible to effect a settlement. We spent the rest of the week travelling through parts of Europe without result. Our sojourn on the continent taught us little respect for the continental legal and judicial system and our mission ended in failure. It was only after we returned to Canada that we were able to effect a full settlement of the dispute. On the continent, we allowed ourselves one evening of relaxation; we attended one of the famous Parisian nightclubs. I thought Dubin was a cosmopolitan, worldly traveller. But Dubin also made a big mistake, although perhaps not quite commensurate with my mistake in the robbery case. He ordered scotch in the nightclub and learned a lesson: never order British liquor in a French nightclub; it is not customary and very expensive!

In contrast with my robbery case, which clearly required the imposition of a strictly deterrent sentence, I dealt with many cases in which I decided that the main object to be achieved in sentencing was the reformation of the offender, particularly in the case of youthful offenders. The appellate courts have repeatedly stated that deterrence and reformation are both proper principles to be considered in sentencing for criminal and other penal, offences. The judging business, in this regard, is like baseball: you win some and lose some. A lawyer of my acquaintance occasionally comes upon me at a gathering of lawyers or judges and invariably asks if I recall a client for whom he acted on charges before me. He proceeds to relate the same account: "Your Honour, you straightened him out. You gave him a severe tongue-lashing but sentenced him with considerable leniency. Do you know, he now has a good job, is married and has a family. He speaks of you with gratitude for what you did for him." I do not recall the offender, the offences or the disposition, but my spirit soars in gratification on each occasion that I hear this report.

I once made a short address about youthful offenders before an august audience: I had the honour of being appointed by the Ontario Provincial Judges Association as its representative to a United Nations Congress on crime that was held in Geneva, Switzerland. My attendance at this conference was a learning experience. It was there, for instance, that I became acquainted with the concept of the "rapporteur," which I adopted in organizing the Judges Special Committee on Criminal Justice in Ontario. At the Congress, the rapporteur took detailed notes of the discussions and prepared a summary that, in essence, was adopted as the final report of the Congress. With few exceptions, all the countries of the world were represented. Meetings were held in the huge assembly hall of the UN, which was equipped with an instant translation service in four or five languages with earphones and dials available at each seat to allow the occupant to listen to the proceedings in the occupant's language of choice.

When the discussion was directed to youthful offenders, I decided to tell this prestigious audience about a proposal that I thought could usefully address the problem in Canada. When the opportunity presented, I shook off my nervousness and addressed this gathering. I stated that I had come to the conclusion that, in Canada, most offences committed by young people between the ages of about sixteen to twenty-one years of age were attributable to a number of causes in combination. Usually the offenders were school dropouts. They were unemployed and uncontrolled. Lacking work or a trade, they were bored. They had no skills and little, if any, money, yet yearned for the rewards usually associated with honest labour. They tended, moreover, to become repeat offenders. It served little purpose simply to process young offenders through detention centres and welfare agencies.

It was my proposal that youthful offenders between the above ages could best be dealt with through the creation of a Youth Corp. The Youth Corp would be organized along military lines; it would provide a military type of discipline but without the weapons. The recruits would be put to work, not as punishment, but for the purpose of self-improvement and service to the country. There are numerous tasks that could be undertaken in the public interest, such as tree planting and pruning, fighting fires in the north, and the control of environmental problems. The tour of duty would provide the opportunity for some limited travel and instil self-esteem, motivation, and pride of country.

In court, if the offender should exhibit an inclination to profit from the experience, the sentencing judge, in his or her discretion, instead of the usual punishment, might grant the offender a conditional discharge on terms that the youth enlist in the Youth Corp for a specified period. In due course, if the offender were to successfully complete a tour of training, the youth could be brought back to court before the same judge. In open court, the judge would then declare that this youth had fully atoned for the offences and that the discharge be made absolute, with the effect that all reference to the offences be deleted from the offender's record. I believe my proposal was well received at the UN Congress. In Canada, while it received some notice in the press, nothing came of it.

Back in Canada, I dealt with a group of young people charged with one of the most minor of offences that, on the facts however, raised major issues of law. Fourteen individuals came before me for trial jointly charged with trespass contrary to the Trespass to Property Act of Ontario. They were a group of anti-nuclear protesters who took up occupation on a portion of Queen's Park, grounds of the Ontario legislature owned by the Crown. They had prepared the location as a campsite for occupation on a twenty-four hour per day basis and remained in occupation for forty days, resisting all efforts of government officials to convince them to withdraw peacefully, despite several formal notices demanding that they leave. Ultimately, the police forcibly evicted them.

The protesters were represented at the trial by counsel who argued that they were legally justified in remaining on Queen's Park in the exercise of the common law right of peaceful assembly and demonstration as well as constitutional rights under the recently enacted Canadian Charter of Rights and Freedoms.

At one stage of the proceedings, I signalled an intention to call a recess. As customary, an official of the court called: "All rise!" As I got up to leave, my clerk nudged me: "The accused are not standing, Your Honour! They remain seated."

I hesitated only momentarily. I considered briefly and dismissed any notion of citing the defendants for contempt of court. I left the courtroom and returned without comment and the trial resumed. At the conclusion of the trial, I convicted all the defendants for the offence of trespass under the provincial statute. Then I lectured them for disrespect. I told them I was not concerned about their failure to show respect for me personally but what was not excusable was to show disrespect for the court and the administration of justice. The Crown was apparently satisfied with my rulings on the law, the vindication of the government and the police, and the convictions, and with regard to sentence, only requested that I impose a small fine on each offender in the amount of $100.00. I considered the issues of law raised by counsel to be important and wrote a lengthy judgement. I concluded that the conduct of the defendants, in their extreme use and occupation of the land at Queen's Park, far exceeded any right of assembly and demonstration or right of expression either at common law or under the Charter. With regard to sentence, in light of the defendants' attitude in court, I doubled the penalty and imposed a fine of $200.00 on each defendant.

Occasionally at the Old City Hall, the docket would list a number of charges of gaming and betting. Often these charges involved new immigrants and others of ethnic origin who, although resident in Canada for some years, nevertheless had little or no facility in the English language. From time to time, the police conducted raids on premises where gambling was suspected to be taking place. They would seize money openly displayed on the tables and gambling paraphernalia, which became forfeited to the Crown, and arrest all the occupants on the premises. In due course, a courtroom would be filled to overflowing. A case would be called, and a large group of people would come forward. One of their numbers, with the assistance of the official court interpreter, would act as representative and spokesman. The spokesman would plead guilty to being the "keeper" of a common gaming house and all the others would plead guilty as "found-ins." I often wondered whether they took turns in accepting the designation as keeper that attracted the heavier penalty. The judges used to regard these cases with a degree of tolerance. These were otherwise law-abiding individuals with a weakness for a mild form of gambling, which was not particularly harmful to the public. The keeper was usually fined $300.00 to $500.00 and each found-in was fined about $50.00. I had my share of these cases and followed the usual practice.

In quite a different category was the case I dealt with on what came to be known as off-track betting. This was a new type of commercial enterprise that began to be carried on in ordinary retail shops. It was a form of betting on the races whose use was rapidly expanding. There were sporadic prosecutions of individual shops with mixed results. It fell to my lot, ultimately, to preside at the trial of the person who conducted the largest operation of the kind with a chain of about twenty-four shops in the greater Toronto area. Gaming and betting and other forms of betting have been criminal offences from at least the earliest years of the Criminal Code in Canada. There are certain exceptions, one of which is betting on the races at one of the officially recognized racetracks. Betting at the track is justified on the rationale, as I understand it, that it is incidental to racing horses and that racing fosters and promotes the breeding of horses, a worthwhile object.

The defence raised at trial was that the bets tendered at the shops were in fact taken to the racetracks and placed at the tracks. The trial went on for several days. At the conclusion, I had no difficulty, on the evidence, in holding that this defence was a sham. The defendant was not merely carrying on a courier service; that was just sheer pretence. The betting took place at the off-track betting shops and the defendant was actually carrying on a gambling business under a thin veneer of legitimacy. I convicted the accused and imposed a heavy fine in the amount of $50,000.00 and, in addition, sentenced him to imprisonment for nine months. That, I believe, was the end of off-track betting as a form of private enterprise in Ontario.

What I did not at all anticipate was that, according to rumour, the Government of Ontario was itself contemplating taking over the off-track betting business. I was considerably upset by these reports, having just done my utmost to condemn this type of activity and imposed severe punishment to underscore the condemnation. Normally, conduct is made criminal under sanction of the law when it contravenes moral standards and is seriously harmful to society. I found it difficult to reconcile that off-track betting was wrong when carried on by individuals as a private business but automatically right when carried on by the government. The government did not take over the off-track betting business. Instead, it went into the hugely more remunerative lottery business and later expanded into the operation of gambling casinos in a joint enterprise with private interests.

There is a wide body of opinion that gambling is addictive and harmful. If one were to seek confirmation, it would be instructive to consider the Moloney case. Moloney embezzled about $10 million, which he spent in gambling. His story is like another version of Dr. Jekyll and Mr. Hyde. Moloney was a highly placed executive of the Canadian Imperial Bank of Commerce at a busy branch on Bay Street near the Old City Hall. During working hours, he was the consummate banker; after hours, he would remove his banking attire, don sports clothing and become transformed into the quintessential, compulsive gambler, with a corresponding adjustment even in his style of speech. He gambled at very high stakes at casinos in Las Vegas, Atlantic City, and Macao in Asia. He was such a good customer that Caesar's Palace in Las Vegas made available a private plane to carry him back and forth for gambling at their casino. He would leave after work in the early afternoon to engage in gambling in the evening and return by plane early next morning, just in time for a change of clothing and resumption of his duties at the bank. It was on one of these junkets that the police apprehended him as returned from the Toronto airport.

I had no dealings with Moloney directly. I heard his story in court in a related matter, which was a preliminary inquiry in a charge against his friend and associate, Mr. Ruggiero. The chief device that Moloney used to steal from the bank was to cause bank drafts to be issued out of dormant and fictitious accounts. To get the money out of the country, in several instances, Moloney transmitted the money to Las Vegas or Macao, payable to Ruggiero, in one form or another, who endorsed the drafts or transferred the proceeds to Moloney.

Ruggiero was charged with possession of stolen property, namely money, knowing it to be stolen. To prove the offence, the Crown had to prove that it was stolen money, Ruggiero knew the money was stolen, and he had it in his possession. Ruggiero conceded that the money was stolen. For purposes of a preliminary inquiry, I had no difficulty finding there was sufficient evidence to show that it came into his possession and that he knew it was stolen. Defence counsel contended, however, that the charge could not be supported because the possession did not occur in Canada. He argued that both at common law and under the Criminal Code no person could be convicted for an offence committed outside of Canada.

This defence raised a complex issue of law regarding the extraterritorial application of the criminal law of Canada. In many instances, a criminal offence may not be wholly committed within the confines of a single state or country. It is not uncommon for one of the elements of an offence to take place in one country and for other of the elements to take place in other countries. Furthermore, even if all the elements of an offence should occur in one country, its harmful effects may be felt in another country. How then should this self-imposed restriction in Canada be interpreted? I examined all the decided cases I could find on the subject both in Canada and England and wrote a judgement on the subject. I found an influential judgement of Lord Diplock in the House of Lords in England in which the judge wrote that it was only the rules of international comity that dictated the limitations or restrictions on the territorial jurisdiction of a country to enforce its criminal laws. This was just an old fashioned way of saying that it was only the rules of public international law that dictated any such restrictions.

Fulfilment

I held that the possession of the money by Ruggiero outside of Canada could not be considered in isolation from the conduct inside Canada. This included his co-operation and assistance to Moloney in getting the stolen money out of the country that resulted in harmful consequences within Canada, for example to the bank from which the money was stolen. I held that the Canadian courts retained territorial jurisdiction in such a case and committed Ruggiero for trial. I thought the case was consistent with my article of years ago, which I entitled "Is International Law Part of the Law of Canada?", and could not resist including a reference to my own article in the judgement. I also made a point of remarking that international crime was becoming increasingly prevalent in the modern world and that, subject to the rules of international law, there was no reason why a state should be inhibited from prosecuting cases of international crime. Indeed, there was good reason to encourage a state to prosecute these offences, which were a scourge upon all states and difficult to prevent or control.

I always tried to be supportive of the police. I often took an occasion in court to stress the importance of their task, the dangers to which they were subjected and the debt of gratitude the public owed to them as protectors of society. In individual cases, however, I appreciated that police officers, too, suffered from human frailties and I did not always expect perfection in their conduct. Police officers testified in almost every case that came before me. I scrutinized their testimony for the usual purposes as I did with all other witnesses. I was not invariably satisfied with their testimony or their conduct. In some instances, I found that a police officer acted in excess of the officer's authority either because of misunderstanding of the law or over-zealousness in the performance of the officer's duties.

Such was a case in which, according to a report in the press, I stated that preventing or stopping political dissent was not part of a policeman's duties. A young woman was charged with causing a disturbance in a public place by shouting. According to the testimony of a Metro policeman, who, at the time, was on horseback in Nathan Phillips Square, the accused was approaching people with left-wing posters and newspapers that she was offering for sale. A crowd was gathering. She was shouting and people were shouting back. The officer asked her two or three times to leave the Square. She was reported to have said that it was her democratic right to sell newspapers and she didn't have to obey a "fascist lackey": "I have my rights. You can't do anything. I have my rights."

I am reported to have held that it was not an offence to sell papers on the streets or in any other public place and no policeman had a duty or right to request the person not to bother people by selling papers. In dismissing the charge, apparently I added: "And if you said 'I have my rights,' you are quite correct, you do have your rights."

I recall another similar situation in which, late at night, a policeman noticed a man standing in a shadow at a side wall of a shop on a normally busy, downtown Toronto street. He shouted at the man: "What are you doing there?" Startled, instead of responding, the man ran away. The officer chased after and caught up with him and a struggle ensued. The man was charged with resisting a peace officer in the execution of his duty in making an arrest. It turned out that what the man was doing was simply urinating against the wall of the building. In this democratic country, a policeman's authority to interfere with the liberty of the individual by making an arrest without warrant is strictly confined to the situations specified in the Criminal Code. In the case at hand, I held that the officer was not in execution of any duty in trying to apprehend or arrest the accused person and dismissed the charge.

In the above two cases, the police officers no doubt acted without authority unwittingly. That is quite different from an excessive, overzealous or abusive exercise of power that I believe is illustrated by the Da Silva case. Every policeman must surely know that an involuntary admission or confession by a person, who is suspected of having committed a criminal offence, is not admissible in evidence at a trial of that person for the offence. A confession is involuntary if is induced by a police officer by the application of physical force, threats or other forms of coercion. The rule was established many years ago and has been refined and confirmed by numerous decisions of the courts. The object of the rule is to eliminate the forms of police brutality all too commonly practised in a police state or dictatorship. It is also intended to avoid the danger of convicting a person on dubious or unreliable evidence.

In Da Silva, the police were investigating an incident in which a man had been knocked to the pavement in a street fight. The victim had sustained serious injuries. Apparently, the police felt certain that Da Silva was the person who had administered the blow and who was said to be the victim's best friend, but they did not have the evidence to prove it. The victim, who made a complete recovery, refused to name his friend as the perpetrator. Da Silva claimed that a complete stranger, who happened to get into an argument with the victim, administered the blow. In this state of affairs, the investigating officer brought Da Silva to the police station where he was kept without food or drink for fifteen hours while interrogated in an effort to obtain a confession from him. In the course of the questioning, the officer suggested that Da Silva, an unsophisticated person, take a lie detector test, and turned him over to an another officer for a test on the polygraph machine.

This officer asked a series of questions, left the room to consider the results, returned and continued the interrogation, prefaced as follows: "Jack, I've looked at your chart. You've had a good test here today, but you haven't told me the complete truth about some of the questions."

Then, in order to get Da Silva to admit he was the person who struck the blow that felled his friend, the officer proceeded to plant in Da Silva's mind that the officer was ready to accept it was all just an accident. Da Silva seized upon this bait as an excuse route to avoid punishment and haltingly made the initial admission. He was then returned to the investigating officer who continued the interrogation, which resulted in a complete confession without which the police could not have hoped to obtain a conviction.

I sharply criticized the police officers for the methods they employed to extract a confession and dismissed the charge. I held that the confession was induced by interrogation over a long period of time in an atmosphere of oppression. The police had suggested to the accused that a lie detector test was reliable when they must have known it was not admissible. Finally, the confession was obtained through an inducement, albeit in subtle form, by holding out the hope or promise that what the accused did was not a punishable offence.

In contrast to the Da Silva case, I recall listening with admiration for the participants of an operation of the Royal Canadian Mounted Police that exhibited work of great sophistication and of the highest calibre. The operation was conducted in exemplary fashion. This was a preliminary inquiry into charges, against a group of people, of conspiracy to import heroin into Canada and conspiracy to traffic in heroin. The persons charged were Messrs. Bennedetto, Zizzo, Bellitti, Cutrona, Codispotti, Asaro and three others. A full account of the operation would at least be equal in dramatic interest to a best-selling detective story. For present purposes, it will be confined to a bare outline of the evidence at the preliminary inquiry.

The tale began with the arrival of a vessel to the port of New York City. RCMP officers, acting in conjunction with counterparts in the US, were waiting for the ship to dock. They had information about baggage being used to smuggle narcotic drugs into the US in transit to Canada. Two large trunks were unloaded, which were suspected of containing the drugs and brought to a storage shed with all other luggage from the ship. The police waited nearby to discover who would come to claim the trunks. A good-looking, youngish man sporting a well-trimmed beard came for the trunks. He was the courier later identified as Bellitti. The police followed Bellitti to the railway station in New York City and later on the train to Toronto. On the train, a plain clothes RCMP constable was seated as a passenger directly opposite Bellitti. At Union Station in Toronto, other officers were on hand to learn who would constitute the welcoming committee to greet Bellitti on his arrival in Toronto. They were not disappointed.

From this stage onwards, officers of the RCMP kept under close surveillance the courier, the people who came to meet him on his arrival, and all other persons with whom they came into contact. One of these, for instance, was Zizzo who, as the evidence disclosed, was apparently the ringleader. On one occasion, at night, an Italian speaking RCMP officer with good athletic ability climbed to the roof of a dwelling where he peered through a window into the kitchen of an adjoining house. He testified that he observed Zizzo in conversation with others of the accused persons. He stated that he saw Zizzo waiving his finger at one or other of them, as if for some failure in carrying out instructions.

When the trunks arrived at a customs warehouse in Toronto, RCMP officers opened them and discovered they had been outfitted with false bottoms and sides. The police tore out the lining and underneath found, as no doubt anticipated, over fifty bags of pure heroin, with a street value in the millions of dollars. The police removed the heroin, except for one bag, which they left in each trunk so that it later might be found for supporting evidence. For the other bags, they substituted bags filled with flour. Then, carefully, they restored the trunks in all respects to their former condition. Then the police waited for whoever might come to take delivery of the trunks. In due course, two of the suspects arrived with a truck to pick up the trunks. In their presence, the trunks were opened for the usual customs inspection. The suspects made plausible but false answers about the contents. They were allowed, however, to take away the trunks, but were followed by the police to their destination — a dwelling in a quiet location in Toronto. During the surveillance in the Toronto area, the police were assisted through the use of electronic devices that enabled them to listen to conversations and noises.

Early the next morning, a squadron of the RCMP attended at this dwelling. At a given signal, they smashed the outer doors with sledgehammers and entered the premises just in time to observe several of the conspirators in the act of opening the trunks and removing the heroin or supposed heroin. All the occupants of the house were arrested. I committed all the accused for trial. Subsequently, I learned that all were convicted on charges of conspiracy or related offences, some after a long trial and some on pleas of guilty, and all were sentenced to substantial terms of imprisonment.

I sometimes wondered if I took a perverse pleasure in raising controversial questions of law or fact at a trial. For instance, a man was charged with a regulatory offence under a federal statute, which arose in the following circumstances. On a lovely warm day in summer, the man took his child for an outing at the beach. A marine police patrol found them floating on an inflated rubber craft about one hundred yards from shore. The man was charged with failing to keep life jackets on board this contrivance. It occurred to me that this charge was an extreme application of the Navigable Waters Act under which the operative word was "vessel". The prosecution referred to the device as a "dinghy." I was disinclined to convict the defendant for this alleged misconduct even though it would only attract a light fine of $50 or $100. I recessed the court, looked up the word "vessel" in the dictionary to ascertain its plain and ordinary meaning, returned to court and dismissed the charge. I held that this contrivance was not a "vessel." To my amazement the conviction was appealed and reversed by another court. I had made a serious error; it appeared that this object was indeed a "dinghy" and hence a "vessel" or so higher authority decided.

A much more important case in which I displayed the same tendency was a trial on a charge of pollution laid under the Environmental Protection Act, a provincial statute. The defendant was the Toronto Refiners and Smelters Limited. The accused operated a plant at the foot of Bathurst Street and had occupied it for many years prior to the enactment of the Environmental Protection Act in 1971. The charge was laid only a few years later and may have been prosecuted as a test case to demonstrate the worth of the legislation. The charge was that between the hours of 12:30 a.m. and 1:25 a.m. the company caused the emission of a contaminant, namely, a "white plume" from the main stack that was "likely to cause material discomfort to any person." The plant was located in an area zoned for industrial uses. The only residential properties nearby were a row of houses on Niagara Street on the northerly boundary of the lands of the company which, curiously, were also situated within the industrial zone and whose use was, therefore, non-conforming.

A lawyer from the Ministry of the Environment vigorously prosecuted the charge. Counsel for the defendant strongly defended against it. The trial occupied two days. As well, both sides submitted extensive written argument. Counsel for the company raised one of the most comprehensive lists of unusual, rare and esoteric defences that I have found collected together in a single case. They contended, firstly, that the Information failed to disclose any offence known to law, based upon a difference of opinion on the meaning of the word "plume." Next, it was argued that the subject of pollution fell within the legislative competence of the federal parliament under the Constitution and was not within the powers conferred upon the provinces; and hence the statute was invalid. Then it was urged upon me that the observations and reactions of the neighbours on Niagara Street at other times than the time of the incident were irrelevant and wrongly admitted in evidence. Next, counsel submitted that the prosecution should be "stayed," in effect dismissed, for what was claimed to be an abuse of process — delay in advising the accused of the violation and delay in launching the proceedings. The final argument was that the charge should be dismissed under the doctrines of "necessity" and "impossibility," much-discussed in academic circles but rarely, if ever, applied in any case in England or Canada. This last argument was grounded on an alleged settlement with the Ministry on terms that the defendant replace the smokestack with a huge chimney to release the discharge high into the atmosphere. The defendant claimed that it was unable to comply with the settlement because it was unable to obtain a building permit from the municipality that would enable it to do the reconstruction.

I wrote a thirty-eight page judgement in which I carefully considered each of these defences. In each instance, I concluded that the defence was not applicable to the circumstances of this case. Then, when it must have appeared I was on the point of entering a conviction, I directed my attention to what I regarded as the critical issue of the case, which was whether, on the evidence, the defendant committed the offence as charged in the Information. In my judgement, I noted that "the written argument for the defendant is relatively silent on this issue." I held that, while there was evidence that on other days and times residents on Niagara Street might have been affected by the fumes, there was no evidence that at the dead of night, between the hours as charged, anyone was affected by the emissions from the chimney. I held this in spite of the evidence of an inspector from the Ministry who testified that he came specifically to do an inspection and deliberately stepped into and out of the "plume" momentarily in order to test it for its noxious effects. I held, therefore, that at the particular times charged, the emission was not "likely to cause material discomfort to any person" except for an official who went looking for it. The prosecutor, who was as much anti-pollution activist as departmental counsel, was furious with me for this decision, which was contrary to her expectations. She promptly appealed my decision and, on appeal, it was reversed. Thereupon, however, it was appealed further and restored by a judgement of the Divisional Court of the Supreme Court of Ontario. According to a report in the press, the prosecutor vowed to appeal the decision once again, but I lost contact with the case and am unaware of any further developments. However, in subsequent cases on pollution, I endeavoured to enforce the provisions of the Environmental Protection Act, which may have restored me to the good opinion of the prosecutor.

I propose to conclude this miscellaneous collection of cases by reference to two cases that illustrate the diversity, on the one hand, and the importance and complexity, on the other hand, of the work that was coming before the Provincial Court. The first case is Trimont Investments Limited. This case came to the Provincial Court in its capacity as an appellate tribunal. Shortly after I came on the Bench, the Provincial Court was relieved of the burden of dealing with minor offences under the Highway Traffic Act. Jurisdiction over minor traffic offences was conferred upon the Justices of the Peace. Then, about midway through my career, this jurisdiction of the Justices of the Peace was extended considerably. The Ontario legislature enacted the Provincial Offences Act, which was intended to relieve the Provincial Judges of the bulk of the caseload resulting from their jurisdiction over all provincial offences. Under this statute, jurisdiction was conferred upon the Justices of the Peace to hear and determine charges of provincial offences, not merely minor infractions, but all offences created by provincial statutes, many of which are very serious and call for heavy punishment upon conviction. However, the relief this afforded to the Provincial Judges was retracted to a degree by provisions in the Act for appeals from Justices of the Peace to be heard in the Provincial Court, which would therefore exercise the usual appellate jurisdiction. The Act also left available a hearing in the Provincial Court in the first instance in complex cases.

Trimont was the owner of an apartment building containing fifteen stories and 342 dwelling units that, as landlord, was mistreating its low-income tenants in a manner that I considered to be oppressive and outrageous. The company was convicted by a Justice of the Peace and fined $5,000 on three charges of failing to keep the building clear of combustible materials by allowing garbage to accumulate by the elevator and in the basement contrary to the Fire Marshall's Act of Ontario. The company appealed on the ground that the conviction was against the weight of the evidence. The defence raised at the trial and on the appeal was that the company had exercised due diligence in difficult circumstances.

On the appeal, I had the assistance of a transcript of the proceedings before the Justice of the Peace. The evidence disclosed that an immense amount of garbage had been allowed to accumulate throughout the building, by the elevator and outside the garbage rooms on each floor, as well as the basement. A dead cat was found in the same place in the building on separate inspections.

According to the main witness for the defence, who was the sole shareholder of the company and could be regarded in a practical sense as the owner of the building, the building was a "problem building" with "problem tenants." He proceeded to describe his tenants variously as "lower-class," a "rough bunch," a "certain element," "tenants not seeming to care," and "vindictive." On his own statement, it was clear that he had caused the garbage rooms on each floor of the building to be locked up. These were the rooms installed on each floor of the building for the very purpose of being used by the tenants to dispose of their garbage. The owner explained his high-handed action in locking all the garbage rooms by stating that he was "training his people" to take their garbage right out of the building to the ground and placing it in the outdoor garbage bins. I had not the slightest difficulty with the case either on the facts or the law. The defence was a complete sham. I wrote a judgement of fifteen pages, only for the purpose of reading it word for word in open court. I wanted to put on record my profound condemnation of this apartment building owner, particularly because he had stated that he dealt with the tenants of his sixteen other "low-end" buildings in the same fashion. I dismissed the appeal and confirmed the fine imposed by the Justice of the Peace. My only regret is that I failed to consider whether I had the jurisdiction to increase the penalty or at least make an order for the defendant to pay the costs of the appeal.

Eighteen
Influencing the Law

According to the common law system of justice that we in Canada inherited from the British, it is the function of the legislature to make the law by enacting new laws or amending or repealing old laws. It is said to be the business of judges, on the other hand, simply to interpret and apply the law. They are not supposed to be making new law. In fact, judges make a great deal of law, incidentally, through their judgements and decisions in individual cases. This judge-made or case law is created mainly by interpretation, refinement of principles and application of the law to new situations. The process is facilitated and controlled by adherence to precedent — what lawyers call the rule of stare decisis. Briefly put, the rule dictates that judges of lower courts must follow and apply the law as laid down by the higher courts. Not all the reasoning in judgements of higher courts is considered to be legally binding, just that part that represents the actual grounds for decision in the case. This is referred to as the *res gesta* of the case. It is distinguished from reasons set out in the decision that may be interesting and may expound on aspects of the law but are not crucial to the actual decision of the case. These reasons are referred to as *obiter dicta* and, although having persuasive value, are not binding upon a lower court judge. This process of law making is ongoing, so that, through the decisions of the courts and the statutes of the provincial legislatures and the Parliament of Canada, the law is continually being modified and adjusted to meet changing social and economic conditions.

When I was appointed to the bench, I entertained no grandiose notions about changing the law. Still, as every judge knows, the decisions and judgements of the courts, in whatever position they may be in the judicial hierarchy, and occasionally even in minor cases, have the potential to influence the progressive development of the law.

In a case I tried while I was still a magistrate, a man named Onuska was charged with a minor offence. He was charged with being a "found-in, without lawful excuse" because of his presence at a party where the person giving the party was convicted of serving liquor to a person who was already intoxicated. I did not deal with the principal offence. I was only concerned with the charge against Onuska. The charge against him was laid under a provision of the Liquor License Act, an Ontario statute. The only point of the case for me was whether a person could be guilty of a penal offence because of his mere presence in a place where another person was committing another offence. I wrote my first judgement as a judicial officer to vindicate the principle that no person by his presence is guilty of an offence unless in some way the person participates in the main offence. I was of the opinion that the words "without lawful excuse" added nothing to the issue of liability. I thought Onuska gave a perfectly lawful excuse in any event. He was invited to attend a party and, when asked why he went, he responded, "Well, there were girls going to be there." In the course of time, I believe that the practice of the police to enforce this type of provision fell into disuse.

I did not consider that there was any possibility at all that *R. v. Cross*, another case I decided in my early years on the Bench, could influence the development of the law. The charge concerned a federal prohibition of the export of silver coins. Apparently, the silver content of the coins was very valuable at this point in time. The accused had been melting the coins and selling the finished product as silver. I held that it was not the coins that the accused was selling, but silver bullion. I wrote a judgement on the subject and then quite forgot the case. To my amazement, somewhat later, I found that my decision had been followed and applied in a judgement of the Quebec Court of Appeal and reported in the law reports, with extensive quotations from my decision. They made one mistake. They must have considered that a lower court judge could not have produced so erudite a judgement; so, they did me the honour of elevating me to the High Court by referring to me as Vanek J. or Mr. Justice Vanek. I was considerably bemused by this error of designation.

R. v. Thornton is a case in which I take a degree of pride. A young man came before me charged with "possession of a weapon for a purpose dangerous to the public peace" contrary to the Criminal Code. The undisputed facts were that, late at night, the accused, about eighteen years of age, was walking along the main street of the Yorkville district in Toronto, which at that time was a hippie haven. He appeared to have a pistol stuck under his belt and displayed in the manner of a western cowboy of the movies. A police officer came upon him and asked, "What are you doing with that pistol?" The youth replied that he was carrying a great deal of money and added: "I have it for my protection." The accused was assisted in his defence by an able lawyer who later became a judge. His strategy was virtually to laugh the matter out of court: "It was a silly little episode; the gun was not even a real gun; it was merely a starter's pistol; it was only in possession for purposes of self defence." On this basis, counsel stated that the charge should be dismissed. Crown counsel concurred. It is difficult, if not extraordinary, to resist the joint opinion of both counsel. Still, I decided to give the matter further consideration, adjourned the case, and wrote a judgement under which I convicted the accused of the offence charged.

In order to convict for this offence, I had to decide that the starter's pistol, was a "weapon" and that it was in "possession for a purpose dangerous to the public peace." I had to do so despite the fact that the pistol was capable only of discharging a pellet and generally could not inflict serious injury and the explanation that it was only in possession for the youth's protection. On the first issue, I had no difficulty in deciding that it was a weapon. A pellet fired from the gun could strike and injure a vulnerable spot on the body, such as an eye, and could be used as a weapon in other ways, by threats, to provoke other persons, or by its mere display. I held, therefore, that the starter's pistol could be used as a weapon, and hence, satisfied the statutory definition of the Code. I had more difficulty with the second issue, whether an eighteen-year-old youth was justified in carrying a gun on the street because he thought he might need it for protection. I searched the decided cases and found a decision of Mr. Justice Middleton, a distinguished judge of the Ontario Court of Appeal when I was still a student, which I believed supported the view that I was favouring. I held that the starter's pistol was possessed for a purpose dangerous to the public peace. In Canada, generally, we enjoy life in a relatively peaceful society. People are not permitted to carry firearms in public except under permit in rare situations. If a person feels the need for protection, the protection should be obtained through the police and not by self-arming in anticipation of an attack. The subjective opinion of the accused himself, particularly in the case of an eighteen-year-old youth of unknown emotional reaction to sudden stress, did not justify the possession.

The case went on appeal to the Ontario Court of Appeal, which overturned my judgement in a split decision. Two of the judges disagreed with me, but it seemed I won over Chief Justice Gale, who dissented. Two or three months later, another case came before the Court of Appeal on very similar facts — no two cases are exactly identical. This was a decision of Judge Greco of Thunder Bay in *R. v. Nelson*. The facts were very much the same except that the accused was in possession of a knife and not a gun. Judge Greco no doubt felt bound by the decision of the Court of Appeal in *Thornton* and dismissed the charge. The Crown appealed the decision to the Court of Appeal. I suspect that the Chief Justice packed the Court. Instead of a Court composed of three judges, the case was heard by a panel of five judges. This time the Ontario Court of Appeal reversed the decision of Judge Greco in *Nelson*. I have felt justified, therefore, in considering that, in effect, they restored my judgement in *Thornton* and established a principle that, in this country, people are not permitted to carry guns, even on the basis of a perceived need for self-protection.

Over the years, I became increasingly concerned about the powers that assistant Crown-attorneys were assuming and exercising in court. A prime illustration is an incident in the *Plumber* case, a case that was on a long daily list for trial. There were three counts: the first charged that the accused unlawfully assaulted a police officer with intent to resist or prevent his lawful arrest; the second was a charge of attempted robbery; and the third, I cannot remember. This fell within a class of offence that we called a "hybrid offence." The Crown has an election to proceed by way of indictment or treat the matter as a minor offence for which the penalty is commonly a light fine. When the accused was asked, "How do you plead to these three charges?" His lawyer responded on his behalf: "On the first charge, not guilty to the offence as charged but guilty to the lesser and included offence of common assault" and, according to my recollection, also pleaded "not guilty" to the other two charges. The Crown indicated its acceptance of this plea, which would have reduced the offence to which the accused pleaded guilty to common assault — a summary conviction offence. Upon conviction for this offence, I would confidently expect the Crown to withdraw the other two charges.

An "included offence," to which the defence counsel referred, is an offence, the essential elements of which are included in a more serious offence. For example, if one assaults a police officer, the lesser included offence is common assault. The offence of common assault is elevated to a more serious offence by the commission of it against a police officer.

However, under the Code, a plea of guilty to an "included offence" required not only acceptance by the Crown but the consent of the Court as well. Generally, the Court almost invariably consented. The judge would not know in advance all of the circumstances that justified proceeding on the included offence, while they would be well known to the Crown. However, I would insist upon being shown a proper basis for the exercise of the discretion of the Court. Thus, my practice was to state: "I shall hear the Crown's statement of the alleged facts and then determine how the discretion of the Court will be exercised."

When I heard the Crown's statement of the alleged facts, I was shocked. I was told that the accused was attempting to deprive a woman of a purse she was carrying. She realized what was happening and held fast to the purse. The accused did not disengage but persisted and tried to pull the purse away by force, which the woman grimly resisted. This conduct of the accused could amount to robbery or attempted robbery — serious indictable offences. The incident attracted the attention of an off-duty police constable who rushed to the scene and addressed the accused: "Stop; I am a policeman; you are under arrest!" In response, the accused turned upon the police officer and began to fight with him.

When I heard this account, I asked the Crown how he could justify acceptance of a plea to common assault on facts indicating the commission of much more serious offences.

The Crown replied, "Well, to tell you the truth, Your Honour, I am just trying to clear the list."

I replied, "What do you mean, clear the list? I don't administer this Court on that basis at all; I apply the law."

"Well, Your Honour," he added, "I have considered all these matters and there are several charges I have to consider. I have also considered the end result as to what the sentence should be appropriate to this act."

Of course, these answers did not satisfy me in the slightest degree. What this young assistant Crown counsel was doing, in essence, was to take the criminal charges before me for trial out of my hands and control and administer justice in accordance with his own opinion of what was a satisfactory disposition. If such a process were permitted, why would I be needed? The judge would become a mere figurehead. Consequently, I refused to consent to the acceptance of the plea to the lesser offence. Both counsel then joined in a request for me to adjourn the case, possibly in the hope that another judge might be more compliant and persuaded to accept a plea to a single charge of common assault as planned. I refused to grant an adjournment. Counsel persisted; I firmly resisted any such ploy. The case was listed for trial that day and would proceed to trial that day. Thus, I forced the matter on for trial and, after hearing the evidence under oath, convicted the accused for one of the indictable offences — I believe it was the charge of robbery. Then I was informed that the accused had a bad criminal record. I sentenced him to a substantial term of imprisonment.

Obviously, I took strong objection to plea bargaining, certainly in the form and manner in which it was regularly being practised in the Provincial Court as a means of programming the judge. In general, I disapproved of the "wheeling and dealing" between Crown and defence counsel and the administration of criminal justice by a "deal," behind closed doors, that effectively removed criminal charges before the court from the control and disposition of the presiding judge.

The *Plumber* case and my views on plea bargaining were disseminated to the legal community in Toronto by way of a non-legal medium. A Toronto newspaper published a verbatim copy of the official court record of a portion of the proceedings under the headline "Judge Refuses to Clear the Lists."

The preceding episode brings me to two cases in which I again dealt with a question of the exercise of prosecutorial authority but in much greater depth and detail. Assistant Crown attorneys are answerable to the Crown attorney, who in turn acts on behalf of the Attorney General for Ontario. Therefore, these cases actually concerned the relationship between the executive and judicial branches of government and their responsibility and powers regarding criminal charges before a court for disposition.

R. *v. Lawson and Slavnick* was a case dealing with the issue of double jeopardy, which, the English might say, has been part of the law since time immemorial. The rules of double jeopardy dictate that no person may be tried or convicted a second time for the same offence, whether originally the person was convicted or acquitted. If the person was previously convicted, our Criminal Code in Canada provides for the defence to be raised by a plea of what is called *autrefois convict;* or if previously acquitted, by a plea of *autrefois acquit.* The accused was charged with the offence of cheating at play, in other words, at cards. At this time, cheating at play was one of a group of offences that, although indictable, fell within the absolute jurisdiction of the Provincial Court. Hence, the accused came before a Provincial Court Judge for trial. Upon arraignment, he pleaded "not guilty." Crown counsel admitted, "I have no witnesses to call, no evidence to put in." Consequently, defence counsel applied to the Court for dismissal of the charge. In the absence of any evidence before the Court, the first judge found the accused not guilty and subsequently issued a certificate of acquittal.

Later, the same charge for the same offence was re-laid and this time the matter came before me for trial. On this occasion, to the charge as re-laid, the accused entered the special plea of *autrefois acquit.* In support of this plea, the accused filed a certified copy of the information under which the accused was originally charged with the same offence, the certificate of acquittal, and a transcript of the previous proceedings. Counsel for the accused argued that the accused had been put in jeopardy on the previous charge on which he had been acquitted and that the second charge should be dismissed or quashed. The Crown contended, in accordance with his view of the traditional law on double jeopardy, that for this defence to apply, not only must the accused have been charged with the identical offence but that a trial must have taken place. This, he argued, necessitated the actual hearing of evidence and the adjudication of the charge "on the merits."

I undertook an extensive research of the case law and found that the decided cases were seriously in conflict and difficult or impossible to reconcile. While I was heavily engaged in this work, however, the Ontario Court of Appeal decided the very point at issue before me in *R. v. Hatherley*. They decided it substantially on the same reasoning that I had already reached. In *Hatherley*, the accused had been arraigned on a charge and a plea had been entered to the charge. The Court of Appeal held that the Crown could call evidence or not in its discretion and the fact that the Crown did not call evidence did not mean that there was any less of a trial. Once the accused entered a plea, the trial began. Hence the adjudication by the judge on the charge was "on the merits" and the defence of double jeopardy was sustained.

Of course, the decision in *Hatherley* rendered unnecessary the continuation of my labours in my case. However, the judgement in *Hatherley* rested almost entirely on a bare two-page statement of conclusions without reference to the supporting authorities. These included an important previous decision in the case of *Karpinski*, a decision of the Supreme Court of Canada by which even the Court of Appeal was bound. I felt it was important for the law to be firmly settled on a delicate and difficult question of the application of double jeopardy and decided to complete the writing of my judgement by a review of all the authorities that supported the conclusions in *Hatherley*. Upon completion, I sent my judgement to the *Canadian Law Quarterly Review*. They published it as an article, prefaced by an editorial note, which I confess I found gratifying: "The issues raised in the case are important and practical ones, and it is hoped that Judge Vanek's scholarly treatment of them will be of assistance."

R. v. Weightman and Cunningham is a case very similar to *Lawson and Slavnick* on the facts. Once again, I was involved in the second go around. At the first court appearance before another judge, there was no plea of guilty or not guilty; the case did not reach that stage. The charge was trafficking in heroin, a very serious indictable offence on which the accused was entitled to an election, whether to be tried in the Provincial Court, or in another court, with or without a jury. If the accused elected trial in another court, the judge would have been required to conduct a preliminary inquiry. A trial date had been set and the case came before the first judge for trial. Crown counsel addressed the Court substantially as follows: "Sorry, Your Honour, one of my prime witnesses is absent; we are unable to go on to today; we request an adjournment."

The judge inquired: "Who is this prime witness?"

"He is a police officer," came the response.

"Why is he not here?"

"He is on his honeymoon."

"Surely you knew about this in advance and could have arranged with defence counsel and the Court beforehand for a suitable date for trial, could you not?"

Defence counsel opposed the granting of an adjournment and the judge heard argument on the subject. Ultimately, the judge ruled against the motion and refused to allow an adjournment of the case. Crown counsel then stated, simply: "The Crown is withdrawing the charge, Your Honour."

The judge noted, "This charge is withdrawn at the request of the Crown."

Again, in this case, the identical charge was re-laid and the charge as re-laid came before me for trial.

There had been a previous decision of Judge Crossland (not considered binding upon me under the rule of stare decisis) that arose in almost identical circumstances. What the Crown was trying to do in his and in my case was entirely obvious. The Court had made a decision after argument in which it refused to grant an adjournment; the Crown presumed to grant itself an adjournment anyway by withdrawing and later simply re-laying the charge. The Crown was claiming the right to adopt this procedure, which, incidentally, raises an issue about the withdrawal of criminal charges as a matter of absolute right.

Judge Crossland held, and I later agreed, that the withdrawal of a criminal charge by the Crown for the oblique purpose of circumventing a ruling or decision of the Court was an abuse of the process of the Court. The remedy for this was to stay further proceedings in the case, equivalent to a dismissal of the charge.

The question of the existence of jurisdiction of a judge to stay proceedings for abuse of process had previously been discussed in the House of Lords in England in several sets of reasons for decision in a case called *Connelly*, which was ultimately decided, however, on other grounds. In *Connelly*, the majority of the judgements inclined to the view that this residual jurisdiction existed in the courts. However, judgements in England's highest court, although persuasive, are not binding upon the courts in Canada. In Canada, the same issue came before the Ontario Court of Appeal in the case of *Osborn* in which it was held that judges did indeed possess jurisdiction to stay criminal proceedings for abuse of process. The decision in *Osborn* was appealed to the Supreme Court of Canada, which, by a majority decision, overruled the Ontario Court of Appeal. Three judges of that Court recognized the doctrine of abuse of process, three judges rejected it and the seventh was silent on the point.

In another case, *Rourke*, a decision of the Supreme Court of Canada released two months before my judgement in *Weightman and Cunningham*, the Court once again dealt with the issue of abuse of process. Chief Justice Laskin wrote a minority opinion that strongly supported the existence of a residual discretion of judges to stay proceedings for abuse of process. The decision the Supreme Court of Canada in the *Osborn* and *Rourke* cases cast great doubt on a judge's authority to exercise a purported residual discretion and dismiss criminal charges for a perceived abuse of the process of the Court.

After giving full consideration to all the judgements in the Supreme Court, I decided that, on the question of abuse of process, the opinions of the majority were obiter and that the actual decisions turned on other matters. I was fully mindful that it might well be considered presumptuous for a lower court judge to fail to follow the majority opinions of the Supreme Court of Canada even in matters that I regarded as obiter. Nevertheless, as lawyers would say, in *Weightman and Cunningham* I distinguished the actual decision of the Supreme Court in *Osborn* and *Rourke*, followed the judgement of Chief Justice Laskin in *Rourke*, and relied upon the decision of the Ontario Court of Appeal in *Osborn*. In my view, *Osborn* still applied and supported the existence of jurisdiction in abuse of process. I do not know whether at the time I was being courageous or foolhardy.

My reasons for decision next dealt with the so-called right of Crown counsel to withdraw criminal charges. I regarded this to be an issue of great importance because the practice was the linchpin in the process of plea bargaining — the withdrawal of charges in exchange for a plea of guilty on a lesser charge involving a lesser punishment. On this aspect, there was a decision of Mr. Justice Lieff that seemed to support a qualified right of withdrawal, a decision that I believed could not be justified by judicial authority and, in any case, was distinguishable. However, no case supported a right of withdrawal as an absolute right of the Crown, that is, without the consent of the Court. The further complicating feature of the case with which I was dealing was that the presiding judge at the original hearing appeared to consent to the withdrawal of the charge by the Crown. I was satisfied, however, that the judge was merely repeating an empty formula, echoing the statement and decision of the Crown without intending to express his actual consent to the withdrawal.

In the result, I held that the persistence in the prosecution of an offence by re-laying a charge, despite the refusal of the judge before whom the matter came for trial to grant an adjournment, constituted an abuse of the process of the Court. I decided that for this abuse, the Court possessed an inherent jurisdiction to stay the proceedings, a jurisdiction that I exercised, thereby effectively disposing of the charge against the accused. I felt that my decision vindicated a constitutional principle established in England years ago regarding the relations between the executive and the judicial branches of government and I closed my judgement with the declaration: *"Rex non est lex; lex est rex!"* Subsequently, in my recollection, the Supreme Court of Canada settled the dispute about the existence of jurisdiction to stay proceedings for abuse of process; it held that the courts possessed this jurisdiction, which, however, should only be exercised sparingly in relatively rare situations.

One of the last cases I was assigned prior to my retirement was the case in which the nominal defendant was a young woman by the name of Squires but the real defendant, so far as I was concerned, was the Canadian Broadcasting Corporation. It is a good illustration of the importance and complexity of some of the work in the Provincial

Court, at least by the time I left the Bench. Squires was a television reporter who was employed by the Canadian Broadcasting Corporation. During a preliminary inquiry in a high profile case in Ottawa, about an act of terrorism that caused the Turkish ambassador to Canada to incur serious injuries, Squires attended with a TV cameraman. She was directing the cameraman to take video pictures as the ambassador, in a wheelchair, was being taken out of the courtroom at a recess in the proceedings. Squires was charged with an offence under a provincial statute, which provides that no person shall take any photograph or motion picture at a judicial proceeding or of any person entering or leaving the courtroom or in the precincts of the courthouse or publish or broadcast it. There are certain narrow exceptions, the most relevant of which is worded as follows: "with the consent of the parties and witnesses, for such educational or instructional purposes as may be approved by the judge."

At the trial, the CBC took the occasion to launch a full-scale attack on the constitutionality of the provincial statute. This they did by making a preliminary motion in which they requested that the charge be quashed on the ground that it infringed upon a fundamental right or freedom guaranteed by the Canadian Charter of Rights and Freedoms, a part of the Canadian Constitution. The relevant sections are as follows:

2.Everyone has the following fundamental freedoms:
(b) Freedom of thought, belief, opinion and expression, including freedom of the press and other media of communication;
11.Any person charged with an offence has the right
(d) to be presumed innocent until proven guilty according to law in a fair and public hearing by an independent and impartial tribunal;

Section 2(b) might well be in conflict with section 11(d) of the Charter.

Moreover, all the rights and freedoms in the Charter are qualified to the extent described in a general section which reads:

1. The Canadian Charter of Rights and Freedoms guarantees the rights and freedoms set out in it subject only to such

reasonable limits prescribed by law as can be demonstrably justified in a free and democratic society.

The Canadian Charter of Rights and Freedoms confers upon the courts an awesome power. They can declare invalid an Act of any of the provincial legislatures or of the federal parliament if it should be held to be inconsistent with a right or freedom guaranteed in the Charter. The substantial issues in this case, therefore, turned on the preliminary motion to, in effect, strike down the provincial statute containing the prohibition about the televising of judicial proceedings and gain recognition that the televising of judicial proceedings was a constitutionally guaranteed right of the electronic media under the Charter.

Specifically, I had to decide whether "freedom of the press" included a right of the electronic media to televise judicial proceedings; and, if so, whether the provincial statute should be allowed to stand, nonetheless, as a "reasonable limit demonstrably justified in a free and democratic society."

The hearing on the motion to quash extended over a period of several weeks and included the testimony of twenty-seven witnesses and the filing of over forty exhibits of documentary and audio-visual materials. Counsel of outstanding ability assisted me. Upon the conclusion of the hearing, I wrote two judgements both of which were published in the law reports — a judgement of twelve pages in which I ruled on the admissibility of documentary evidence, and a forty-five-page judgement on the main issues. With regard to the nature of the evidence, I wrote:

A great deal of the testimony was devoted to the effects of television on the conduct of fair trials, the impact on participants including the defendant and victim, the consequences in the field of law enforcement, and generally the proper administration of justice. The *viva voce* evidence included the United States experience with televised proceedings in the courts and the process whereby the rules prohibiting television have been relaxed in a number of states and the inquiries, surveys, studies and reports on the strength of which changes were made in these rules. This evidence is largely of a sociological nature and includes testimony of well-qualified experts in the fields of social psychology, psychiatry, criminology and scientific methodology and research in the social sciences.

Early in the hearing, counsel for the Applicant simply tendered several bundles of documents, which he claimed were admissible in evidence without further proof as a "Brandeis Brief" according to a practice instituted in the United States. The materials included attitudinal and opinion surveys, learned articles, statistics, and briefs on legislative history, and were supplemented later by additional similar documents. Counsel maintained that in a constitutional case under the Charter, the rules of evidence were relaxed in order to allow the admission of evidence of a sociological nature to underlie the issues. I was shocked by the submission that bundles of documents not properly proved through the testimony of a witness could be admitted contrary to the normal well-established rules of evidence. I really did not know quite how to deal with this issue. It was a new problem in my experience. I probably did not realize at the time that it was relatively new in the experience of others as well and that I was actually treading on new ground.

Early in my career, however, I learned an important facet of judicial life. Although I, as judge, am in charge of my court and the proceedings before me, I cannot be expected instantly to know the answer to every problem by which I may be confronted. A convenient safety mechanism is to call a recess and retire to chambers for calm reflection or, if necessary, adjourn the case to another day. What I did, ultimately, was to allow the materials to be filed on a provisional basis. Upon the conclusion of the hearing, I reviewed the documents and ruled on the admissibility of each item tendered. I held that some relaxation of the rules of evidence was warranted in a constitutional case where the validity of legislation is challenged under the Charter. The nature of the evidence in a constitutional case is different from the evidence in an ordinary criminal case. On a criminal charge, the evidentiary facts involve matters of perception, feeling, motivation and the like. In a constitutional case, the relevant evidence is more of a theoretical and abstract character. It includes the opinions of experts, which often can not be adequately shown except through surveys setting out the full range of professional opinion. In general terms, I held that the inherent reliability or unreliability of the tendered material determined the degree of liberalization of the rules and that the ordinary rules of evidence were not to be abandoned at trial merely because a constitutional issue was raised.

On the main issue, I held that section 2(b) of the Charter (e.g. freedom of thought, belief etc.) did not include any right of the electronic media to televise judicial proceedings. Further, if it did, the provincial statute prohibiting the televising of judicial proceedings fell within reasonable limits demonstrably justified in our Canadian democratic society. Therefore the statute was not inconsistent with any constitutional right or freedom and remained in full force and effect.

The Ontario Court of Appeal dismissed an appeal from my judgement on the main issues and the Supreme Court of Canada denied leave to appeal the decision further.

My decision only dealt with the question of a constitutional right or freedom. The provincial legislature, if so inclined, could amend the statute to permit judicial proceedings to be televised, subject to controls governing the nature and placing of the equipment in the courtroom, just as has been allowed in a number of states of the United States. For my part, however, I am content that the provincial government has not seen fit to relax the prohibitions in any way.

The trial of Paul Bernardo in St. Catharines, Ontario, on charges of murder, has served as a virtual demonstration of the worth of the provincial statute. It aroused an immense amount of interest, excitement, and concern within the general public. The trial included evidence of rape, sexual perversion and brutality of an unspeakable nature, much of which was deliberately captured on videotape by the accused himself. Patrick LeSage, the then Associate Chief Justice of the Ontario Court of Justice (General Division), presided at the trial. According to report, at the opening of the case a motion was made to permit the proceedings to be televised, presumably on the ground it would serve an educational purpose. The application was refused. In the conduct of the trial, the learned Associate Chief Justice was able to avoid the excesses of sensationalism that have been labelled a "media circus," such as those that contaminated the O.J. Simpson murder trial in the United States. The Bernardo trial was a fair and public hearing, held in a calm atmosphere, with due regard for the rights of the accused and consideration for all the participants. In the courtroom, members of the media and the public who secured seats were able to follow the proceedings in all its lurid details of sexual depravity, including the scenes on film. Out of the courtroom, the public likewise was able to follow the proceedings but were spared the trauma of viewing on their television screens the scenes of sexual sadism that added nothing of significance to their understanding and knowledge of the trial.

Nineteen
The Rule of Law

If anyone wishes to learn about the rule of law, it is helpful to visit a country where the rule of law does not exist. I had this experience in about the year 1983, when Joyce and I joined a group of American judges and their spouses on a tour of mainland China. This came about after I became a member of the American Academy of Trial Judges, which sponsored the tour. Cy Perkins, who preceded me as president of the Ontario Provincial Judges Association, had introduced me to this organization.

We were a relatively small group of about thirty people. Joyce and I were the only Canadians on the tour. We travelled at an exciting time in Chinese history. It was approximately fifteen years after the end of the so-called "Cultural Revolution" in China and less than that after the historic first visit to China of President Nixon. Ostensibly the tour was a fact-finding mission; the object was to study the justice system in China at this time.

We landed first in Tokyo. We spent a day sightseeing in the Japanese capital. The next day our tour was taken by bus about one hundred kilometres into the Japanese countryside to the Nikko Toshogu Shrine, a famous Shinto shrine located on a substantial tract of land. The site was swarming with Japanese people who had been brought to the shrine in countless buses.

At the shrine, I managed to disgrace myself by getting lost. It was a most unnerving experience. It happened when I was busy taking pictures of a representation of the three mythical monkeys — "see no evil, hear no evil, and speak no evil." I did not realize that all my companions had returned to our bus. I was left surrounded by a multitude of Japanese, with whom I had no means of communication. All of the buses on the grounds looked alike and it seemed that I was in grave danger of being abandoned deep in the heart of Japan. Ultimately I was rescued. My companions sent out a search party who, by good fortune, came upon my woeful person and brought me back to our bus.

The tour was on a tight schedule and I had delayed our departure by at least an hour. I had to make amends for my carelessness that was the cause of annoyance and discomfort to my companions. To seek forgiveness for my transgression, I produced my only bottle of scotch whiskey and passed it around the bus, which may have helped to restore their goodwill. It was, nevertheless, a long ride afterwards to the coast, where we remained overnight.

As a group of judges, we travelled under prestigious auspices and were welcomed with particular warmth in each centre that we visited. The warmth of the welcome was due to the presence in our party of a person who needed no special introduction to Chinese officialdom. Allison Cameron, accompanied by her husband William Cameron, a retired colonel of the American Air Force, was the daughter of General Joseph Stilwell who, during World War II, was the special representative of the United States for south-east Asia and in charge of the administration of the American lend-lease program for this area. Universally known as "Vinegar Joe" Stilwell, he was very popular with the Chinese people. Allison had been brought up in China and was perfectly fluent in Mandarin. As the daughter of the famous and well-loved friend of the Chinese people, she was invariably greeted with fondness everywhere we travelled, especially by officials of the older generation with personal recollections of Vinegar Joe.

In every major centre that we visited in China, we were received by representatives of the Organization for Friendship with Foreign Countries, an official or perhaps semi-official governmental entity, and given a formal banquet. A Chinese dignitary would propose a toast to the United States to which Judge Hugh Stewart, the president of the American Academy of Trial Judges, who was one of our party, would naturally respond with a toast to the Chinese nation. Once it was made known that the tour also included a Canadian judge, who gave the tour an international flavour, I was also called upon to propose a toast to the great people of China. Indeed, as a Canadian, I found myself to be quite popular in China because of Norman Bethune. He was an expatriate Canadian physician who fought a battle with tuberculosis, participated in the Spanish Civil War, joined Mao Tse Tung in the Long March from Shanghai, and became a hero of the Chinese revolution. It seemed as if every reference to Canada produced amongst Chinese people, by reflex reaction, the response, "Ah, Norman Bethune."

We flew from an airport on the coast of Japan into Shanghai en route to Beijing. However, we did not reach Beijing. Upon arrival in Shanghai, still weary from strenuous travelling, we were informed that there would be some changes. All hotels in Shanghai and Beijing were filled to capacity and our itinerary had been changed; instead of going direct to Beijing, we were to spend the day in Shanghai and, in late afternoon, we were to take a five-hour ride by train to Nanjing. We finally arrived in Nanjing in a state of utter exhaustion and were booked into a huge hotel complex, which had accommodated President Nixon, in time only for a late supper.

The next morning, I awoke with a serious physical disability. I was unable to move my head from side to side without excruciating pain. In distress, I turned for help to Allison who, with her mastery of Mandarin, made inquiries on my behalf of available remedies. She returned to report that I could choose between treatment by acupuncture or by massage interspersed with frequent immersions in the bathtub. I chose the latter. So, while the rest of my party spent the day sightseeing in and about Nanjing, I submitted to the ministrations of a local barber who also served as masseur. He seated me in a regular barber's chair in his barbershop and massaged my neck with hands of steel. The next day, still not recovered, I got my chance to go sightseeing with the others of my group. Seated beside my wife in the bus, without turning my head, I would catch a glimpse out of the corner of my eye of something that attracted my interest. Our conversation was somewhat as follows: "Joyce, what are those objects in the fields to the right?" "Just water buffalo, water buffalo pulling a cart or plough, that's all, dear." It was the first time I ever went sightseeing in a foreign country with a stiff neck.

However, a day or two later, I was fully recovered and ready to enjoy the rest of the tour. Still, by this stage, we had learned nothing about the Chinese legal system. It was only when we returned to Shanghai that we were given any information on this subject. In Shanghai, the judges on our tour met with a judicial officer who explained the system of justice in China: "Of course we have a justice system; it is much the same as yours. There are judges, lawyers and courts; and they administer the law." But we were scrupulously excluded from witnessing anything resembling a trial and I do not recall even being shown the inside of a courtroom. I found the opportunity to ask a question. I told the official of our concept of habeas corpus. I explained that it applied when a person was being held in a prison or other confinement. By serving the applicable document, the jailer or custodian was bound to produce the person in court before a judge to ascertain by what legal authority, if any, the person was being held. If no legal authority could be shown, the person was required to be set free. I asked the official if there was anything like it in China. The official did not appear to know about what I was talking.

In Shanghai, our party was given a sumptuous banquet by the Organization for Friendship with Foreign Countries. It was hosted by Li Hi Quin, the president of the High Peoples Court of Shanghai, and held in an historic hotel situated at the waterfront. I was seated beside a big, stolid woman as my dinner companion, who could not speak a word of English. Later, I was informed she had been a colonel commissar of the Red Army, was given a thirty-day course in training for the judiciary, and was immediately appointed vice-president of the High Court of Shanghai. At dinner, I distinguished myself by spilling my wine, some of which may have soiled her garments, but without seeming to cause any offence. Ultimately, I proposed my usual toast to the great people of China, which was well received. After the banquet, our tour was scheduled to depart by plane for Xian, the ancient capital of China, to be followed by a visit to Beijing, the modern capital. Li Hi Quin accompanied our party to the airport. I must have made a very good impression upon him, no doubt thanks to the memory of Norman Bethune and his contribution to the Chinese revolution. In an extraordinary gesture of friendship, despite my protestations, the president of the High Peoples Court of Shanghai insisted on personally carrying my luggage on the way to the airport.

A day or two following our arrival in Beijing, Joyce and I were able to play hookey. We were scheduled to visit the head office in Beijing of the Organization for Friendship with Foreign Countries, an event in which we had no interest. Instead, through the good offices of our tour guide, who operated the telephone for us, we got in touch with a young woman of our acquaintance. She was the daughter of Ron Haggart; a newspaperman of established reputation who used to write for the *Toronto Evening Telegram*. She was spending a few years in China as a columnist for an English language newspaper in Beijing. She invited us to join her at the Beijing Hotel where she was to meet with a large circle of her friends and acquaintances. The Beijing Hotel was a modern edifice, a hotel of superior quality, located in the heart of the capital, near Tiananmen Square and the Forbidden City.

We passed a very pleasant and interesting afternoon in the company of this broad assortment of young people who were studying and working in Beijing. From them, at last, we learned about the system of justice in China. They were surprised that we knew nothing about it. They told us about the posters, prominently displayed, not on the main streets such as the one fronting the hotel, but throughout the residential areas adjoining main streets. The posters contained lists of the names of persons, occasionally with photographs. Opposite each name appeared the letter "X." Everyone knew this meant that these people had been executed or were about to be executed in mass executions open to the public.

Altogether, my experience in China helped to provide me with a much better appreciation of our justice system in Canada, where justice is administered on the basis of law and in accordance with the rule of law.

In our democratic country, the rule of law is inextricably bound up with the constitutional doctrine of the separation of governmental powers. The doctrine holds that governmental powers are divided amongst three branches of government, the legislative, executive and judicial, each with its special functions. It is a fundamental part of the doctrine that the judiciary must be independent of the executive and legislative branches. The cornerstone of the rule of law is the principle of judicial independence. It underpins our entire system of law. The principle has been part of the law since at least the Act of Settlement in England of 1701. It is now enshrined in the preamble to the Canadian Constitution in the Charter of Rights and Freedoms, which provides that every person charged with an offence has the right to be tried "according to law in a fair and public hearing by an independent and impartial tribunal."

The object of the principle is to provide that a judge shall be free from external pressure and influence of any kind, particularly political or governmental influence, in order to ensure that the judge's decisions will be impartial and in accordance with the law. There have been isolated incidents in Canada in which cabinet ministers or other officials of government have intervened in a case before the courts. In general, when these incidents have come to light, the offending cabinet minister or official has been forced to resign from office or has otherwise been brought to account and punished. It is particularly important to uphold the principle of judicial independence of provincial judges in Ontario and the other provinces of Canada because of the special relationship between the provincial judges and the provincial governments. The provincial governments appoint the provincial judges, pay their salaries and pensions, and administer their courts. This necessarily involves a degree of governmental control over judges and courts. In addition, the provincial government is the prosecutor and hence a litigant in almost every criminal or penal case in the provincial courts. It is essential, therefore, to guard against interference and even the appearance of interference by the executive or legislature with the functions of the provincial judges.

On the whole, our judicial system has been remarkably free from the taint of corruption. In part, this is attributable to the fact that all of our judges, be they appointed federally or provincially, are appointed for life, subject to a set age for retirement. They are not dependent on periodic election to office and are not subject to the influences that affect elected governmental officials. This is unlike the system that prevails in some other countries; for example, even in the United States where some state judges, in contrast to the federal judges, hold office through election by the public.

At least of equal importance in maintaining a fair and responsible judiciary and the assurance of impartial justice is the principle of judicial independence. In the Universal Declaration of the Independence of Justice, internationally adopted in 1983 and to which Canada is a signatory, the principle has been expressed in the broadest of terms. Part II states: "Judges individually shall be free, and it shall be their duty to decide matters impartially in accordance with their assessment of the facts and their understanding of the law without any restrictions, influences, inducements, pressures, threats or interferences, direct or indirect, from any quarter or for any reason."

The financial conditions affecting a judge have also been held to affect independence. The late Chief Justice Dickson, in a judgement in the Supreme Court of Canada, stipulated that "the salaries and pensions of provincial court judges shall be adequate, commensurate with the status, dignity and responsibility of their office." The Supreme Court also approved the creation in each province of a commission to make recommendations on the salaries and pensions of provincial judges as an objective means of fulfilling the constitutional requirement of maintaining "independent and impartial tribunals." This is the device, which originated and was developed in Ontario, to which I have referred elsewhere in these memoirs.

The Supreme Court also has held that in addition to the independence of judges in individual cases, the principle extends to the administration of the courts as an institution so as to ensure that the judicial process shall be free from executive or legislative entanglement.

A breach of a judge's independence usually takes the form of some interference when a case is before a judge for adjudication. I was very much distressed on one occasion by an extraordinary governmental intervention in a case I had already decided and considered closed. The incident occurred in the days when Arthur Klein was still the Chief Judge of the Criminal Division of the Provincial Court. I came to work one morning at the Old City Hall and, according to my custom, met with other judges in the judges' common room for conversation and coffee prior to commencing my activities in court. I was seated beside the Chief Judge at the long rectangular table used by the judges. In the course of the usual joking at the table, the Chief Judge abruptly turned to me and, with a laugh, asked: "Tell me, Dave, what are you doing, going about sentencing Crown witnesses?"

"What do you mean?" I countered, puzzled.

By way of response, the Chief Judge tossed a letter to me. It was from the Ministry of the Attorney General, addressed to Arthur Klein as Chief Judge and inquired almost exactly: "What business was it of Judge Vanek to be sentencing Crown witnesses?"

The letter referred to a case, of no special importance that I had all but forgotten. I had dealt with it two or three months previously in Richmond Hill, an area just north of Toronto. Furious about this type of intervention, punctuated with a few choice expletives directed at the author of the letter, I reacted: "You can tell that ... person ... he should look up some law, particularly on the inherent jurisdiction of a justice of the peace to do preventive justice." I included in my remarks a reference to the leading case on the subject.

Previous to my attendance in Richmond Hill, a judgement was reported in the law reports that attracted my interest. It reminded me of the jurisdiction, to which I have referred, which somehow had been neglected over time. I began regularly to use this inherent jurisdiction of a justice of the peace. I found it to be a useful tool in the resolution of a particular type of case when it appeared that something had to be done, short of applying the full force of the criminal law, to defuse a matter and prevent or circumvent a threatened breach of the peace. The remedy afforded by this jurisdiction was to make an order, without conviction for any offence, requiring a person whose conduct was in question to enter into a recognisance in a small amount of money to guarantee that the person would keep the peace. I used to make the terms as little onerous as possible. Generally, I would not require the actual deposit of any amount of money and would limit the order to a period of one year. Basically, I relied upon the written undertaking itself and the psychological effect of an order of the Court as a means of resolving conflict. I found this to be a reasonable way of dealing with a number of cases.

In Richmond Hill, I encountered a situation that I considered eminently suited to the exercise of this jurisdiction. It was a case involving a group of adolescent youths, about sixteen years of age, which, in those days qualified them to be dealt with as adults in an adult court. They had been making a considerable nuisance of themselves in a local shopping centre after it had been closed for business for the day. An altercation occurred between one of them and a shopkeeper as a result of which the youth caused the shopkeeper to be charged with the offence of common assault.

After I heard the testimony of this complainant and his associates, in accordance with my practice, I made my usual announcement about the inherent jurisdiction to do preventive justice. I cautioned the people in court that, at the end of the trial, when all the evidence was in, I would consider exercising this jurisdiction. I would exercise it, in order to maintain the peace, against anyone involved in the case, whether defendant, complainant or other witness, as I deemed necessary according to the evidence.

At the termination of the trial, I convicted the shopkeeper for common assault. Any application of force to a person in anger is held to be sufficient in law to constitute a common assault. It was a mild case of assault such as a mere slap to the face. I believe I imposed a light fine. Then I dealt with the complainant, referred to in the Ministry's letter as a "Crown witness." I lectured the complainant and his companions regarding their rowdy and unruly conduct in the shopping centre after closing, which I considered contributed to the situation described in the evidence. I made my typical order requiring the complainant to enter into a recognizance without deposit of any money on terms that he must keep the peace and stay out of this shopping centre for a period of one year. I believed that I was doing no more than a good parent might have done as a disciplinary measure.

I was very upset by the letter from the Ministry of the Attorney General to the Chief Judge of the Criminal Division of the Provincial Court that complained about my exercise of a judicial function. I considered it to be a blatant attack upon my independence. As a judge, I fully appreciated that I was answerable for my legal decisions on appeal, and, if found to be in error, I welcomed correction through the appellate process. However, I did not expect, nor would I accept, that I was also answerable to someone in the Ministry of the Attorney General, the Attorney General himself, or the Chief Judge of the Provincial Court.

Apart, perhaps, from a follow-up letter, the next I learned about this affair was by receipt of a copy of a Supreme Court of Ontario judgement. It appeared that the Crown had appealed my disposition on behalf of the complainant. I was under the impression that the person who considered himself prejudiced by my order would have launched his own appeal. Although the Crown appeals on behalf of the prosecution, I considered it to be very strange for the Crown to appeal on behalf of the complainant.

Mr. Justice Lerner delivered the judgement on appeal in the case, later reported in the law reports as *Re Shaban*. He held that there did indeed exist an inherent jurisdiction of a justice of the peace to do preventive justice by binding over persons by a recognizance to keep the peace. He went on to hold, however, that I should have afforded anyone that I contemplated dealing with in this manner the opportunity to make full answer and defence. He stated that I should have adjourned the case and given the complainant the opportunity to obtain legal advice, retain counsel, and present evidence. I believe the Crown made the only submissions on the appeal. I am unaware of anyone who was present to make submissions reflecting my reasons. I might have wanted to explain the object and intent of my order and the impracticability of providing all the usual safeguards as if the order was directed against a person convicted of a criminal offence. For failure to provide these safeguards, however, the judge on appeal held that I had acted without jurisdiction.

This result, in those days, immediately left me open to a civil action for damages. However, Mr. Justice Lerner was empowered to make an order protecting me from liability and, fortunately, exercised this authority by an order of protection. Federally appointed judges have always been immune from civil liability when acting as judges. Protection from liability in a civil action is basic to the principle of judicial independence. Some years after the decision in *Re Shaban*, the legislation governing provincial judges was amended in Ontario and certain other provinces to give provincial judges the same immunity as federal judges. In some other provinces and territories, the protection is qualified or limited to an extent.

Notwithstanding the above amendments, the decision in *Re Shaban* produced this effect on me: never again did I exercise the inherent jurisdiction of a justice of the peace to do preventive justice.

My experience fully confirmed my belief that judges and the public should be vigilant to support and preserve the principle of judicial independence. If judges err, there is always an appellate court to correct them. The principle of judicial independence is not for the protection of judges, but for the protection of the general public, in order to ensure equal and impartial justice in accordance with the rule of law.

Twenty
Regina v. Susan Nelles

Undoubtedly, my single most important case was the Nelles case. Susan Nelles was a young nurse who worked in the cardiac section of the Hospital for Sick Children at Toronto, one of the most prestigious hospitals in Canada. She came from a prominent family in Belleville, a city on Lake Ontario, about thirty-eight miles east of Toronto. Her father was a respected paediatrician and her brother was also a physician. One day, two police officers knocked on the door of her residence and, when she came to the door, abruptly told her she was under arrest for murder. She was charged with four counts of first degree murder in connection with the death of four babies who were patients at the Hospital and who died from poisoning alleged to have been caused by the deliberate administration of massive overdoses of the drug digoxin. It was thought that Susan Nelles had been given the responsibility for the constant care of the infants at or about the time that they died. I was assigned to conduct a preliminary inquiry into the case.

The object of a preliminary inquiry is to determine if there is sufficient evidence to require a person accused of a serious criminal offence to be put on trial. According to a leading decision of the

Supreme Court of Canada, the test of the "sufficiency" is whether there is any evidence upon which a jury properly instructed could find the accused person guilty of the offence charged. In recent times, defence counsel have used the preliminary inquiry for the purpose of acquiring a thorough disclosure of the Crown's case through the examination of the Crown's witnesses, rather than to obtain a discharge at this early stage of the proceedings. In this case, however, it was abundantly clear from the outset that the defence was challenging the Crown to show a sufficiency of evidence to warrant committing Susan Nelles for trial on the four counts of first degree murder. At the beginning of the hearing and as required by law, I made an order prohibiting publication of the evidence until the termination of the proceedings.

When I commenced the hearing, I had no knowledge about the case except that it concerned the offence of murder. In a criminal case, prior to commencement of the proceedings, any information about the facts and circumstances of the case is deliberately withheld from the judge. The judge is required to decide the case wholly on the basis of the evidence submitted in the proceedings.

The circumstances surrounding the deaths of the four babies charged to Nelles were described mainly through the testimony of the nurses who worked in cardiac wards 4A and 4B at the hospital. Cumulatively, they were responsible on a full-time basis for the care of the babies and had the most continuous contact with them. All the nurses testified about their particular involvement from their individual perspectives. Their evidence was generally delivered in a factual manner that only tended to enhance the harrowing and emotional effects on them of their experiences. The four babies were Janice Estrella, Kevin Pacsai, Allana Miller and Justin Cook. They were all sick babies but were not expected to die when they did. They were expected to have a substantial number of years of life, although not the full life of a normal healthy child.

Kevin Pacsai was probably in the best physical condition of the four babies. He was admitted to the hospital on March 11, 1981, and assigned to a bed in room 431. Susan Nelles came on duty for the night shift, which was for the period from 7:30 p.m. to 7:30 a.m. the next morning. She was assigned to care for baby Pacsai but was also given the duty of looking after other children. Nevertheless, Susan Nelles tended to baby Pacsai without incident until 1:30 a.m.

At 1:30 a.m., there was a sudden emergency in room 438. Baby

Manoglovich had suffered a seizure. Nelles ran to assist other nurses in an effort to stabilize this baby. However, at about 2:35 a.m., baby Manoglovich went into cardiac arrest. A Code 25 was called. This sounded an alarm throughout the hospital. An arrest team came running. A crash cart was wheeled out packed with all the medications and equipment needed for such an emergency. In the ensuing excitement, turmoil and confusion, nurses on the cardiac wards flocked to render assistance. The arrest team worked on the child in a strenuous effort to save his life, to no avail. At 3:35 a.m., the baby was pronounced dead. Susan Nelles assisted in the effort to save the baby during the entire two hours of the emergency.

Meanwhile, other nurses looked in on Kevin Pacsai in room 431 from time to time and relieved Nelles of her duties with the other children in her care. Upon her return to room 431 to resume her care of baby Pacsai, Nelles noticed a change in his condition. She asked doctors who happened to be on the floor to examine him. She was holding the child when, suddenly, he became rigid in her arms. The child stopped breathing momentarily but was stimulated and revived. The chief resident arrived and arranged for the child to be transferred to intensive care to which he was moved at 6:00 a.m. At about 9:50 a.m., baby Pacsai suffered a cardiac arrest. A Code 25 was called, to the same effect as previously described. All efforts to resuscitate the child failed. Kevin Pacsai was pronounced dead at 10:00 a.m. This baby had been treated by the administration of digoxin, a prescription drug commonly in use for children suffering from heart disease.

Shortly after the death of baby Pacsai, an autopsy was performed on his body in the course of which samples of blood were taken. An analysis of the blood revealed a blood level of digoxin of 26 ng/ml (i.e. 26 nanograms per millilitre of blood). This was a level of twenty-six to thirty times the therapeutic dosage and a strong indication that the seizure that brought on the death was caused by a massive overdose of digoxin. Doctors at the hospital contacted the coroner who arranged for an inquest to be held. Word of the pending inquest circulated and created a great stir of confusion and concern amongst the nurses.

Understandably, staff doctors at the hospital were very upset with the likelihood that one of their babies had come to his death by digoxin poisoning. This concern was considerably heightened a few days later when it came to light that back on January 11, 1981 a resident in pathology had performed an autopsy on another baby who had also died on the cardiac ward. This was baby Janice Estrella. The resident had taken a sample of blood that, on analysis, disclosed a reading of 72 ng/ml — an astonishingly high level, vastly in excess of the therapeutic range.

The next sequence of events occurred on the weekend from Friday March 20 to Sunday March 22 and included the deaths of babies Allana Miller and Justin Cook — about ten days after Kevin Pacsai died.

Allana Miller was a cyanotic or blue baby about one year of age. She was admitted to the hospital on March 19 at about 7:00 p.m. and put in room 423. On the next day, Friday March 20, Susan Nelles was again on the night shift. Nelles was assigned to care for Allana Miller. She was also to tend to two babies in room 418. At about 10:30 p.m., Justin Cook arrived at the hospital and Nelles was assigned to attend to all of the details concerning his admission and to care for the child. Justin Cook was placed in a bed in room 418 between the beds of the other two children in the room. Nelles looked after Justin on an almost continuous basis while other nurses helped to look after Allana Miller in room 423.

While Nelles was busy with Justin Cook, Allana Miller exhibited signs of distress. Between 1:00 and 2:00 a.m., her cardiac monitor kept going off, and on one occasion the baby vomited. Her condition deteriorated sharply and Nelles was called back to room 423 and resumed her duties with Allana. At 2:40 a.m., Allana Miller suffered a seizure. A Code 25 was called. The arrest team arrived amidst all the accompanying confusion. All efforts to save the child failed. At 3:30 a.m., Allana Miller was pronounced dead. A sample of blood taken at an autopsy shortly after her death showed a blood level of digoxin of 78 ng/ml.

Next day, Sunday March 21, on the day shift, Sui Scott was the nurse assigned to Justin Cook in room 418. Justin was a very sick child. At 10:30 a.m., he underwent a diagnostic examination. As a result of the findings, an operation was scheduled for the next day. At about 6:30 p.m. he suffered a severe blue spell. A Code 23 was called. This Code signals a call for a specific doctor. The cardiac fellow attended. A crash cart was brought into the room. There was the usual commotion. With medication, the baby recovered at this time.

For the night shift, 7:30 p.m. to 7:30 a.m. Sunday March 22, Susan Nelles was again on duty. Nelles was assigned to look after Justin Cook. He was to be given constant nursing care. Nelles remained with this baby during the night and early morning hours except for the usual breaks for coffee and food and to relieve herself, on which occasions other nurses took over. At about 3:00 a.m., Nelles suddenly called out in alarm. The baby had taken a turn for the worse. A Code 23 was called and a drug was administered but without effect. The child went into seizure and a Code 25 was called. All the excitement of previous calls of Code 25 was repeated, possibly intensified. Dr. Jedaiken, a cardiac fellow, arrived with the arrest team. Every effort was made to save the child, without success. The child died and was pronounced dead at 4:56 a.m.

In the course of the attempt to save the child's life, Dr. Jedaiken took a sample of his blood. After death, an autopsy was performed and a sample of blood was again taken. Upon analysis, the digoxin blood level in the pre-mortem blood was 72 ng/ml; the blood level of digoxin in the post-mortem sample was 91 ng/ml. Ominously, this baby was never on digoxin. In his case, digoxin was *contra* indicated.

It was at about this stage in the story that the staff cardiologist under whose care baby Cook had been placed for treatment was awakened at his home in the early hours of the morning and came rushing to the hospital, breathless, in great excitement. He described himself as a senior physician with expertise both in paediatrics and cardiology. He arrived at the hospital at about 5:00 a.m. He testified: "When I walked in, I came into the nurses' station and observed Nelles. She was sitting at the desk with a strange expression on her face, no sign of grief at all, quietly writing up her report."

"What emotions did she exhibit?" he was asked.

"None at all."

"Did you find that usual or unusual?"

"Very unusual conduct of a person who had just been present where there were two deaths of babies" was the answer.

I found it curious that, apart from this testimony, most, if not all of the evidence of the doctors about the occurrences at the hospital came from interns and residents rather than staff physicians, who appeared to have been kept out of the limelight.

This was the state of the evidence on what I regarded as the main facts of the case when Crown counsel announced that there were not just four, but twenty-four, babies who had died on the cardiac ward in the same time frame and in suspiciously similar circumstances. Suddenly, I felt the impact of all the evidence I had heard, and the full weight and pressure of presiding over a murder case involving the likelihood of a large number of deaths of babies caused deliberately by digoxin poisoning. It seemed to me that all the stress, strain and trauma of the nurses and doctors was being transferred onto my shoulders. Someone was going about our beloved Sick Children's Hospital killing babies! Was it this tiny young woman who almost sank out of sight seated alongside her tall lawyer?

Immediately, however, I had the task of ruling on the Crown's application to admit into evidence all of the circumstances surrounding the deaths of twenty additional babies. The evidence would be as "similar fact evidence" in support of the contention that Nelles was guilty of the murder of the four babies as charged. On a question of the admissibility of evidence, the same rules apply on a preliminary inquiry as at a trial. If the issue is the identity of the perpetrator, evidence of similar acts and events at other times and places are only admissible under this doctrine if they tend to be logically probative that the accused is the guilty party. A usual illustration is where a person who commits a number of similar acts happens to be disfigured by a scar or does the acts in a particular way that tends to identify the person as the one responsible for the commission of the offence charged.

I was relatively satisfied that the evidence of the additional deaths did not qualify for admission under this rule. As I stated at the time, and confirmed later, the application appeared to be an effort to prove one mystery by evidence of several other mysteries. Nevertheless, upon reflection, for purposes of the preliminary inquiry, I allowed the evidence to be admitted. However, I specifically reserved my decision as to the significance that might be attributed to this evidence. The inquiry was prolonged, therefore, and I heard detailed testimony regarding the deaths of babies in the additional cases, as well as a considerable amount of forensic and scientific evidence to show the significance of all the evidence relative to the four counts of murder before me.

In the realm of the mysterious and inexplicable, as well, were certain strange and unusual happenings that occurred after Nelles was arrested and, while on bail, not allowed back into the hospital. The incidents included a large number of threatening telephone calls and "X" marks imprinted with lipstick on doors, windows and lockers. Then there was the bizarre incident of propanolol in the nurses' soup and salad. Propanolol was another drug used in the treatment of babies at the hospital. At about 2:00 a.m., the nurses brought their soup and salad from the refrigerator to the nurses' station for their late night meal; and, just as they began to eat, they discovered that the food was laced with pills of propanolol. The bare facts concerning these incidents added measurably to the level of tension and apprehension of all the nurses in the cardiac wards but disclosed nothing about the person responsible for them or the identity of the person who poisoned the babies.

The Nelles case attracted counsel of exceptional quality. Robert McGee for the Crown and Austin Cooper for the defence were senior counsel on the case. They were lawyers of considerable experience and established reputation and ability in the law. Robert McGee presented the case for the Crown in a thoroughgoing and creditable manner. Austin Cooper had the more difficult role of demonstrating that the evidence was not sufficient to justify the accused being committed for trial. In a preliminary inquiry, it is not customary for the defence to call witnesses or present any evidence. From a defence viewpoint, it would serve no useful purpose and lead to needless disclosure of its case. Hence, defence counsel is generally restricted to cross-examing the Crown's witnesses.

The strategy adopted by Austin Cooper contained a positive element as well as the negative object of neutralizing the damaging effects of the testimony of the Crown witnesses. The Crown produced all the nurses who had any contact whatever with the four babies who were the subject of the charges before the Court. In cross-examination, the questioning of each of the nurses by Austin Cooper took substantially the same form.

"Did you know Susan Nelles? What kind of person was she? Did you get along with her? How did she get along with the other nurses? Did you notice anything unusual or abnormal in her behaviour?"

This cross-examination of the nurses was obviously intended to show, on the positive side, that the accused was a normal stable person, emotionally and mentally. It was further intended to show that she got along reasonably well with her peers and displayed no behavioural abnormalities that would lead anyone to expect that she would go about deliberately murdering babies entrusted to her care.

On the other hand, Austin Cooper cross-examined with crushing effect the staff physician. This was the physician who testified that he came rushing to the hospital after the death of Justin Cook and observed Nelles seated at a desk in the nurses' station with a strange expression on her face, no sign of grief, quietly writing up a report. Cooper wanted to know, however knowledgeable that doctor was in paediatrics and cardiology, just what qualifications and expertise did he possess in the field of psychiatry. What did he actually know about this young woman? What prior contact or acquaintance did he have with her? What opportunities did he have to study her behaviour in normal circumstances, her emotional make-up, and her reactions to stress? By the time Cooper finished his cross-examination, the testimony of this physician had been torn to shreds as indicative of probative guilt. On the contrary, it tended to show that Nelles was simply a good, conscientious nurse.

Pursuant to my ruling regarding the introduction of similar fact evidence, the Crown called witnesses who related the circumstances surrounding the deaths of other babies in addition to the four babies in respect of which Nelles was charged. The defence took a most ingenious step in the proceedings; the defence prepared a chart and, with the consent of the Crown, filed it as an exhibit. The chart contained a list of the nurses who were on duty on each of the days when the twenty-four babies died in the hospital in mysterious or unexplained circumstances. To my surprise, the list disclosed that Susan Nelles was on duty on most but not all of the days when babies died and that another nurse was on duty on *all* of the days when babies had died.

The chart constituted a very important, if not critical, piece of documentary evidence in the case. It highlighted a major defect in the case for the Crown. It confirmed that Susan Nelles was not even on duty on the day of the death of baby Estrella — one of the four babies included in the charges of murder laid against Nelles! Both the Crown and the defence assumed that one person was responsible for killing all four babies. Neither side believed there was a conspiracy between two or more people to kill babies at the hospital. It was certainly unlikely that people would be going about in concert with this object and, more importantly, there was no evidence at all of conspiracy. Therefore, if Nelles did not kill one of the babies, it followed that she could hardly be found guilty of killing the others.

In this dilemma, the Crown called as one of its final witnesses a distinguished physician from the United States, regarded as an expert in the use and effects of digoxin. Previously, scientific evidence had

292

been produced, through the testimony of personnel of the Centre for Forensic Studies, about the effects of digoxin in relation to the death of the four babies. It appeared, however, that although there were some studies on the effects of digoxin in therapeutic use, little was known of its effects when used as a poison. The expert witness on digoxin sought to resolve the conundrum regarding baby Estrella in singular fashion. Nelles was on duty at the hospital on the night prior to the day baby Estrella died. The expert postulated that Nelles could have inserted a lethal dosage of digoxin into the intravenous equipment attached to the baby on the night before she died so as to cause her death by a slow infusion of digoxin. Upon reflection, I considered this scenario to be quite unlikely and, moreover, without any foundation in evidence.

I believed that the investigating officers made a sad error in the early stages of their investigation. They approached a supervisory nurse to ascertain which of the nurses were assigned to care for the four babies. The supervisory nurse produced her assignment book. It showed that Nelles had been assigned to care for only three of the babies. It seems probable that the investigating officers misread the data in the book or otherwise received the impression that she was given the duty of looking after all four babies.

When all the evidence was in, counsel were given the usual opportunity of presenting oral argument. Austin Cooper's opening was most dramatic: "Your Honour" he thundered, "the Crown has charged the wrong woman!" He proceeded to demonstrate all the defects in the case for the Crown. For his part, Bob McGee, in an address that took up the better part of two days, argued convincingly that there was an abundance of evidence to require that the accused be committed for trial.

The preliminary inquiry occupied forty-one days of evidence from over one hundred witnesses and four days of argument by counsel. At the conclusion of the hearing, I adjourned the inquiry about three weeks for judgement. I soon discovered that I had not allowed myself enough time to deal with the matter and had put myself under extreme pressure to honour what I regarded as a commitment. I had to review the evidence and come to a decision on whether to commit for trial or discharge the accused. It would have been expedient, and not unusual, simply to hold there was sufficient evidence for committal, offer a few words to this effect, and leave the issue to a judge or judge and jury for disposition at a trial. I realized that if I held there was an insufficiency of evidence and discharged the accused, as a generally perceived lower court judge I would be taking it upon myself to foreclose a decision on a question of guilt or innocence. I would remove four, and possibly twenty-four, charges of murder from consideration by a judge and jury. I appreciated, moreover, that if I found the evidence insufficient for committal, I would be bound to prepare written reasons for judgement to fully justify my decision.

It seemed to me that an inference of guilt for the murder of babies could not logically be drawn against Nelles from the mere fact that the babies had been assigned to her care — in one instance, constant care. On the other hand, it appeared to be highly unlikely that another person could manage to slip into rooms occupied by babies entrusted to her care and murder them in separate incidents by the deliberate administration of a lethal dosage of digoxin. The ultimate issue in the case, however, was whether there was any evidence before the Court within the test laid down by the Supreme Court of Canada that required an order to be made committing Susan Nelles for trial on the four counts of murder. I found the test to be simple in its wording, but complex and difficult in its application. I had to determine whether there was "any" evidence on which a jury "could" convict. My task was further complicated by the admonition by the Supreme Court that it was not the function of the judge at a preliminary inquiry to "weigh" the evidence as if the judge were dealing with the matter at trial. Accordingly, I drew a distinction between "weighing" and "assessing" the evidence. I examined each aspect of evidence to determine whether, in this case, based wholly on circumstantial evidence, it was evidence that was legally probative of guilt and, finally, whether, on all the evidence, there was a sufficiency of evidence requiring committal for trial. I devoted a substantial section of my reasons for judgement to a discussion of the law and its application to the facts in this preliminary inquiry.

I agonized over my decision. Ultimately, I decided what I wished to do and spent the rest of the period I had allotted myself working feverishly to prepare reasons for judgement.

I worked under very trying conditions. The fact that I was engaged in writing a judgement did not automatically relieve me from my regular schedule of duties in court. The Provincial Court was overburdened with a load of cases awaiting disposition. The executive branch was reluctant to make additional appointments of judges and assistant Crown attorneys; and there was no provision for sabbaticals or time off or relief from a judge's ordinary duties. I soon realized that it was impossible for me to meet my self-imposed obligation to deliver judgement by the date I had set unless I was given some relief from my regular schedule. I telephoned Chief Judge Hayes. He immediately appreciated my problem and responded: "Sure Dave, take as much time off as you need," and I was relieved from my regular assignments. This did not fully resolve my problem, however, because the overloading of the courts still remained an obstacle. Day by day, it seemed, I was being called by whomever was administering the caseload: "Say, Dave, we are short of judges today; can you help us out? We need a judge today for court No. 21," or "Perhaps you can give us an hour or two in the afternoon."

One Saturday, I decided to work in the quiet and seclusion of the Old City Hall instead of labouring at home. I found it difficult to do the work at home. My chambers contained about fifty books of transcripts of the testimony, the exhibits, and my own notes, all of which were laid out on my desk and every available flat space for my assistance in examining and reviewing the evidence. I worked through the day until about 4:00 p.m. and then packed up to leave for home.

On Saturdays, the building was closed after the single court held to process prisoners brought in from the activities overnight had been completed, usually by early afternoon. As I was leaving, all was quiet in the building; no one was present except, I presumed, for the caretaker. He was probably cavorting with the ghosts of the Old City Hall who, according to local legend, occupied the large attic on the fourth floor of the building where large amounts of old furniture were stored. I walked to the ground floor and found the outside doors to be locked. I was able to obtain access to the courtyard where my vehicle was parked but the huge wrought iron gate was securely locked and blocked my car from leaving the compound. I left my briefcase, containing the court records that I had been examining, in my car as I still intended to use them at home in continuation of the work I had been doing. Then I tested the east door that led out of the building to James Street and was pleased to find that it opened.

However, I knew from experience that the door was attached to a very strong spring and when opened, it was likely to be pulled back and locked from the outside. While testing the door, I cautioned myself not to let go of the door. Somehow, I failed to heed my own advice. Absentmindedly, I must have lost my hold on the door; it slammed shut and I found myself effectively barred from the building with my car and documents still inside the building enclosure. I was upset by my own clumsiness and the ridiculous situation in which I had put myself. It was then I remembered that I had been distinctly asked, before leaving that morning, to come home early. I had to attend a family gathering — I believe it was to honour Sam, my well-loved brother-in-law, on his birthday. I looked about and found an outside buzzer, which I pressed in order to summon the caretaker who I felt certain would be somewhere in the building. It was to no avail. After engaging fruitlessly in this endeavour for several minutes, I gradually became more and more excited and overwrought.

Finally, I ran in a panic to the front of the building on Queen Street and along both Queen and Bay Streets looking for assistance while there was still some daylight. Finally, I spotted a policeman, who was standing in the intersection; he was probably directing traffic. At all events, I interrupted whatever he was doing by shouting wildly: "Officer, officer, I need help!"

The officer inquired: "What is the trouble?"

"I can't get into the Old City Hall," I replied, in great excitement.

The police officer must have puzzled why a member of the general public would be wanting so desperately to gain admission to the main courthouse in Toronto of the Provincial Court after it had been completely closed for business on Saturday afternoon. Astonished, the officer asked: "Why do you want to get into the Old City Hall?"

Stuttering and stammering, I made known to the officer who I was and the singular circumstances that had brought me to this pass. At last, he realized this was a serious matter. He said, "I will come with you."

The officer accompanied me back to the Old City Hall, but he had no better means of gaining access to the building than I had been employing. So, we simply took turns knocking on doors and pushing buzzers. Finally, after about an hour thus engaged, when we were both about ready to give up hope, we succeeded in alerting a sleepy caretaker who finally came to open the door, and the gate enclosing the courtyard, to enable me to regain my car.

I worked under difficult personal circumstances. In addition to being called away intermittently on other judicial duties, at this time I was in poor physical condition because of a problem with my eyesight. I suffered from a condition of double vision that was a consequence of an over-active thyroid. My wife became very alarmed when she was a passenger in the car I was driving and I asked her if the vehicle ahead of me was one car or two. I could read fairly well in the morning but my ability gradually deteriorated as the day wore on. I could barely see the printed page when I became particularly fatigued. The first time I examined my reasons for judgement in their entirety occurred when I arrived in court to deliver judgement and found them on my desk. Thus, in the process of examining the evidence and producing a judgement, I worked feverishly and under pressure.

On the day to which the case had been adjourned, I delivered judgement in a large courtroom, filled to capacity, in a pervasive atmosphere of tension and emotion. No doubt, the audience included close relatives of the deceased babies as well as relatives of the accused. I was aware that both Nelles' father and brother had died during the course of the preliminary inquiry. I wondered whether the stress and strain of criminal proceedings against a daughter and sister was a contributing cause of death in each case. For the rendering of judgement, the case had been moved from the Old City Hall to one of the courtrooms at College Park, probably to ensure better security. In fact, security was tight. Police officers stationed at the door controlled the admission of people seeking to enter the courtroom. One of the officers in charge asked me, if at all possible, whether I could bring matters to completion by about 1:00 o'clock; the police wanted to avoid the necessity of a second investigation of people who might want admission to the courtroom for a session in the afternoon. I promised to do my best to meet the 1:00 p.m. deadline.

I delivered the opening part of my judgement orally, without reference to the written reasons for judgement I had prepared. I read the rest from my written reasons. However, I did not read aloud my detailed discussion of the law; there was no necessity, or time, to read those portions aloud. I held that the evidence did not reach the low threshold of the test set by the Supreme Court of Canada to justify committal for trial. Accordingly, I finished my judgement by directing that Susan Nelles be discharged on all four charges of murder. It was almost exactly 1:00 o'clock.

Fulfilment

My decision struck the public, concerned about unexplained deaths of infants at its Hospital for Sick Children, like a bombshell. It created an explosion of agitation and excitement. As a result of my order prohibiting publication of the evidence until termination of the proceedings, it was the first substantial account of the events to reach the public. The newspapers published long extracts from my written reasons. A colleague of mine commented that my judgement drove coverage of a war off the front pages of the newspapers.

In the climate of turmoil and emotion engendered by my judgement in the Nelles Case, the Government of Ontario appointed a Royal Commission of Inquiry under Mr. Justice Samuel Grange of the Ontario Court of Appeal to examine the circumstances surrounding the extraordinary number of mysterious deaths at the Hospital. The hearings in the Royal Commission extended for a period well over a year. A host of lawyers participated. The Commissioner allowed the proceedings to be televised. At the conclusion, the Commissioner issued his report. It contained statements expressly agreeing with my decision in the preliminary inquiry and generally approving of my handling of the charges against Susan Nelles.

I believe I should clarify two matters. The first is that I never intended to express a firm conclusion that the four babies had been murdered, despite an unfortunate observation I made as an aside in the course of reading my judgement, an aside that received headlines in the press — "This is a whodunnit!" Of course the case was prosecuted and defended on that basis and there was substantial evidence that led to that conclusion. I recall that it was the opinion of the Crown's expert on digoxin that it had to be a deliberate administration of an overdose of digoxin that caused the death of the four babies. However, for purposes of the preliminary inquiry there was no need for me to make any such finding. There was a sufficiency of evidence on that aspect of the case. All I had to decide was, if the babies were murdered, was there also a sufficiency of evidence that Nelles was the perpetrator.

The second matter concerns the "other nurse" who was disclosed to have been on duty on all days when twenty-four babies died at the hospital, including the four babies referred to in the charge against Nelles. In my judgement, I confined myself to the observation that the evidence of guilt "tended in another direction." I felt that this oblique reference was sufficient to show what was relevant, that other nurses had access to the babies and one nurse had as much opportunity as Nelles and was equally or even more likely to be the guilty party. I did not elaborate, however, as the other person was not before me charged with any offence. I did not wish to make any statement that could be harmful to her if she were not charged or prejudice her or the police if the police decided to pursue the matter further as against her.

In the end, how twenty-four babies, who were not expected to die, came to their death at Toronto's renowned Hospital for Sick Children remains a mystery.

A defining moment, in my opinion, is an occasion when one is called upon to bring to bear the full force of one's life-experience in the solution of a difficult problem. My decision in the Nelles case was a defining moment in my career as a judge.

Twenty-One
Final Thoughts

I am sometimes asked about humour in court. The short answer is, there is none, except, perhaps, in the occasional rare situation. The disposition of a criminal charge is serious business. The judge should not tolerate levity in the courtroom or indulge in humorous remarks. They will not be appreciated by the accused. Occasionally an amusing incident takes place but it should happen only unintentionally. A judge should also avoid any exhibition of arrogance or sarcasm or speaking down or up to people in the courtroom. I recall a young assistant crown attorney who would address an obviously disreputable female person who appeared in court as "this lady." I thought it was sufficient courtesy to refer to her simply as a "woman."

The closest I ever came to being amusing in court took place when I was trying a case of possession of instruments suitable for the purpose of breaking and entering into a place — the possession of burglar's tools. A major piece of evidence was a pair of rubber gloves. Twisted and rolled, they lay beside me on my desk as defence counsel argued that they were of no use to the accused for they were obviously too small for him. As counsel spoke, abstractedly I picked up the gloves and was trying them on. "Hmm," I mused, in what was intended as a comment to myself, but which unconsciously I uttered in a voice that filled the courtroom, "A perfect fit!" Of course, that provoked considerable laughter.

The closest I came to sarcasm occurred in a case of breaking and entering in which the facts were positively ludicrous. The accused had pleaded guilty. Crown counsel informed me that a policeman found the accused late at night in the act of disengaging an air conditioner at the second floor of a retail establishment. When he noticed the officer, he got to the ground and began to run, still holding the air-conditioning unit. He stood before me, woebegone, awaiting sentence. The Crown produced a criminal record, which, as we used to say, was "an arm long." His counsel made a very good plea for leniency: "He was only recently released from the penitentiary for his last offence. He is now just an old 'lag', past the age for the commission of a serious crime; at most, he is now just a nuisance. There is a child to look after. So why not give him one last chance to enjoy some of his life on the 'outside'?" I was convinced. "What was the use," I asked myself, "to send him back to the penitentiary from whence he had just come?" I wound myself up in righteous indignation and addressed the accused as follows: "Michael Gruczek," I began (not the real name), "As a criminal you are a complete failure. Why don't you try some other occupation?"

Ultimately, my sentence was a simple order of probation, which was a highly unusual disposition in the circumstances. I left the courtroom followed by my court clerk, an older man of considerable experience in the criminal courts. Still glowing with an inflated sense of my own humanity, I asked my clerk what he thought of my sentence. "Your Honour," he replied, "he'll be back in court tomorrow!"

For the most part, court-related humorous situations occurred out-of-court, not in court. As an illustration, I was involved with a case that used to be known as off-track betting. I had never been to the races and there were constant references in the trial to terms and procedures in wagering on the horses with which I was quite unfamiliar. I decided upon an expedition to the Woodbine racetrack in order to acquire a measure of familiarity and background on this subject. When Sam, my brother-in-law, learned about this project in self-improvement, he insisted I accept two tickets that he held entitling the holders to watch the races from the dining room overlooking the track.

Armed with these tickets I took Joyce with me to Woodbine and began placing bets in moderate amounts. To my discomfort, I found that I was a steady loser. We were seated in the dining room over dinner when I glanced casually at a party seated at the front window.

"Say, Joyce," I asked. "Isn't that Curly Posen seated over there?" She agreed it was and we approached Curly at his table. He presented his usual genial demeanour and cordially invited us to join him at his table, which we did. I confided to Curly that I was discouraged about my betting and losing on the races. When Curly learned my system of wagering, he convulsed in laughter.

"No wonder you are losing; you are betting in reverse of the odds," he explained. From an obvious wealth of experience, he gave me a full lesson about betting on the horses that he claimed should lead to success.

With a show of pride, Curly told me he was the owner of a horse which, as it happened, was entered in one of the races. He showed me a list of the total of eight races and, sure enough, Bob-tail Nag (not the real name) was listed to run in the seventh race. At the finish of the sixth race, after I lost again despite his advice, Curly drew his rotund frame to its full height, and suggested:

"Let's go down to the paddock and find out how my horse is doing."

Of course, I followed Curly while we filed past a number of stalls with horses that looked rather strong and sprightly to me. Finally we came to Bob-tail Nag. Horse and I mutually regarded one another with interest. Curly examined his horse and engaged in a brief conversation with the trainer. Then, brimming with satisfaction, he turned to me and said:

"Let's go to the wicket and lay our bets."

Again I followed and, despite an inclination to the contrary, in his presence felt honour-bound to place a wager on Bob-tail Nag — to win. We then returned to our table overlooking the track.

The seventh race, for us, was a sad event. Bob-tail Nag hesitated as the other horses were off. He was last, moved up, fell back, and finished behind all the other horses. He came in last. Poor Curly! He was crestfallen, but bravely survived the event. Once again he drew himself to his feet and said:

"Let's go down to the paddock and find out what happened?"

Once again we descended to the paddock and found Bob-tail Nag remarkably subdued. The horse seemed to realize that he had disappointed his proud master and seemed to promise to do better next time. Curly again engaged in conversation with the trainer after which his happy, jovial nature was fully restored. Curly confided to me that the trainer told him why Bob-tail Nag lost the race: "It was only because, before engaging in a race, a horse had to have a good bowel movement and this horse had not done so." I found this information very interesting and my day at the races most enjoyable, but neither this knowledge nor indeed anything I learned about racing and betting helped me decide my off-track-betting case.

The appointment to the Bench changed my life in a number of ways. The appointment did not bring about a mere progression in the legal profession from practitioner to judge. It made an abrupt change in my life equivalent to a full change in the nature of my occupation. An immediate effect was that, in addition to a reduction of income, which I had anticipated, I suffered a considerable financial loss, which was quite unexpected. This came about because I had adopted a year end in my legal practice of January 31 in place of the usual December 31. The result was that I became liable in one year to pay income tax on the totality of my earnings over a period of two years. I discovered later, in conversation with other judges that this was a common consequence of appointment to the judiciary. In a sudden panic, however, I sold a very promising investment that I had every intention of retaining. Not long afterwards, we managed to sell our lovely bungalow on Mead Court just prior to the dramatic escalation in the value of residential properties, which, nevertheless, put us in sufficient funds so that we could have avoided the necessity of selling my prized investment. We rented a suite in an apartment building for a few years and then purchased an apartment in a high-rise condominium complex where we have been residing ever since.

Another immediate effect of the appointment was a rise in personal status, whether real or apparent. An appointment to judicial office is generally regarded as an "elevation" to the Bench. In addition to a huge volume of congratulatory statements and letters, I received a great deal of playful bantering from personal friends. I was immediately dubbed "the hanging judge" and given a coin marked on one side "guilty" and on the other "not guilty," which I was invited to toss as an aid to decision-making. A further consequence was an enhancement in the courtesy and respect that was extended to me by members of the Bar, the general public, friends and acquaintances alike. I confess, I rather enjoyed being addressed as "Your Honour," and the elaborate manifestations of respect I received as a judge. I had to caution myself from time to time that any excess beyond normal was addressed more to the office than to the person and that my becoming a judge did not automatically transform me into a superior or exalted being.

On the other hand, it tended to isolate me from other people, not merely by their attitude towards me but by my own reaction to them in my altered circumstances. I probably overreacted to the need to ensure that I would not be unduly influenced in my legal decisions. I tended to avoid association with lawyers — particularly those who regularly appeared before me as counsel in court. I resigned as a director and president of the Credit Counselling Service and became inactive as a member of Temple Sinai. I compensated for this self-imposed isolation by enjoying the collegiality with the members of the court and the fraternization and socializing with judges with whom I became particularly friendly.

I was particularly fortunate in my posting to the Old City Hall in Toronto as my base court for service as a judge because it exposed me to the benign and beneficial influence of travel. The Toronto judges were frequently dispatched to hold court in other parts of Ontario as the need dictated. This enabled a judge to visit towns and hamlets in a variety of locations throughout the province. There used to be a television program called, "Have Gun Will Travel." I used to arrive at those destinations with my court gown slung over my shoulder and announce my presence to the local secretariat with the words "Have *Gown* Will Travel."

Unfortunately, not all the occasions for travel were enjoyable. I was given the assignment one day in the summer to hold court in North Bay, about 250 miles north west of Toronto, fronting on Lake Nipissing. I was to relieve the local judge, who was scheduled to be away, probably on vacation leave. My friend, Chief Judge Fred Hayes, took pains to suggest: "You might take Joyce with you and make something of a holiday out of it as well."

So, I made inquiries to ascertain the best hotel in the area near the courthouse, reserved a room in the hotel, and made all the other appropriate arrangements. On a Sunday morning, anxious to make an early departure, I called to Joyce, who was still fussing in our bedroom, "Are you ready yet, dear?"

"In just a minute. Take out the garbage, dear." She called back from the bedroom.

"Where is it?"

"In the kitchen."

I walked from my study to the kitchen, picked up a plastic bag with its contents, transported it to the hall of the building and dropped it down the garbage chute. Moments later Joyce appeared, ready to go, looked about and asked, "Where is the parcel?"

"What parcel," I inquired.

"The lunch I prepared for the road and the other things I was going to take along with us."

"Oh no!" I exclaimed in consternation. "I must have thrown it down the garbage chute!"

"What?" She uttered incredulously. "You threw away the lunch I prepared for the trip?"

"Well," I had to defend my action and I have always understood that the best defence is a good offence.

"It was packed in a plastic bag just the way you always put out garbage in a plastic bag. It looked just the same."

In rising vexation, she listed the full contents of the parcel, I had destroyed: the sandwiches, the orange juice, the bottle of gin — "and my knitting, and my two library books!"

Nothing would serve but that I must run down four flights of stairs to the ground floor and rescue these articles from the incinerator. Sadly, the parcel was lost, irretrievably. Disconsolately, I now picked up the plastic bag containing the garbage and dropped it as well down the chute as we made our way to our car for the drive to North Bay.

In this unhappy state, we drove to North Bay, with an armistice only long enough to enable me to buy a large bottle of tonic water so we could have a drink of gin and tonic upon our arrival at the hotel. It was a hot and sultry day. We arrived at the hotel ready to make peace, but exhausted by the argument, the long trip and the state of the weather. We checked in at the hotel. There was no one to help with our luggage. We had to carry our bags up to our room. Inside, the heat was overpowering. There was no air conditioning. We were both in great need of some libation. I produced the bottles of gin and tonic water. As I began to open the bottle of tonic water, it exploded in my hands and the contents spilled in a flood onto the floor. I called down to the desk and got into an argument with the management. We left the hotel to find a restaurant where we might obtain some refreshment and regain our composure. On the way, we came upon a motel situated at the waterfront. We reserved a room at the motel, returned to the hotel, packed the belongings we had started to unpack and, over the objection of the management, who wanted to hold us to our reservation, moved to the motel.

Overnight, from unbearably hot and humid, the weather turned cold. For the rest of the week of my working holiday, I had to take my car for transportation to and from the courthouse. Joyce was left to entertain herself at the motel. She noted: "I have no one to talk to. Nothing to do. Not even a book to read. No transportation; so I spend my time walking to the only shopping centre in town and back." After I finished my daily sessions in Court, we found we both had nothing to do. The only movie theatre in town featured cowboy films, which did not attract our fancy. It was too cold to go swimming and there was still no one to talk to. It seemed that while we were enjoying a vacation in North Bay, everyone we knew in North Bay was on vacation in Toronto.

Although, on that occasion, everything seemed to be conspired against us, there were many other occasions in which travel to areas outside of Toronto was quite enjoyable and during which all went smoothly.

After I became president of the Ontario Provincial Judges Association, my opportunities for travel increased measurably. I attended out of the province meetings of the Association of Provincial Court Judges and, upon invitation, conferences of the judges associations of other provinces. Thus, I was able to meet, confer, and fraternize with judges of the other provinces and gain a much better appreciation of the various regions of Canada and of the country as a whole.

In the course of my career as a judge, I have dealt with people from all or most racial, social and economic segments of our Canadian society. I have encountered thieves, robbers, embezzlers, prostitutes, thugs, cheaters, liars, and numerous other unsavoury characters — separated from me in space by the distance from the dais to the well of the Court. I doubt that the experience has made me cynical, left me with a jaundiced view about human nature, or affected my observations as to how people conduct themselves and interact with one another. Prior to my appointment to the Bench, I believe I had a good opinion about people generally — that on the whole, people are honest, diligent, hard working, and helpful who try to make something of their lives and avoid harming others. I like to feel that after retirement, I am left with the same attitude and regard for human nature. Beyond this, I have casually wondered whether my experience as a judge has changed me to any appreciable extent as a person. Recently, I asked my wife the very question: "Not at all!" was the immediate response. I have accepted her answer as conclusive on this subject.

Elsewhere in these memoirs, I mention occasionally being asked: "What kind of judge were you? Were you a law and order judge or a lenient judge?" The question assumes that the alternatives are mutually exclusive. I sometimes have been tempted to reply that I was both, or neither. It is not modesty that prevents my answering the question. I am not a disinterested or impartial party, so I leave the matter to the opinion of others. However, I believe I could accept a description by Harold Levy, a well-known Toronto lawyer who used to write an occasional column about legal matters for the Toronto Star. In the context of my conduct of the Nelles case, he observed: "And she drew a crusty, tough-minded, fiercely independent provincial court judge, who was determined to call the shots as he saw them instead of passing the buck to the judge and jury at trial."

I retired from office at a ripe age. I did not object to being required to retire. I felt it was time to go. It would not be correct to state that I enjoyed my career as a criminal court judge. It is not an occupation intended to provide pleasure to the judge or joy and comfort to the people affected by the judge's decisions. It is also a highly stressful employment. Despite the letter from a disgruntled customer that I quoted earlier, I believe my work has received a degree of recognition and approval. The maintenance of law and order depends upon the approval, consent and support of the public. In the absence of public acceptance, society descends into anarchy. I have had the benefit of exposure to the benign influence of several good people and the privilege of affecting the lives of many others. I am grateful to have had the opportunity to make even a modest contribution as a judge to the general welfare of the public.

Index